Revolution In The Affluent
Society

Erik Dammann

Revolution In The Affluent Society

With a Foreword by Thor Heyerdahl

Translated from the Norwegian by Louis Mackay

heretic books

First published as *Revolusjon i velstandssamfunnet* by
  Gyldendal Norsk Forlag, Oslo 1979
English edition first published in June 1984 by Heretic Books
  (GMP Publishers Ltd), P O Box 247, London N15 6RW
Copyright © 1979 & 1984 Erik Dammann
Foreword copyright © 1984 Thor Heyerdahl

British Library Cataloguing in Publication Data

Dammann, Erik
  Revolution in the affluent society.
  1. Social change
  I. Title   II. Revolusjon i velstandssamfunnet.
  English
  303.4'01   HM101

  ISBN 0-946097-06-2

Heretic Books would like to thank the Norwegian Cultural Council
for their generous help towards this translation.

Cover art by Louis Mackay
Photoset by Shanta Thawani, 25 Natal Road, London N11
Printed and bound by Billing & Sons Ltd, Worcester

Contents

Foreword by Thor Heyerdahl

The explorer Thor Heyerdahl was among the first to support the Future In Our Hands, Norway's grassroots movement for social change guided from below. In response to questions put to him by Lars Erik Mellqvist, editor of the FIOH magazine Folkevett, he explains what he thinks is fundamentally wrong with today's society and how the ideas presented in *Revolution in the Affluent Society* can help point the way out of the labyrinth.

Repaying our debts

We must pay back a little of the debt we owe to those many countries which today, largely on our account, are poor and in difficulties. We cannot conceal the historical fact that these countries were the cradle of civilization – from them came our written language, art, architecture and religion. But we used these gifts to turn ourselves into bloodthirsty warriors. By way of thanks, we conquered their countries – we are still doing it, exploiting their labour to maintain our dominance. We have gone forth into all parts of the world with violence and power. It's time we tried to make some reparation for this and went out to parley. For a third of humanity, the catastrophe is here already.

Stemming the poison

The *Ra* voyages proved that the oceans are threatened by pollution. Every single town on this planet is by an ocean, a river or a lake. Directly or indirectly, all pollution ends up in the sea. Poisons remain at or near the surface – they don't sink. 90 per cent of the plankton which is the seed of all life on earth, and a major producer of the oxygen we need, is found where these poisons end up. Our planet will not be habitable for many more generations unless something is done about this problem immediately. Humanity must be seen as a part of nature in its entirety, part of the ecological system. Our planet is built in the only way it can be if it is to function as a perpetual motion machine. We humans are merely an offshoot at the top of the tree; the rest has to be there: oxygen, soil and vegetation. We're sitting on a vulnerable branch of our globe. Both rich and poor countries are rapidly destroying the environment. There is no alternative that will get everything to function perfectly. The first rule is to keep within the ecological limits.

Armaments and the artificial economy

In talking about a balance of power, we are trying to make one another believe the greatest nonsense. I remember the last year of the war, when the Allies had got the atom bomb. We were boasting then that we were the strongest, that we had the power. Now it's the other way round. Western propaganda tells us that the USSR is the strongest. If this is true, we must have had a balance of power at a certain point. Why did no one say stop? The truth is that there has been a balance of power all the time. What one has, the other gets. That is why we don't stop. History demonstrates that we have had a balance of power countless times during the last 5,000 years – to no purpose. With bows and arrows. With nuclear weapons. But who is to determine *when* the balance of power exists? We're never going to agree on that. Talking about a balance of power is to blow smoke in people's eyes. It can't continue! Let us come to an agreement and admit that we're stuck in a cul-de-sac because we can't make our artificial economy balance unless the armaments industry keeps going. Rearmament is both completely insane and absolutely necessary in order to carry on with the dead end of our economy. Millions will be out of work in most industrial countries the moment the arms race stops. We must endeavour to find alternative employment for those who are directly or indirectly employed in the arms industries.

The poverty of riches

To me, the distinctive feature of Western civilization is that everything involves making simple things complicated. Instead of going out oneself with a fishing rod, catching a fish in the stream and eating it, we sell the fish to someone who packages it, who in turn sells to someone else who stores it and who sells it to a third person who then sells it to a fourth ... and when it is thoroughly deep-frozen, old and bad, then we buy it for a high price. That, in symbolic terms, is modern Western civilization. We complicate everything we can complicate. We have entered a labyrinth which ends in a cul-de-sac.

The developing countries, however poor they are, still have a great deal to teach us, for example when it comes to a philosophy of living and the enjoyment of life. It is immensely important to make people ask themselves, 'What is it in my surroundings that makes me happy?' It isn't owning a lot or living in the utmost luxury. It is within oneself – as many great men and women have said – that one must seek riches. They are easier to find in a tiny hut than in a big room in a great palace. Here I'm speaking from experience. I've often been in both places – and I know very well in my heart where I am happiest.

Breaking the vicious circle

There is no universally effective medicine that can be prescribed. And none of us can command nations or even families. But I've encountered sound common sense everywhere in the world. The Future in Our Hands movement can open people's eyes. People don't think enough. Public pressure has to be created. And either people listen – as when you talk to your children and say mind that red hot stove – or else they have to burn themselves before they can understand.

Our society has ten to twenty years left to change its course of development.

'It sounds scornful to demand something so remote from us as that we return to a reflection on the meaning of life, since people's passions and follies have reached such proportions and such an intensity, poverty and unemployment are rife, the powerful all over the world maltreat the powerless and humanity has in every respect gone off the rails. But only through reflection do those strengths grow that have some power against all this destruction and all this misery.'

Albert Schweitzer, 1923

Introduction

The aim of this book is to contribute to the discussion of the need for a fundamental change in our social system and an evaluation of the conditions that would make such a change possible. It is therefore addressed particularly to those who are, rather more than most people, concerned with political and social questions. This perhaps seems self-contradictory, since what is proposed emphasizes the importance of a broad process of change, *guided by the majority*. The way the politically involved relate to this process is, however, important. With their influence on opinion, they may either advance or stifle the possibilities of change for the majority.

This book is therefore an attempt to contribute to increased understanding among those with an interest in politics of the popular revolt that is already developing in all 'affluent societies' — a revolt that is manifesting itself in the increasing number of popular movements and grassroots protests against the inhumanity of industrial society.

What are the distinctive features of this revolt? What changes does it point towards – in the conditions of power and control, in technology and work, and in the control and ownership of the means of production?

The title of the book – *Revolution in the Affluent Society* – has been chosen for two reasons. Firstly, it expresses a conviction that the problems that have been created by the development of industrial society are too deeply rooted to be overcome by reforms on the system's own terms; for every problem this social system solves, two new ones seem to arise. This means that the change we need, and which a great many people support, must lead towards something wholly new. This is not to say that this change can or must occur overnight, but that the process of transformation must build on principles that stand in opposition to the fundamental characteristics of our present. The transformation must be radical, that is to say, revolutionary.

Secondly, it should be stressed that it is the transformation of the *affluent society* that is the subject of this book. The opening chapters discuss the most common theories for change and justice in the Third World, but this is only to provide the basis for what follows. The real theme is the need for a change of system in the rich world; a revolution without historical parallel. All previous revolutions have occurred in countries where the decisive motivation for change was the poverty of the majority, and the traditional theories of revolution have been built on this premise. Despite all attempts to make classical revolutionary strategy fit our present situation, it seems clear that it is inapplicable in a society of abundance.

It is necessary, however, to make two qualifications regarding the meaning that may easily be read into the title of this book.

Firstly, the concept of revolution is commonly associated with ideas of violence, whereas the proposition here is based on a non-violent approach.

Secondly, we repudiate the élitist viewpoint which is at the root of so many theories of revolution. Our proposition represents a protest against what the French New Philosopher, André Glucksmann, calls 'master thinking': what is best for people is decided *for* them, not allowed to be developed *by* them. An essential element in this is the hidebound theory that in practice becomes a means to power for the dogmatic élite, as it is too advanced to be evaluated by the majority of people.

The authoritarianism of thought that this expresses has ideological roots on both major political wings. In bourgeois circles and among conservative social-democrats a great deal is derived from Keynes's thinking – the usual short-sighted self-interest of the bourgeois must be channelled and guided by an élite with a higher social consciousness. The same view of the majority is expressed in Lenin's theories which have to some extent influenced more moderate circles on the Left – the revolution must be directed by an élite group of party cadres, because the ordinary worker can never rise above the primitive 'trade-union consciousness' of short-term material interests.

There is much to indicate, however, that the impending revolution is based on an increasingly conscious, popular protest against all the forms of élite control and monopoly of thought that are exercised by many experts, planners, bureaucrats, possessors of economic power, cultural and organizational leaders, and by dogmatic theoreticians. What is brewing in today's pyramidal society is a revolution from below – a revolt for the right of the majority to responsibility and for the legitimacy of the common sense and the values of ordinary people, which many theoreticians have clearly lost sight of.

If this revolt is to amount to more than a scattering of protests, it must build on cooperation between all free-thinking people who share a common view of the fundamental human values and are open to a free debate about their consequences. This demands, among other things, a willingness to put oneself at other people's political points of departure. Talks with members of various parts of the political spectrum suggest that they often lack this sort of general familiarity with the fundamental viewpoints of their political adversaries. Conservatives often know little about Marx's analysis, socialists may have little understanding of conservatives' (and anarchists') fear of unfreedom and state power, and both may be unfamiliar with new ideas that break with the classical theories.

As an aid to communication between these groups, we have included brief accounts of various political theories, including Marx's social analysis, economic liberalism, anarchism, and ideas of Galbraith, Illich and others on making a break with the society of industrial growth. This will not bring anything new to those who are at home in the theories in question, but for others it may.

In order to do these ideas justice, they are introduced by means of quotations, then followed by an evaluation on the premises of this book. This method of presentation has made it necessary to use considerable space to give an account that is at all coherent of Marx's wide-ranging work, *Capital*. Quotations have been used not in order to present the authors as incontrovertible authorities, but rather to allow them to present their ideas on their own terms in the first instance.

It must also be said that the ideas developed in this book should not be seen as an attempt to present a fixed 'ideology'. On the contrary, the book's aim is to contribute to an analysis that is as free as possible – on the basis of a set of values and view of humanity that is its single point of departure.

1. What Is the Real Purpose of It All?

The late Teddy Dyring, a leading Norwegian politician, once considered raising a very elementary question in the Norwegian parliament: 'Herr Statsminister, what is the real purpose of it all?'[1] Unfortunately, the question was never put. But if it had been, it would hardly have been taken seriously. At best it would probably have prompted some platitude to the effect that the goal of politics is to create the best possible society for all, and with that the debate about individual political matters would have continued as though nothing had happened.

What Dyring intended with his question was no doubt to put the political debate into a context which would compel politicians to spell out their view of the fundamental purpose and meaning of existence and of the way in which social conditions could promote the development of that purpose and meaning. It would in any case have obliged not only the politicians, but perhaps all of us, to ask ourselves which values we set highest and what direction we want to move in. It would then have been clearer that even those of us involved in politics and social development are faced with a *choice* of values. We would perhaps have seen more clearly that if conditions are arranged to favour competition for material gain as the most important factor, we cannot *also* achieve maximum freedom and equal opportunities for all – because competition means that some must lose the advantages and opportunities that others gain. We would also have to admit that if we regard freedom for all as the highest value, we cannot at the same time support more freedom for the few that reduces basic freedom for the many; and that, if we believe that people's sense of spiritual values such as the experience of art and nature, living together and fellowship, are more important and more profound than their materialism, we cannot gauge social progress as an increasing craving to work for material values.

And if we put any value at all higher than narrow materialism as a goal for social development, we cannot claim that the majority of people are incapable of working for anything other than precisely that material self-interest. For who is then to steer the majority in the direction of the higher goals we have set ourselves? The answer can only be that one must then regard oneself, and people like oneself, as a human type with a higher moral value, chosen to *lead* the more primitive masses in a positive direction. Such a view, which is not uncommon in political élites, is often based on the idea that 'people' never consider anything but immediate material objectives because that is how the social structure has conditioned them. But the result is the same: one thinks that only one's own élite group can liberate itself from social conditioning and lead the common horde towards something it is not qualified to see the value of. People who are themselves concerned with ideas of a future based on greater solidarity say arrogantly that one must be realistic about people's short-sighted egoism. They are entitled to such a view of 'ordinary people', but then they should openly acknowledge that their view of humanity is based on élitist discrimination.

A political debate such as Dyring wished to provoke – founded on a declared view of the purpose of life and the possibilities facing the human race – would show the ordinary voter what politics is actually about. It would make it possible and necessary for the majority to take a position in relation to the direction and aim of social development. Democracy would be more real, as elections would be a means for ordinary people to exert influence where it really counts, instead of having to take political stand-points on the basis of individual short-term issues, divorced from any overall context.

But the fundamental question of the meaning of it all , of the view of people and values that every political position stands in relation to, is seldom if ever brought into political debate. So we never know what overall development or what fundamental values we are furthering when we vote for or against a certain party, a new traffic scheme, new tax laws, a planned energy expansion or a plan for investment support for industry. And because no one asks us to consider what we actually want to do with our lives and our society, everything is arranged for it *as it is,* and development rolls on blindly towards a future that no one has taken into consideration.

The widespread fear of the future is no doubt due to exactly this, the fact that the question of purpose and meaning has been regarded as out of place and unrealistic for so long that we have stopped believing that taking an overall view of where we want to go plays any part in the course of development.

'The question of the meaning of life and the true nature of human beings is not considered permissible in our culture,' wrote the writer Jens Bjørneboe.[2]

It's like bad language in good company. It's like relieving oneself on the carpet. We have grown used to the fact that the most central question of our lives, about 'the meaning of life', is almost an obscenity – an immoral question that no one with their intellectual virginity intact would be so lacking in decency as to mention. Question meaning and purpose, and one is not a serious person. Yet we cannot live without raising this question which is surrounded by such formidable taboos. And what we must achieve, is to consider our – or our time's – political, social and economic dilemmas in relation to it.

Admittedly, certain disconnected value statements are still used as labels by individual parties. But always in a non-committal way, never as the starting point for a free debate about the overall consistency of these ideas. The voters are obliged to choose between ready-made theoretical systems, marketed with ideological slogans about Socialism for solidarity and Conservative government for the freedom of the individual. But those who try to see these labels as expressing a general moral and philosophical perspective, those who dare to ask whether the party programmes really are the only correct answer to the questions of solidarity or freedom, find that they have played themselves over the sidelines. Such people are regarded quite simply as communist sympathizers or supporters of reaction.

Those who 'sit on their ideologies' want no questions that might upset the house of cards they have constructed once and for all out of opinions and assumptions. They obviously start from a general view of human nature and values. For the more dogmatic among the ideologues (and there is no shortage of them), the only starting point and the only measure is the ready-made ideology itself.

Two examples will be enough to illustrate this point. Try, at a right-of-centre political meeting, to raise the question whether it really contributes to the *majority's* opportunities for free development that a minority of property owners and controllers should have a decisive influence over the majority's working conditions and changing needs. The question will almost certainly be dismissed on the grounds that the only alternative is increased state control or, in the worst case, communist dictatorship. A discussion of possible solutions involving the distribution of power and property, and hence freedom, without élite control is not acceptable because it upsets the established truths of bourgeois ideologies.

Or try, at a meeting of dogmatic socialists, to question whether the traditional wage struggle by workers earning above-average incomes in a rich country really *is* the best way of expressing solidarity with the low-paid in that country and with the poor majority of the world's population. You can rely on being branded a reactionary, or at best naive, for the sole reason that the traditional wage struggle is the only means of weakening the economic power of the property owners, and the only way to a future society based on solidarity. Here too, a free discussion of *other* alternatives, such as, for example, an intensified wage struggle to the benefit of some form of solidarity fund which contributes to the equalization of incomes, is not permitted. The entire question is dismissed by the dogmaticians not because it demonstrates a lack of solidarity, but because it threatens the established truths concerning the correct socialist strategy; because it threatens the master thinkers' monopoly of opinion. Social transformation will be brought about by the struggle of the masses for their own self-interest — and this self-interest has been defined for them by the monopoly of opinion: in all circumstances and at all levels, it is their economic and material growth. Don't try to suggest that the well-paid might see a deeper self-interest in using the proportion of surplus-value they have won back to the benefit of the common interest and the equalization of incomes.

These examples are chosen at random and could be backed up by others from most areas of politics. A truly open discussion of the fundamental questions of values and morality in relation to which most people could take a position is pushed aside on the grounds of what the ideological élite *knows* – a knowledge that others cannot possibly be equipped to judge. And this applies to virtually all political camps.

Naturally the élite of the radical Left will claim that there is an essential difference between what *they* are defending, an ideology favouring the majority and the weak, and the theories of liberal and conservative ideologues, whose sole purpose is the protection of their own economic interests. But it is questionable whether this assertion is tenable in all circumstances. For one thing, there are liberal and conservative ideologues who have no economic or proprietorial interests to defend. It is too easy to defend political beliefs on the grounds that the motives of one's adversary are necessarily more base than one's own. In any case, it is certainly not an acceptable starting point for a debate on what is to be the object and meaning of politics. Of course, it is equally idiotic to suggest, as is often done on the Right, that all socialists want dictatorship and an end to freedom.

But if there are leaders with equally worthy motives in many areas of the political spectrum, and, no doubt, many political opponents who in a debate about fundamental values would find they had the same point of departure, why then are the front lines so absolute? Why do people not defend the elements of their ideology in terms of the fundamental questions that would be understood by their opponent, and by the common voter? Why is the question of 'the purpose of it all' so intolerable?

The experience of many years spent trying to open a debate of this kind seems to show that those who oppose a fundamental rethinking of the issues are certain groups in all parties who have arrogated for themselves a decisive power over popular opinion. These are the ideological élites, the defenders of prefabricated theory, those who think the 'insight' they possess is so absolutely 'correct' and complete that it's simply a matter of teaching people what they have thought out. These dogmatists do not base their discussion on a view of values but on a total ideology. Their position of power depends on their ideology being acknowledged as something absolute, since it is their knowledge of it that raises them above the majority. This form of power is not built on property or material privilege, but on intellectual, theoretical 'superior knowledge'. The contributions these guardians of opinion make to social debate are not intended to help people understand and evaluate the moral basis and general view behind their theories, but to create respect for their theoretical superiority. Indeed, much of this debate, perhaps most of it, is not in any way directed towards the majority the theories treat as their subject, but towards others in the contenders' own élite groups. It is for this reason that hundreds of political books and articles are written giving sophisticated interpretations of existing thought structures, for every single book or article that tackles the fundamental political questions faced by people outside the political-intellectual élite. It is for this reason that what is discussed is not how the values and feelings of the majority can shape development, but how the majority can be influenced and led. It is for this reason that questions concerning values are dismissed as expressions of naivety and a lack of ideological grounding. And it is for this reason that social debate has turned into trench warfare between different theoretical fronts whose defenders never dare to climb out of their trenches to ask each other what they are actually fighting about – a word war above the heads of the silent majority in no-man's-land.

Of course, this lack of respect for ordinary people and their basic outlook is not characteristic of all intellectuals. In intellectual and political circles, too, there are many, perhaps a majority, who want to climb out of the trenches of rigid ideology. But it is the dogmatic élite that dominates the debate and the party apparatus, inspires the humble admiration of the party press, and secures so many column inches for its analysis. And the élite's contempt for what is 'ideologically unsound' frightens most questioners into silence. The élites occupy positions of intellectual power and their weapons are all-embracing ideologies.

The appetite for power and the arrogance of the ideological élites is found on both Right and Left, says the French New Philosopher and post-Marxist, André Glucksmann, in his book *The Master Thinkers*.[3] 'Someone will perhaps suggest that the Right hopes to build its rational society from above, while the Left promises to build it up from below. The fact is, the master thinkers take their point of departure neither in the grassroots nor at the top, but in themselves and their science. They are waiting only for one thing – for people to listen to them.'

The increasingly complex structure of political theory has become the élite's exclusive property. Its premises are the basis on which social debate is conducted. By convincing the majority that a set of ready-made opinions represents the only answer to questions of values, the élite prevents people from developing a personal basis and standpoint.

In her book *Economic Philosophy*,[4] the British economist Joan Robinson shows how throughout its history economics has been marked by constant attempts to dismiss the fundamental moral questions. The influential economists have taken pains to make clear that their analyses are 'purely scientific', objective and independent of any moral judgment. But in reality science always builds on a given assumption – an assumed answer to certain fundamental philosophical questions. Science itself does not provide answers to such questions. It is simply a method for analyzing objectively the consequences and connections that can be derived from the given suppositions. It is only with the consciousness that the scientist has *chosen* one of several possible suppositions that the research can be called objective. If scientists refuse to realize or admit that they have made such a choice – because they think their point of departure is the only one possible – their conclusions will be subjective, camouflaged and actually unscientific.

Classical economics in particular has been strongly characterized by false objectivity of this sort. For example, it has been generally assumed, as though it were an indisputable fact, that narrow material self-interest will always be the basic motivation for people's actions and that the exploitation of this motive is the only possible means of creating a good society. This, Joan Robinson suggests, is an ideology to end ideology, because it does away with the moral problem. In this analysis, all that is necessary to achieve the best for all is for everyone to act egoistically. It is an idea, Robinson points out, which goes back 'to Adam Smith, if not to Adam.'

As a rule, the unequal distribution of power and property is regarded not as a moral question but as a sort of natural law – an expression of qualitative differences between the social classes. In other words, economic theories of this sort rest on a basic view of human nature, without any doubts being raised as to the validity of this view in relation to other possible views.

Similarly, current neo-classical economic theory builds on the presupposition that a rising level of consumption will always represent social improvement (which is, to be sure, assumed to diminish gradually).

That growth in consumption above a certain level might *reduce* people's contentment because other values are injured, is not taken into consideration. In analyses of this sort, suggests Robinson, the analysts pretend that ethical judgements are excluded. Everything is presented as a piece of pure logic.

Two generations ago the Swedish economist Knut Wicksell was already maintaining that to camouflage moral standpoints in this way is scientifically indefensible. The fundamental assumption which the theories are based on should at least be stated unequivocally:

> If, for example, we regard the working class as creatures of a lower species, or if, without going so far, we regard them as not yet ready for full participation in what society produces, then we ought to say so clearly and base the rest of our reasoning on this premise. Only one thing is scientifically unworthy – to conceal or suppress the truth, i.e. in this case, to represent the situation as though this class had already achieved everything it could reasonably want or expect, or to rely on unfounded optimistic convictions that economic development inherently tends in the direction of giving the greatest possible contentment to all.

The tendency to suppress the underlying philosophical or moral standpoint that all human values are based on has been dominant in European thought since the breakthrough of the natural sciences in the eighteenth and nineteenth centuries. The objective scientific analysis which was apparently able to find technical and organizational solutions to all human problems seemed to make the question of choosing values obsolete and unnecessary. In the enthusiasm for the scientific method and its necessary claim to objectivity in analysis itself, it was often forgotten that science, too, is used to achieve a chosen *objective,* on the basis of one of several possible general views of existence. Society's ideal figure became the analytical intellectual who disdainfully dismissed all awkward questions concerning the object and purpose of research. Later, watertight bulkheads were built between scientific investigation and value judgements. The stewards of objective truth arrogantly consigned all moral questions to isolated niches outside the reality in which political and practical decisions were taken. Moral judgement became a harmless private concern for dreamers, for the religious and other romantics cut off from life.

Whereas existence had formerly been seen, in general, as a whole in which spirit and matter were parts of the same complete reality, it was now split. On one side was the 'actual' physical reality which could be calculated and explained; on the other, the unreal world of spiritual 'illusions' concerning the purpose and meaning of existence, morality and choice.

Obviously, this separation was never absolute. But even today it represents the main starting point for ordinary social debate. The scientific élite has used it to secure its position and influence. Ordinary, general evaluation in which the majority would be able to participate (and which is perhaps more accessible to non-specialists than to specialist-educated intellectuals) threatened the hegemony of science. By pushing fundamental but 'unscientific' questions aside, the experts have been able to claim exclusive right to all society's important decisions.

One reason for this was unquestionably the weakness of the church and Christian leaders. With its influence over people's values, the church could have contributed to social development built on a clear moral standpoint. Instead, throughout the centuries it has consistently shut its eyes to the revolutionary implications of its ideals of neighbourly love. Instead of demanding the transformation of society in the direction of justice for the weak and the oppressed, the church has maintained the existing split between morality and politics, thereby giving full freedom of manoeuvre to the amoral exercise of power. Christian duty became limited to a question of religious experience and private belief, while the church supported existing injustices, the slave trade and colonization, the military maintenance of oppression, class differences and the power and privileges of a minority.

The Norwegian bishops' unanimous declaration in favour of a new international economic order suggests that the church's view of politics and religion is changing, but many – perhaps most – Christian leaders still uphold the division between personal morality and politics. One of the leading representatives of the Norwegian Missions Association expressed an extremely common attitude among Christians when he said, in 1977, 'It isn't the task of the church or the mission to draw social conclusions from the message one is preaching ... It isn't its task to pronounce on political models for a new world order ... '5

Perhaps it is not surprising that those who are working for social change have largely rejected moral premises. The complacency of the church has led to the very concept of morality becoming associated with efforts to turn interest away from social injustice. The struggle for social justice has had to dissociate itself from such narrow moralizing. But instead of pointing to the actual and full implications of the moral imperative, people have tried to argue from scientific objectivity. As a result, the debate over social conditions and power relations has been left hanging in the air as a matter of unquestionable belief in various theories concerning economic laws. On one side, we have the liberal view of social development as a consequence of the leadership that arises through natural selection in the blind and naturally determined struggle of individuals for economic gain. On the other, the conviction of capitalism's predetermined crisis, collapse and replacement by socialism/communism – brought about by the radical leadership that arises in the same blind and naturally determined struggle for narrow, material objectives.

In practice, both attitudes imply that the majority of people are deprived of power and responsibility, since they are assigned a predefined role in a process governed by economic laws. The suggestion that a consciousness of moral options might strengthen the demand for social change is usually regarded as unscientific and unrealistic on both political wings.

One thing that has gained currency as a result of this tendency is a one-sided interpretation of Marx. As a protest against the camouflaged class-based view (i.e. the particular choice of values and attitude to human nature) which lay behind the claimed objectivity of the classical political economy,

Marx sought to create a 'really' scientific, objective economic analysis. His analysis was based on *historical materialism,* an understanding of history and social development as a process obeying certain laws, where naturally determined conditions shape particular modes of production which in turn determine the main direction of a development proceeding stage by stage, constantly creating new structures of society and production.

In the Preface to his main work, *Capital,* Marx wrote (in 1867) that 'It is the ultimate aim of this work to reveal the economic law of motion of modern society.'[6] The scientific character of his analysis is stressed at several points in *Capital* as a counter to the concealed moral standpoint that characterized the economic theories of the time: the outrageous exploitation of labour and a completely inhuman view of working people were largely represented as a matter of 'economic necessity'. This is the context in which Marx's wish to state clearly his moral neutrality must be seen. Nevertheless, it is not hard to see that Marx had a moral and value-based starting point from which to write his principal work. It is said that Marx was the first social-economic theoretician to acknowledge openly that he took a class-based position. Inherent in this, there is of course a choice of values. And large parts of *Capital* burn with moral indignation at the circumstances of life which working conditions of the time forced on the majority. A single example is enough to illustrate the background to his indignation and to justify it. Marx refers to a report from the health inspector in Manchester which showed that, owing to high infant mortality, the average working-class life expectancy in Manchester was seventeen, and in Liverpool two years lower than this. If a consistent attitude to values had been the basis of the economic debate, who could possibly have objected to the idea that revolutionary change was necessary, without disclosing their self-serving motives? Marx certainly shook many people's convictions, but if he had challenged the false defenders of morality on the clear premise of values, he might *perhaps* have forced people into a debate about the just transformation of society that would have blown even deeper breaches in his opponents' front lines. Instead of the century-old discussion concerning belief in various 'objectively determined' lines of development in the economy, it might have been possible to have a discussion about what we actually want. But the basis which Marx chose for his work on social transformation was not moral, but historical necessity. This is no doubt one of the reasons why Marxists today still avoid the fundamental confrontation between opposing moral systems and their social implications.

Was Marx himself willing to admit that a choice of values and attitudes to humanity lay behind his analysis? Is it right to claim that Marx believed humanity has a predetermined historical destiny that is independent of any moral standpoint?

Certainly, Marx's own statements can be interpreted in various ways. On the one hand, he says: 'It is not consciousness that determines life, but life that determines consciousness ... Consciousness is, therefore, from the very beginning, a social product, and remains so as long as men exist at all'.[7] Such statements, of which there are several in Marx's writings, give no clear indication of how they are to be understood. If they are interpreted as expressions of absolute determinism, then the human being is assigned a passive role in the historical process. They *can* be understood to mean that people are for ever limited to an unconscious struggle for the most primitive material self-interest without the capacity to set themselves higher objectives and to accept the consequences. But this, of course, was precisely the premise of the classical economics which Marx strongly attacked. Why was it important to Marx to work for an alternative analysis which pointed towards change and justice? Why was he not content to let *history* show that the old economists' ideas were unscientific?

Marx's constant insistence on the existence of laws governing the development he was sketching must be understood, as has been said, against the background of nineteenth-century social debate. On the one hand, it was necessary to show what was untenable in the claims of classical political economy as to the permanent and naturally determined character of class differences – and it was necessary to do this on the premise of the overwhelming belief of the time in objective, scientific analysis. At the same time, it was important for Marx to give the working class a belief that it was useful, that history was on its side and that a transformation not only was possible but would come. Ernst Fischer is among the commentators on Marx who think that quotations from Marx such as the above, put forward in a period of heated debate over opposing scientific theories of evolution, should not be taken as assertions that people have no possibility of choice. In Fischer's view, Marx did not regard the evolutionary laws he was outlining as something absolutely determining for human actions, but as laws with the character of *tendencies*. In other words, people themselves decide how historical tendencies are realized, a decision that cannot be made without a conscious or unconscious moral standpoint. In support of this view, Fischer quotes the following passage from Marx's book *The Holy Family*:

> History does *nothing* ... it 'wages *no* battles'. It is *man,* real living man who does all that, who possesses and fights; 'history' is not, as it were, a person apart, using men as a means to achieve *its own* aims; history is *nothing but* the activity of man pursuing his aims.[8]

This view of Marx's, which according to Fischer he never abandoned, clearly gives the human being moral responsibility for choosing ends on the premise of a basic ethical outlook, in the historical situation that exists at any given time. A less dogmatic interpretation of Marx, in other words, ought to allow considerable room for discussion of the values on which our social objectives should be based. Seen in this way, Marx's analysis of historical lines of development may be regarded simply as a tool for a more realistic, goal-directed social reconstruction than those based on pure utopias. Or, as stated in Erling Falk's Preface to the first Norwegian edition of *Capital* (1938): 'The working class had to achieve a realistic knowledge of society and its evolutionary tendencies if it was to be able to advance feasible programmes and mobilize around future goals that development would confirm, instead of constructing ideal societies which are constantly and repeatedly revealed as unrealistic speculations.'[6]a

In other words, a less dogmatic interpretation of Marx might open the way to a more fruitful debate than the hopeless deadlock in the alignment *for* or *against* Marx, which is often taken as though it accounted for all standpoints. It should be made clear that the front lines are not drawn merely by pinning on the labels Marxist or anti-Marxist. Both sides must be willing to make clear their human goals and the values on which they base their suppositions. Only then can the real contradictions be seen. The battle for change that is needed now cannot be defined by words and concepts of which both supporters and opponents have the most divergent understanding. Opposing values are the real issue today. Whether one calls oneself a Marxist or not says little about which side one stands on. 'Marxism?' asks André Glucksmann'. 'Can one seriously use the definite article (*le marxisme*) to denote a single spiritual treasure that is regarded as common property by the deadliest of enemies: the Russian authorities, the Chinese authorities, traitors within the country's frontiers, revisionists without?'[3]

The belief that Marx's historical analysis determines the sort of society that *must* come relieves us of all responsibility for thinking through what we really consider to be 'the purpose of it all'. Only on the basis of such a standpoint, and a willingness to accept its consequences, can the widespread desire for a society built on other values than today's be focused as a powerful force for change in a human direction.

This has probably never been more necessary than it is today when more master thinkers than ever are trying to convince us that a continuation of the existing course of development is an 'objective economic necessity'. It is time to make clear that their 'scientific' conclusions are only valid on the basis of a premise that is becoming less and less probable as time passes, namely that we, the majority of people, *if faced with a choice,* would choose greater material wealth rather than a society based on other values – cooperation and fellowship, equal access to responsibility and personal development, human contact, freedom, peace and stability.

Unrealistic, say the master thinkers, not thinking it worth the bother of even asking people to choose. Who has told us that this is what everything ultimately boils down to? When did we last hear a leading politician state clearly that social development depends entirely on what we ourselves consider to be 'the purpose of it all'?

The choice we are facing of course is not (as the opponents of change often claim) an absolute either/or. Putting human fellowship and spiritual consciousness higher than materialism does not mean denying all value to the material. It does not mean that we must renounce all technological and material goods and go 'back to the stone age'. And above all it does not mean that the disadvantaged and poor must abandon their just demands for material improvement. Such simplifications only serve to camouflage the significant point – the need to take a stand on the values that are to be the *principal* guidelines for our own and society's development. A choice between the motives of economic self-interest and solidarity is only relevant where there is a question of conflict between values; i.e. where an economic objective obstructs or weakens human solidarity and fellowship. Or *vice versa,* where solidarity requires a renunciation of those elements of material wealth which hinder solidarity.

Now it is often claimed that this choice is unnecessary, that encouraging people to work for economic gain creates an economic surplus that society can use to the benefit of other values. But this assertion illustrates exactly the contradiction we are discussing. The narrow *motive* of self-interest that is thereby strengthened, the competition for private material wealth that this presupposes in an affluent society, serves in itself to separate people from one another, both physically and emotionally. In such a society, individuals and groups must be increasingly encouraged to regard one another as competitors, as means serving their own relative status or economic power. There is a clear contradiction between such a view and seeing one another as fellow human beings, as is necessary in a close community. Precisely because the economic criterion is chosen as the *highest* if not the only value in our society, we experience an increasing poverty in the values representing the opposite of materialism – togetherness, common responsibility, social trust. The result is a growing feeling of isolation, neurosis, alcoholism and violence. With economic objectives dominant, this damage can be repaired superficially, but not at the root. The cause cannot be removed because it lies in the choice of values of which this objective is itself an expression.

The alternative to this is not a society without material values, but one in which another *motive* for work and production is encouraged. Such a motive, and the social reorganization it implies, will not occur overnight. It will not be brought about by a political decision alone. But there are many reasons for thinking that it exists in most of us as a repressed wish for a more human life and society. It is not a question of renouncing self-interest, but of making room for other types of self-interest than the material. It goes without saying that the greater our wealth becomes, the lesser interest there is for further material growth in relation to other values – such as having something more profound to live for. And if this is ever to be expressed as a force for change from below, the contradictions between underlying values must be drawn into the debate in such a manner that the choice and its principal implications are clear to the majority of people. A fundamental transformation from below is only possible if ordinary people are respected as being responsible for the basic choice of direction, and not regarded merely as passive tools for the élite groups' control models.

What follows is an attempt to analyze the consequences of such a view of change. Our social development today is driven principally by motives of economic self-interest. This does not mean that values such as human solidarity are absent, but that they are subordinated. And the conflict between economic and human values seems to be ever more clearly marked as development continues. It is today creating such obvious problems for most people that the time for change must surely be here.

The question to raise is therefore this: what fundamental conditions seem to conflict with and weaken the development of such values as human solidarity, fellowship and equal access to freedom, a voice in society, personal and spiritual development? How can the majority of people, by acting and taking a stand on the basis of these values, contribute to a fundamental change of political course? And how can this process be encouraged without élite control?

2. Broadening Perspectives

In the eighteenth and nineteenth centuries, public discussion of economics and social development was, generally speaking, a concern for the upper class alone, and perspectives were limited to the interests of this class. The great majority of wage-labourers and peasants were regarded almost exclusively as tools for the economic objectives of the ruling class. Positive 'social development' was a question of exploiting the remainder of the population as efficiently as possible to the advantage of a minority who, in their own view, represented 'true' society. What could be done for 'the poor' was always a matter of charity, practically never of real changes or transfers of wealth which might have threatened the ruling class's obvious privileges.

Marx cites a quotation from Bernard de Mandeville, writing at the beginning of the eighteenth century, which illustrates the contemporary view of those groups that stood outside the small circle of the privileged:

> Those that get their living by their daily labour ... have nothing to stir them up to be serviceable but their wants which it is prudent to relieve, but folly to cure. The only thing then that can render the labouring man industrious, is a moderate quantity of money, for as too little will, according as his temper is, either dispirit or make him desperate, so too much will make him insolent and lazy ... knowledge both enlarges and multiplies our desires, and the fewer things a man wishes for, the more easily his necessities may be supplied.[6]

What is characteristic in this and other similar statements from the same period is not just the contempt they expressed for ordinary working people, but the narrow perspective underlying them. Economic development was judged exclusively from the perspective of the privileged. Political economy was the economy of the ruling class and what was 'rational' was what served its interests. Contributing to the majority's knowledge and freedom was foolish, because the ordinary worker represented a necessary production expenditure and nothing else.

During the first decades of this century, perspectives gradually broadened. At least the intelligentsia developed a limited insight into the situation of their own fellow citizens. 'The poor' were no longer judged merely as tools, it was now possible to see them as individuals with certain feelings and rights, even if they were biologically destined for a given place in the social hierarchy. In 1932, the Austrian Robert Eisler, then a world-renowned economic historian, expressed this attitude in his book *Stable Money,* where he claims that it is unnecessary and incompatible with modern civilization that there should be widespread poverty in any social stratum. 'With reforms, we can steadily improve the masses' standard of living, without overturning the historical and biological stratification of society, and without any such moral transformation in human nature as one can never hope for.'[9]

But already in Eisler's time, the official social perspective was beginning to show signs of a further broadening. During the thirties, more and more intellectuals grew to regard all citizens as of equal human value. Social stratification was no longer an expression of biological differences but of changeable, social ones. As a theoretical principle, at least, it began to be accepted that all citizens of the same country ought to have something approaching equal opportunity. On the other hand, nationalism flourished. The general sense of common identity within the narrow confines of national frontiers could be turned into outward-facing enmity. The result was five years of war between neighbouring European states.

Today it is difficult to imagine a war within Western Europe. Perspectives have again widened. Even though economic competition between nations continues, there is now a considerable sense of common identity within the major groups of nations. On the other hand, the formation of blocs has created new lines of conflict, between East and West and, even more profoundly, between North and South – between the rich, highly industrialized countries and the poor countries on which the industrialized countries are increasingly dependent for the raw materials of their continuing growth.

The limited global perspective that has prevailed in the rich countries during recent decades is in many respects reminiscent of the ruling class's narrow view of the nation in earlier times. In the first decades following the Second World War, the poor majority in the non-industrialized countries were still largely regarded as people of a different type from us; an inferior race whose want it might be 'prudent to relieve', but only to the extent that there was no obstruction of national economic goals. The poor countries' destitute plantation labourers and the underpaid workers in their industries, dominated by the rich countries, were regarded as the tools of our economic development. Up to the present day, a 'healthy world economy' has been an economy in which the majority of countries and people are exploited to the utmost to the benefit of the dominant nations and their growth. Typical of this are all the representations of our time as the 'age of prosperity' in spite of the fact that an overwhelming and growing majority live in poverty.

Over the last ten years there has unquestionably been a certain change in this narrow global view – a certain further broadening of perspectives. Now it is perhaps more usual to see the world majority in the terms in which Robert Eisler described his own country's working class before the war; it is inconsistent with civilized thinking that there should be poverty in any layer of the world population. The situation of the poor must only be improved 'without overturning the biological stratification' between the world's races and peoples.

The clearest indication that there is still a long way to go to a fully developed, egalitarian, global perspective is perhaps the difference between the ways in which the concept of solidarity is used when it is a matter of nations within one's own region, and when it concerns nations in other parts of the world.

During the United Nations Conference on Trade and Development held in Manila in 1979, Norway's foreign minister made the point that the problems of economic stagnation in the industrialized countries provide an unfortunate background for discussion of the needs of poor countries. In the matter of shipping, in particular, where Norway has powerful interests of its own to consider, it was revealed that the country's previous role as a 'bridge builder' between poor and rich countries had been based not on an expanded global perspective, but on the fact that until then Norway had not had much to lose from such bridge building. Press reports from the negotiations stated that 'despite our generally positive attitude to the under-developed countries, we cannot ignore obvious national interests.'[10]

But as far as the Western industrialized countries are concerned, the demand is precisely that we must *not* let obvious national interests stand in the way of solidarity and common responsibility. Despite the fact that Norway has enough oil and energy for its own use, it is often stressed that saving and perhaps rationing must be accepted as an expression of solidarity with the community of Western industrialized countries and so that our partners may avoid unnecessary shortages. It will no doubt be some time before saving and perhaps rationing become Norwegian policy in order that *poor countries* may avoid unnecessary shortages.

Even among progressive groups in the rich countries, the approach taken in discussions of the right that people in poor countries have for support in their liberation and self-determination is different from what is accepted as a matter of course for underprivileged groups at home. While major transfers of resources to regional development and social security for citizens in difficulty are regarded as just demands, similar transfers of wealth to the populations of poor countries are often depicted as unacceptable charity. When it is a matter of fellow citizens in one's own country, the public expense of assuring everyone's right to education, decent nutrition, health care, work and security is acknowledged without question – and reactionary protests against 'mollycoddling the weak, small farmers, the unemployed and artists' are contemptuously dismissed by a radical élite which eagerly maintains that similar economic aid towards covering the most basic needs of the oppressed in *poor countries* only 'hinders their liberation and self-determination'.

Of course, it is true that the basic problem for people in poor countries is not poverty alone, but the fact that they are oppressed by the propertied class of their own country, with the support of powerful concerns based in the rich countries. But the important point here is that a similar argument is never used against existing attempts at redistribution and public expenditure within the nations. Here, the same radical groups argue the opposite: that a fair sharing of national wealth is a necessary step on the road towards the abolition of oppression and inequalities of power. To maintain that a national equalization of income by means of progressive taxation must wait for a complete restructuring of society would be regarded as cruel and reactionary.

A common argument for this double standard in relation to disadvantaged groups in one's own and in other, poorer countries is that transfers of wealth to poor countries are usually under the control of the rich élites of these countries, and therefore do not contribute to the self-determined development of the poorest. This argument is in many cases correct, but it ought surely to be an argument for directing such transfers towards the basic needs of the majority, on their own terms, rather than for opposing the principle of transferring wealth at all. A willingness to exert political pressure of this sort on the government of countries supplying raw materials presupposes a greater understanding of the price of solidarity – also in our external economic relations.

Tanzania's president Julius Nyerere has argued tirelessly that our perspectives must now be broadened from national and regional solidarity to embrace solidarity with the world's poor majority. If we accept progressive taxation for the benefit of the disadvantaged in our own country, why can we not also accept a progressive taxation of the rich countries to the benefit of the poor countries? Why should levelling of this sort be regarded as charity in the international context, when nationally it is accepted as common justice? 'The fact that in a nation state there is a government which arranges the transfer of wealth, but that in the world there is no equivalent authority to do this work, makes a difference as to how the transfer should be effected. It does not make any difference to the requirement that a transfer be made,' said Nyerere in his address to the Commonwealth Conference in London in 1975. 'Nations which are already wealthy have to accept that they are members of the world, with the right to a fair share of the world's resources, but no more. They have to bend their minds, and their economic and political systems, to achieving a fair internal distribution of their existing wealth. They should not expect to deal with the problems of comparative poverty within their own nations at the expense of people abroad who are poorer than the poorest.'

But we are still unable to see other world citizens with the same eyes as we see our own, says Nyerere: 'The difficulty is, of course, that aid to the poor countries is still looked upon as voluntary and generally as charity, which the government should only give after all the demands of its own citizens have been met. But serious people would not expect poverty within their own country to be dealt with only through charity.'[11]

Socialists in the industrialized countries like to maintain that their perspective is and always has been global, because the social system they are fighting for will put an end to exploitation, both domestically and in relation to the Third World, thus giving the people of the poor countries the means of liberating themselves. But their limited perspective is revealed in the *means* that are chosen on the road to socialist society. No true socialist would accept that the struggle for socialism should take place at the expense of the poorest in his or her own country. But the same consideration is not shown for the far more oppressed and impoverished world majority. Demands for immediate transfers of wealth to ensure the poorest of the world the barest essentials that we take for granted, always come second, after the national wage struggle. Indeed, in practice these workers in poor countries are to a great extent *victims* of the strategy for change followed by the majority of socialists in the rich countries.

President Nyerere underlined this point in his 1972 *Appeal to the Socialists of Europe,* in which he demonstrated the need for a transformation of the world economic ystem structured by the competition between rich countries to increase their own wealth, and the exploitation of poor countries' cheap labour and raw materials. The greatest advantage from the current situation he says, goes to 'the national economies of the rich nations – which include the working class of those nations. And the disagreements about division of the spoils, which used to exist between members of the capitalist class in the nineteenth century, are now represented by disagreement about division of the spoils between workers and capitalists in the rich countries.'[12]

Because the national struggle for justice lacks a world perspective, it is not a struggle for the internal distribution of a fair share of the world economy, but one for shares of the growth that takes place at the poor countries' expense. Because the strategy of socialists in the rich countries takes national economic growth for granted, they in practice act in support of the exploitative international economic system, says Nyerere. 'At present they are the beneficiaries of it – their nations are, and therefore a great deal of the wealth about whose distribution they quarrel with their own capitalists. They must face up to the implication that they are supporting the continued exploitation of the world's poor by their national economies.'

What Nyerere is speaking for here is precisely the broadened perspective in which *both* ends and means are chosen with regard for the weakest, regardless of which part of the world they live in. 'The socialist parties of Europe have to carry over into the international arena that struggle for equality which they have conducted and are conducting within their own nations,' says Nyerere. The point, of course, is not that efforts towards national justice should be reduced, either in the short or the long term, but that the relatively affluent, indeed even the relatively poor in a rich country, should not be given *priority* over the absolutely poor in the rest of the world.

A narrow national and regional perspective is also current among the advocates of the capitalist mixed economy. Although it is supposed in these groups that differences of wealth and income are a necessary incentive to work, it is nevertheless accepted that the state has a duty to provide for the basic needs of the losers in this competition. But this acknowledgement of the most elementary needs of the weakest is not extended to people outside the Western industrialized countries. In dealings with countries in which the majority have not secured even the most fundamental *material* human rights, it is demanded that the rich countries' own growth must be assured before anything else.

Seen in the context of a longer time-scale, however, there can be no doubt that we are on the threshold of a new and final broadening of perspective. A clear historical line runs from the ruling-class view of previous centuries, via the perspectives of nationalism and later bloc formation, towards a real understanding that the ends and means of regional development must be subordinated to consideration of the *human race's* situation and future.

No doubt it seems unrealistic to suggest that, for example, material sufficiency for the unemployed of the poor world should carry as much weight in our national economic debate as our own unemployment problem – but in the longer-term view it is scarcely more improbable than our present social security system and distribution of power and wealth would have seemed a couple of generations ago.

There are also many signs that a global view is developing, not least in public opinion. In all rich countries during the sixties and seventies, countless grassroots movements and groups have arisen with global solidarity as their primary objective. Third World problems, colonial history, the distribution of resources and education about other cultures are all on the way to full acceptance in schools and they will affect the thinking of the coming generation in a way which is quite different from that of their parents. Equitable trade with local producers in poor countries, direct contact between communities in rich and poor countries, local development projects, long-distance adoption, solidarity movements and support groups for liberation movements, study groups and research into the position of poor countries and their development, contact with immigrants in the West as well as peace corps, development aid and missionary work in other parts of the world have all created a network of connections and contacts which are already changing our view of the world. And because this broadened perspective does not weaken but, on the contrary, seems to strengthen our understanding of the qualities of our own culture and other cultures, it also gives us a great deal of feedback from societies that have preserved more of the values we must now try to rediscover.

And even though UNCTAD conferences are still clearly marked by the self-interest of the industrialized countries, the fact that this dialogue is taking place at all is itself an indication that perspectives are broadening.

The increasing and destructive influence of the multinationals on the economies of poor countries may seem to invalidate the assertion of increasing global responsibility. The same can be said of the luxury life of tourists from rich countries in the Third World and their effect on local culture, and the exploitation of poor countries' underpaid labour that results from our investments in the Third World. But what is new and significant is that the negative aspects of these things are being understood by increasing numbers of people in the rich countries. Even those sections of the press that ten or fifteen years ago one-sidedly defended these conditions are now giving voice to an increasing scepticism and debate. And world problems have at least been gaining a steadily growing position on the platforms of political parties.

Certainly, a world perspective has not yet been adopted by the majority in the rich countries, and a globally responsible politics is therefore not yet a reality. It may even seem a long way from being realized. But it is important to see that we are at a turning point. Our feelings of human solidarity and fellowship, and our self-interest in the broadest sense, both point in the direction of a struggle to hasten the creation of a globally responsible politics. And historical development suggests that this struggle is realistic.

3. Development From Above

Given the broadened perspective discussed in the last chapter, it would be meaningless to discuss future objectives for the rich societies without first outlining the framework which consideration of the world majority obliges us to adopt. What changes are needed in the Third World if the human rights that have been mentioned are to be realized in the broader perspective, and what will these changes mean for us?

It is generally accepted today that the most immediate, *tangible* problem the world majority faces is poverty.

In 1976, the Director-General of the International Labour Organization produced a report on conditions in the Third World.[13] The report contained an analysis of the income and cost of living of various population groups. Because of differences in the prices of basic necessities, the actual poverty line is estimated differently in different parts of the world. In Western Europe, anyone with an annual income of less than 500 US dollars per head (1976) was defined as 'very poor'. In Latin America, the corresponding poverty line was put at 180 dollars, in Africa at 115 dollars and in Asia at 100 dollars. According to this method of calculation, the report concluded that the 'very poor' constituted 71 per cent of the population in Asia, 69 per cent in Africa and 43 per cent in Latin America. In all, there were in the Third World more than 1.2 thousand million people – i.e. more than the total population of the industrialized countries — who fell below this severe poverty line. Although this says nothing about other problems, such as lack of access to health care, education, water, hygiene, etc., it is a more than adequate indication of where the human race's main problem lies today.

What has to be changed if these problems, which overshadow everything, are to be solved?

It has been said that the poor countries' population growth and over-population is their basic problem. Although it is of vital importance to stop population growth, making it into a fundamental *cause* can help to conceal the deeper social and political problems which have been shown to lead to a high birth rate. Moreover, there are now clear signs that population growth in the Third World is in the process of levelling out, partly because of the efforts that have been made in this respect in the Third World countries themselves. But the most important reason for not taking overpopulation as a cause of poverty is the fact that the poor countries actually have enough resources and enough cultivated land to feed their populations adequately. The researchers Lappé and Collins,[14] from America's Institute for Food and Development Policy, think they can prove there is not a single poor country that does not have enough food resources for the local population. In relation to this, it should be mentioned that Norway, West Germany and Britain all have less cultivated land per inhabitant than any of the three poor continents.

The conclusion, in other words, must be that there seems to be a lopsided and unfortunate use of national wealth and income in the individual poor countries, and that this lies behind the problem of poverty. The ILO report mentioned above also states that, 'In most developing countries the richest 10 per cent of households typically receive about 40 per cent of personal income whereas the poorest 40 per cent receive 15 per cent or less, and the poorest 20 per cent receive about 5 per cent.'

But income from production in the poor countries is not only distributed unevenly within those countries. A disproportionate part of the wealth that is created goes out of these countries to investors in rich countries and as a contribution to the growth of the industrialized countries. For example, for every pound the rich countries invested in the poor countries during the sixties, *two* pounds were going back to the rich countries as profit on previous investment.[15]

The uneven distribution of income is, of course, also an indication of an uneven distribution of property and political power (an inequality that is largely a historical inheritance from the colonial period). It is evident that in countries where, notwithstanding the poverty of the majority, income is primarily to the benefit of others, the population cannot have any significant influence on political development. In fact poverty, the all-pervading struggle to live, the illiteracy that affects the majority of adults in poor countries and the reduced political activity that is its consequence, have generally speaking given economic élite groups the sole right to determine the poor countries' politics and economies. And this tendency is strengthened by development. In a lecture given in Tokyo in 1976, the Nobel Prize winning economist Gunnar Myrdal said:

Being rather independent of formal constitutions, the underdeveloped countries are governed by an upper class which has seen to it that all egalitarian reforms have been stopped or watered down ... In recent years there has been a marked increase in the number of purely authoritarian regimes which in most cases has meant that countries are ruled by a military junta or a civilian élite which is usually supported by the army. With few exceptions, they have followed the same inegalitarian political line. This has held development back.[16]

Today this economic upper class owns, together with the multinationals, a considerable part of the land in the poor countries, and is almost wholly responsible for determining industrial production and the distribution of the results of that production. In most poor countries, therefore, development takes place 'from above'. It is especially those areas of economic activity which are already most highly developed that are developed further. And this applies in particular to the enterprises that are owned by, and operated to the advantage of, the poor countries' ruling class, alone or in league with the rich world's major companies. The effect of this is clearly damaging for the poor majority in most parts of the world.

Development from above in industry

Development from above leads to both the country's own capital, and capital brought in from abroad, being invested in the élite-controlled major industries rather than in local crafts and small industries. Large-scale industry presupposes an 'infrastructure'; and it is therefore usually established where there are already transport routes, railways or harbours for raw materials and for distribution of finished products. There must be electricity and energy available, water supplies, access to service institutions for banking services, etc., good accommodation and living and working conditions for the élite that administers the enterprise, whether this élite is local or from a rich country. All this leads to major industries being established more and more in industrial centres, thus contributing to the urbanization and centralization that is one of the main problems for the poor population. The capital that is needed for the development of the urban infrastructure is necessarily obtained at the expense of investment capital for the villages and smallholdings where 75 per cent of the poor countries' inhabitants are employed, thereby reducing the possibility of improving the efficiency of important local food production for local use. The resulting migration into the cities has led to an enormous and increasing number of slum dwellers, for whom very few poor countries have the means to provide reasonable accommodation and employment. A secondary effect of this is that more and more people lose contact with the culture and traditions of their own country and become the rootless victims of a bewildering conflict of cultures.

Technological development from above

Because the most important industries in poor countries are usually owned by the upper class or by concerns based in the rich countries which have profit as their highest objective, production is obviously oriented towards sale on the markets with the greatest purchasing power. In other words, production very seldom contributes to the basic needs of the poor majority who lack purchasing power. It is geared to the luxury demands of the élite, or to the manufacture of more advanced goods for export to the rich countries. As a result, this industry enters into competition with the rich countries' highly developed production apparatus and is compelled to develop a correspondingly advanced and automated technology. In practice, this means that more and more has to be invested in machines and energy which replace human labour. And this means that the price of each industrial job steadily increases. According to Robin Clarke, editor of *Science Journal,* each job in a society with advanced, capital-intensive technology costs 350 months' or twenty-nine years' wages, whereas in a labour-intensive economy with simpler technology it requires perhaps the equivalent of six months' wages to buy the necessary equipment for one job. The combined investment capital therefore provides for very few jobs and comes nowhere near creating employment for all those seeking work in expanding urban areas. Even according to standard economic criteria, this is uneconomic in a country with unemployment and a shortage of capital. According to the 1976 ILO report, 'the performance of small units, employing a combination of traditional and intermediate technology generally compares favourably with large-scale units on the efficiency indicators of particular relevance – capital/output, capital/surplus coefficients ... and personal propensities to save and invest.'[13]

The increasing degree to which energy and capital is tied up in urban centres naturally hampers corresponding investment in rural areas where the same capital might have provided work for many times more people in local agriculture and craft production. Production by the poor for their own food and other needs stagnates, the increase in population is channelled even more towards the towns, where unemployment often rises to disastrous levels. According to the ILO report, in 1975, a total of 40.4 per cent of the poor countries' combined population was wholly or partially unemployed.

Another effect of élite-controlled, technological development from above is that its complex production equipment requires a highly educated administration which is largely brought in from the rich countries, thus increasing the dependence of the population, further reducing the majority's possibilities for control of national development, and weakening their national culture and self-confidence.

Development from above in agriculture

As we have seen, the major landowners in poor countries are multinational firms based in the rich countries and an upper class which willingly cooperates with them. To an increasing degree, these landowners have been using modern, capital-hungry machinery, artificial fertilizers and equipment for increasing efficiency and production, which are unavailable to small farmers. Moreover, new high-yield crops such as have been developed by the 'green revolution' have mainly benefitted these landowners and big farmers, because these new crop varieties need more in the way of artificial fertilizers, plant protectants, machines and irrigation systems than the small farmer can possibly provide. The result has been that the small farmers have, on the whole, lost in the competition with big farmers. Many can find no market for their surplus production. They have too little capital to maintain their own operations, they are compelled to sell their land to big landowners, and they join the underpaid army of farm and plantation workers. Because poverty and illiteracy has reduced their occupational and political influence, the proprietors have largely been able to hold wages down to a level which does not even allow workers to buy the food they once produced themselves. And because the majority's purchasing power is too weak, the big landowners prefer to produce for the luxury market of the local élite and the industrialized countries.

Contrary to what is often claimed, this mechanization and large-scale production results in a lower production per unit area than equivalent subsidies to more labour-intensive small farms could have yielded. Here, the ILO report says: 'Small farmers are likely to utilize land more fully than large farmers ... Output per hectare tends to rise as the size of operational holding falls. Agrarian reform is thus likely both to increase the supply of basic food and to ensure that it is distributed to some of those in greatest need.'[13] (Here it is assumed, of course, that the capital input per hectare is the same in both instances.)

Development from above in education

The ruling class in poor countries have generally obtained their position by trading and collaborating with enterprises based in the rich countries. In many cases, this has distanced them from the culture and the problems of the majority. Instead many have been influenced by the norms and development objectives of the rich countries. One result of this is that the élite's increased access to higher education on the industrialized countries' pattern is often given priority over basic education for the majority. The means that could have been used for simple, cheap and practical education for the many are largely used for the élite education of the few. In this way the élite's position in politics and cultural life is further strengthened at the majority's expense. Because this investment in costly higher education has mostly been dominated by the rich countries' cultural outlook and social objectives, it has also been largely useless to the poor countries, being to the benefit of the rich nations instead. Admittedly, highly educated specialists are constantly going from rich to poor countries, but emigration in the opposite direction, the 'brain drain', has been far greater. At the beginning of the seventies, for example, 16,000 technical advisors went to poor countries each year, whereas 40,000 graduates from the Third World emigrated to higher-paid jobs in the rich world.

Development from above in health care

With the help of rich countries, many Third World governments have spent a great deal of money on extending modern hospitals and training doctors according to the pattern of rich countries. Considering the enormous unmet need for medical aid in all poor countries, this too has been done at the expense of providing simpler means of health care for the majority. China's simple but extensive system of 'barefoot doctors' has had a certain influence in some places, but development from above still predominates.

Some people claim that the poor countries' élite-controlled 'development from above' in industry, agriculture and education will have secondary effects that will later benefit the poor, the bases of this argument being that it was precisely this type of development that created affluence for the majority in the industrialized countries.

The non-industrialized countries are, however, in quite a different situation from that of preindustrial Europe. In the first place, a considerable part of the surpluses of capital and raw materials that were the basis of the industrial revolution were procured through the exploitation of other parts of the world. For several generations, the 'triangular trade' was an important, capital-generating element in the European economy: the export of cheap industrial products to Africa, the transport of slaves from there to America, and their exchange for American raw materials which were brought back to Europe. This, and the immensely profitable exploitation of the colonies, unquestionably quickened the pace of our industrial development. At the same time, it was possible to reduce our population growth, which incidentally was greater than it has ever been in the Third World, by emigration to other continents.

The peoples of the Third World have none of these possibilities. Their capital and raw materials are mainly *exported* and contribute to growth in other societies. Unlike the rich countries, which in the industrial revolution were able to arrange world trade to suit their own objectives, the poor countries today are confronted by an international market economy dominated by the industrial countries which channels a large part of their resources and trade surpluses to other parts of the world where purchasing power is located. This entire pattern subjects the poor majority to a *double* oppression, by a national governing élite which contributes to uneven distribution and development within the country, and by the rich countries and their powerful concerns which, economically and often with military threats and interventions, oppose revolutionary changes that might lead to the takeover by the people of their property, or to a popular government which might weaken the rich countries' trading privileges and access to raw materials. (According to press reports in June 1979, both France and the USA are specially training troops to intervene, if necessary, to secure oil supplies from abroad. A little earlier, the chairman of NATO's military committee had stated that 'people in military quarters are very concerned for the security of NATO's vital raw materials ...).[17]

Development from above is clearly a most inappropriate means of helping the impoverished masses of the Third World. Brazil's conspicuous development from above under its military regime, for example, raised the annual growth in gross national product from an average of 1.4 per cent to over 10 per cent — meantime, real wages for an ordinary Brazilian worker *dropped* by 32 per cent between 1964 and 1968. The problem of poverty remains as acute as ever. This is no isolated example: the 1976 ILO report states, 'There is no doubt that the numbers of the poor have increased, in spite of the rapid economic growth in most developing countries. The calculations were made for 1963 as well as 1972, using the same income distribution.' The report's tables show that the number of 'very poor' increased during this period in all three underdeveloped continents by a total of 119 million.

This should be sufficient to show that the existing model of development for the Third World at best leads to such a slow alleviation of the majority's poverty and oppression that it cannot be acceptable to anyone who takes a world view of human solidarity and fellowship.

It therefore seems clear that we must support a fundamental transformation of social conditions in most poor countries and that this transformation must start from the right of the poor majority to freedom, to a reasonable share of their countries' production, and to control over their own countries' development. Control over one's own circumstances and social development is synonymous with an equal right to freedom and personal development, and is also likely to be the best means of eradicating poverty.

When the majority have the political and organizational strength to determine the ends and means of their national development, problems resulting from development from above will be effectively counteracted.

As the peoples of poor countries are mainly involved in agriculture, they will in all probability make a more just distribution of landownership a priority. It is also likely that they will want to invest their social resources in more appropriate technology that can benefit them through increased food production and the greatest possible number of jobs in local crafts and small industries producing for their own use.

Similarly, there are reasons to suppose that a truly democratic government would want to meet the population's own needs before using any surplus for more advanced, export-geared development. It also seems probable that the majority would prefer export and trade to be directed more towards equal partners in the Third World than towards the highly industrialized countries that have hitherto dominated the terms of trade.

Finally, it is reasonable to suppose that decentralized popular administrations, far more than the élite regimes dominated by the rich countries, will want to take over foreign-owned property hindering their own development – and that they will demand radical changes in the current economic world order.

One thing should be made clear at this point: development from below does not automatically commence when a new élite group takes power and calls its regime a 'people's' or 'socialist' government. The decisive factor is whether the new government is willing to decentralize its power by giving people the opportunity and means of directing development according to their own local needs and interests. And this voluntary relinquishment of power does not seem likely as long as illiteracy and organizational weakness presents people expressing their demands and wishes. Of course, every Third World government will make the eradication of poverty a *verbal* priority, but the voluntary relinquishment of power is not a common phenomenon, as Gunnar Myrdal said in his address to a symposium on the economic world order in Sweden in 1978:

> I know of no developing country where official policy has set out to abandon the masses to poverty, to the advantage of other layers of the population. But in the existing conditions of power, development is confirming the historical experience that no ruling-class group has ever climbed down from its privileges and let go of its monopoly position simply because of its good intentions and ideals. There has to be pressure from below to give the ideals power. For the most part, this pressure is absent or ineffective in underdeveloped countries.[18]

So how can the necessary development from below on the premises of the majority in the poor countries be supported by the rich countries that up to now have mainly obstructed or restrained such changes? And what will the broadened perspective on solidarity and common responsibility mean for us?

Let us look briefly at some of the theories that are most commonly discussed in this context, and the possibilities and problems they present – in the light of the basic values we have set out as fundamental to any change.

4. Four Types of Theory Concerning World Problems

New International Economic Order theories

Many people discuss the 'New International Economic Order' as though it will automatically remove poverty and oppression in the Third World. So far, however, it has been very unclear what this change in the existing world order will eventually come to mean.

The principle is to improve the economies of poor countries by giving them greater opportunities to profit from the international market economy through various attempts at regulation. For example, a commodities fund is to be set up to limit fluctuations in price of raw materials produced by the poor countries which result from variations in supply and demand. Proposals have also been put forward for cheaper loans, provision for the devaluation of poor countries' currency, improved exchange conditions, greater access to rich export markets, support for industrialization, and the processing by developing countries of their own raw materials.

Some advocates of the New International Economic Order regard it as much as a means of increasing the rich countries' wealth as of increasing that of the poor countries. By making certain concessions which hasten the development that is already taking place in poor countries, they hope to increase their purchasing power, thereby creating new markets for the rich countries' products. In practice, this means that the changes are likely to reinforce rather than undermine the property relations and the development from above which secures our interests and suppresses those of the majority in the poor countries.

Other NIEO supporters undoubtedly have a broader outlook and regard these proposals as steps on the way to a fairer distribution both between rich and poor countries and within the poor countries themselves.

If the NIEO strategy is to be the only, or the dominant, approach to change, there is, however, much to indicate that it may conflict with the demand for 'development from below'. Taken in isolation, any of the measures mentioned above would seem to strengthen the economic élites in the poor countries, who have up to now opposed a just distribution of wealth, income and social control. If no other changes occur, the improvement of the national economy is likely to be taken in hand by those who own the poor countries' export and trading concerns – i.e. precisely those groups that support the politics of development from above. It would therefore be only a minority who obtained increased purchasing power. And because the global economy is still seen as basically a market economy – that is, one directed according to maximum profit for big business – increased world production would simply continue to be channelled to the privileged groups with the greatest purchasing power.

The problem is that, with few exceptions, those who negotiate on behalf of the poor countries in the tug of war over the new world order are in no way representatives of the majority's interests, but rather of ruling-class interests. As Gunnar Myrdal has clearly pointed out:

> All negotiations and transactions with developing countries have to be conducted with the ruling, upper-class élite, which obstructs or distorts the reforms that are needed in order to promote equalization of incomes and greater economic growth. They are representatives of the élite who take part in conferences between states, where they have pressed for a new international economic order. But none of them has said a word about the need for a new economic order at home in their own countries.[16]

The same scepticism is expressed in the 1976 ILO report,[13] which states: 'The very poverty of the poor, and their lack of resources, insulates them from most of the benefits flowing from the faster currents of world commerce ... a rearrangement of international trading relations of the type discussed is unlikely to have a significant and immediate impact on mass poverty and inequality.'

Another problem is that proposals for a New International Economic Order contain very little pointing towards a reduction of the multinationals' property and power in poor countries, or of their undesirable large-scale production, their appropriation of vital agricultural production for export and their profit at the expense of the underpaid majority. This is not particularly surprising, since the Third World's negotiators often belong to groups whose political and economic power rests on collaboration with the multinationals.

One further, important problem with NIEO is that if it is based on the international market economy, it will contribute to a big increase in global industrialization, in large-scale production, in the exhaustion of natural resources and the ecological consequences that this involves. Even when it is regulated, the driving force of market-based economic activity is the profit motive, whether the profit is the nation's or the company's. If this driving force is to be maintained, enterprises must be given opportunities for expansion through competition for large-scale production profits, in which NIEO will increase the poor countries' opportunities for participation.

This is not to say that the New International Economic Order under discussion is necessarily worthless if combined with attempts to support liberation and self-determination for the majority. Whatever we may wish, the change in nutritional structure that is needed in over a hundred poor countries in the world can scarcely be brought about in the next few years. This means that for some years millions of the Third World's poor will probably be dependent on employment within the *existing* terms of world trade. It is imperative that in the short run they should be given support for a takeover of power in order to start development from below and build a more equitable distribution of national wealth and income. But how much income there is to be distributed will, no doubt, initially depend on the advantages that individual countries can secure through new structures within the established forms of world trade and division of labour. Certainly, countries that have already achieved social control by the majority and an equitable distribution of income regard the New International Economic Order as a contribution to their immediate economic objectives. Tanzania's President Nyerere has expressed the view that both a short-term change in the world's economic order *and* a total transformation of the structure in the long term are necessary, even if the individual Third World country is pursuing a policy of internal redistribution: 'The truth is that however much we reorganize our economic system to serve the interests of the mass of the people, and however much our government tries to weight the income distribution in favour of the poorest people, we are merely redistributing poverty, and we remain subject to economic decisions and interests outside our control.'[11] With regard to levelling the inequalities between poor and rich countries by means of changes in the economic world order, Nyerere says: 'Measures to make the world system work automatically in the direction of reducing the gap are, to our way of thinking, absolutely crucial.' But he also states that, 'In truth, the problem of poverty, and of the national dependence and humiliation which goes with it, will only be tackled at the root when the endless pursuit of economic growth for the sake of growth ceases to be the major objective of national and international policies.'

The New International Economic Order may therefore be one among many simultaneous steps on the way to a world with equal rights for all. But only one step. The long-term solution demands a change in the actual goals and content of world trade, making it able to meet the most basic needs before the demands of the wealthiest. And this appears difficult or impossible without a transformation of the economic objectives and social systems of the rich countries themselves, to which we shall return later.

Theories of revolution

In their most consistent form, these are based on the assumption that gradual economic changes, both national and international, only serve to reinforce an unjust system, while obstructing the decisive, popular takeover of social power, land and the means of production. Therefore we in the rich countries should concentrate our efforts on supporting socialist liberation movements.

There are, however, reasons for wondering whether this theory, if advanced one-sidedly, does not conflict with the demand for solidarity and equal rights on a world scale. As we have seen, scarcely any of the rich countries' revolutionary theorists would regard efforts towards redistributing income to the benefit of the low-paid and disadvantaged in their *own* countries as inessential or a hindrance to a just future society. Should not, then, a demand for similar transfers of wealth directly to the really poor of the world be a natural expression of the principle of equality? (Although this kind of transfer is very difficult, there are many instances of direct contact and transfers between grassroots groups in rich and poor countries which show that it *is* possible. If there was more political pressure, it would grow. Both Myrdal and Nyerere have recently made statements on this.)

The question is, does not one-sided work for revolution in the Third World without a parallel attempt to meet the basic needs and education of the majority lead to just another form of 'development from above' – an élite-controlled social upheaval on behalf of a majority lacking the strength and developmental background to take part in the determination of new social objectives and the new 'people's' government?

Would not a majority that has been given support and time to develop its health, its own strengths, political activity and organization be able to carry out more quickly and more effectively the revolution that *it* needs, and would it not be better assured of freedom in the post-revolutionary society?

If our solidarity with the poor countries is also expressed in terms of economic support for development from below and for the preparation of a *majority-guided* revolution, would this not reduce the need for violence in the takeover of power?' And would not a non-violent, majority government be much more likely to ensue? Why then should any local, economic support for self-determined development of this sort outside the often limited scope of the liberation movements, if it is based on sincere solidarity, be branded as reactionary – as it is in practice by so many theoretical models of revolution?

This question should not be dismissed with the usual dogmatic arguments. It is important because this one-sided outlook on the process of transformation creates unnecessary conflict between groups in the rich countries which are trying in different ways to work for the same end, on the same premise of international solidarity. The development of *broad* support and participation in the rich countries, which globally responsible politics must ultimately rest on, is thus held back.

The question of cooperation between those supporting development from below and those supporting revolution is also important because there is much to indicate that revolutions without a previous strengthening of the majority's ability to participate lead not to liberation but to oppression. 'Long after one has got rid of the parasite, the bourgeois,' says André Glucksman, 'there remains the public person who puts things in order by organizing and sharing out the socially necessary work, and the private person who becomes the victim of this.'[3]

The idea that the revolution and future society must be formed *for* the people, and not *by* the people, has again and again created revolutions which have developed into a parody of popular freedom and democracy. Even the Chinese revolution, which without doubt rescued hundreds of millions from material need and capitalist oppression, has shown itself to be wholly dependent on the varying objectives of the revolutionary élite. And who can guarantee that new Chinese leaders will not reintroduce the economic inequalities of the past? In his book *China – Return Ticket to Revolution*,[20] Jan Bredsdorff shows how, time after time, his Chinese friends have changed direction, following new leaders and then condemning them, only to idolize them again later, following new ideological principles and then similarly turning 180 degrees, all at the slightest signal from the cadres and the party leadership.

China's revolution was unquestionably necessary, but can its instability be explained in any other way than by the denial of the people's right to develop their strength and consciousness as the basis – indeed the precondition – of introducing a people's government? Does not the same one-sided theory lie behind the belief that the revolution alone is all that is needed and that any other expression of solidarity though support for self-determined development and popular participation is to be seen as reactionary?

It must be asked whether this dogmatic belief in revolution as the only solution to all problems may not also express a theoretical alienation, a lack of insight into the situation of the people with whom one wishes to show solidarity. When theory replaces reality, when an interest in people's actual needs, wishes and immediate objectives is dismissed as something unimportant, then what is also dismissed is the ordinary sympathetic solidarity that can and must be developed among the general public in the rich countries. In this way, participation in a broad development in the rich countries on the basis of solidarity between all peoples is reduced to a question of learning to think according to élitist models.

Revolutionary theory points towards a change that is necessary, and probably inevitable in some form, in most poor countries. But when it is presented one-sidedly and dogmatically, its effect is counterproductive and it can in reality be inhuman and lacking in human solidarity.

Ecological theories

The growing consciousness in the industrialized countries of the long-term consequences of continuing our industrial growth on the present lines has itself helped to broaden perspectives – both in geographical and chronological terms. Biologists have shown how our technological interference is upsetting the finely balanced interdependence of innumerable life forms over the whole earth. Ecology, the study of wholeness and interrelationship in nature, has created a general understanding that we are approaching limits where the cumulative effects of our interference in nature are beginning to interact with one another, creating unforeseen natural catastrophes and ecological crises.

Ecology knows no national frontiers. When our national economic objectives, for example, lead us to support bauxite production in Brazil, we are contributing to the current destruction of the forests in the Amazon basin. Experience from other parts of the tropics shows us that interference of this sort can start processes which gradually reduce vast areas of forest to desert. As a result, we risk climatic changes with effects on our biological environment. Ecology demonstrates that, biologically, the human being is not an external 'user' of nature, but part of it like other mammals. This understanding gives human beings a responsibility for all life, for the totality and for the future.

The solutions that have been proposed for ecological balance are also relevant to our main economic problem, the poverty and oppression of the majority. Here, eco-Marxists use a model which describes both the world community and the individual nations in terms of a division between growth centres (metropolises) and exploited peripheral areas (satellites). According to this model, certain parts of the world, the industrialized centres, are degenerating through overdevelopment. These centres, which exist in both rich and poor countries, base their growth on the exploitation of peripheral areas (in both rich and poor countries), which, as a result, remain underdeveloped, being obstructed in their own natural development. The rich countries, which are the dominant national centres in this development, draw people away from primary production in their own peripheral areas in order to satisfy the demands of industrial growth, and in so doing they become increasingly dependent on raw materials from other parts of the world. The battle for sources of raw materials which thus arises makes it necessary for industries in the rich countries to maintain bridgeheads in the form of collaborating centres in the Third World and to protect these with an enormous and growing military apparatus.

This situation, however, creates increasing problems for ordinary people both in the exploiting centres and in the exploited peripheries. Not only are ecological problems created by the plundering of nature and resources; workers in centres of growth also suffer from the inhuman social and working conditions that result from mechanization and centralization, while workers and peasants in the peripheries gradually lose their independence and the basis of their lives.

The solution that is proposed is based on, among other things, the development of a more environmentally appropriate, small-scale technology in both rich and poor countries – a technology to replace complex, automated, impersonal large industry with smaller and more labour-intensive local industries, crafts and agriculture. More surveyable activity of this sort would allow room for individual creative development, it could more easily be controlled locally and it would consequently be organized to produce for local use, using local resources.

This solution presupposes and would promote a greater sense of values other than the narrowly material, not least in the industrial countries' centres of power. As well as restructuring our way of life and economy, and developing our own independence and self-sufficiency, we have to withdraw from the existing international structure of production and trade, especially in relation to the exploited Third World countries. We must also actively oppose the multinational concerns and their allies among the wealthy of the Third World, and free ourselves from the great economic and military blocs that obstruct new development. This would reduce the pressure on the impoverished masses and make possible their own liberation and cultural development, from which we have a lot to learn.

This theory, in its pure form, often leads to a negative view of transfers from rich to poor countries because such transfers create economic and cultural dependence, and conflict with the principle of self-reliance. Reference is often made to the many instances in the Third World in which aid has reinforced development from above.

This ecological theory nonetheless raises a number of important questions. As a model for a future solution it seems to accord with the basic principles of solidarity and human fellowship, since it opposes giving support to oppressive development from above in countries of all types, and gives all individuals greater access to freedom and development on their own terms. The question is, however, whether *in the short term* it protects the interests of the poor majority to the same extent as those of our own populations.

Any restructuring presents social and economic problems. The transformation the ecological theory would like to see in the individual *rich* countries involves public investment in new types of activity while old social structures are gradually altered. This means concentrating on new planning and research. New institutions must be built at the same time as the old ones are maintained, in order to avoid an economic collapse injuring our own populations. There will probably be costly conflict between different interest groups in the country. The champions of change will not be able to risk turning the population against them by allowing the disadvantaged to suffer. It will always be a matter of rebuilding the ship as it travels. We have the national economic strength to achieve this, if the population is willing to share the costs and the problems according to their different abilities to do so.

The poor countries, however, lack this economic surplus, and their poor have no political means of securing themselves in the same way against the short-term problems of change. For generations, they have been forced into activities and conditions of work based exclusively on trade with the industrialized countries. Their production apparatus is built for export to rich markets and every drop in demand instantly reduces its need for labour – while it necessarily takes time and money to set up new jobs.

The ecological theory presupposes precisely this sort of reduction of our trade with the Third World and of our consumption of Third World goods. If this is not combined with economic support, the immediate effect would be catastrophic for the many poor countries whose entire economy is based on exporting a narrow range of raw materials for our major industries. At the same time, they lack the social apparatus and workers' organizations needed to prevent the repercussions from striking the weakest. Indeed, the existing élite, who will still hold power when any such change begins, have enough power to make sure that the decline hits the majority before themselves.

What conclusion can we draw, then? Must not the answer, assuming basic principles of worldwide solidarity, be this: the ecological objective seems correct and necessary for the liberation and self-determined development of the majority, and it clearly provides an important supplement to the theory of revolution, – but we do not have the right to sacrifice the *most* disadvantaged in the process. If we neither can nor will abrogate our responsibility for ensuring that the transformation does not harm disadvantaged groups in our own country, then equally we cannot deny our responsibility for avoiding similar harm to the world's weakest.

This suggests that the ecological theory could be inhuman in practice if it were followed dogmatically as a model for change allowing no room for other approaches which are able to compensate for short-term damage.

Admittedly there are, even in the poor countries themselves, liberation theorists who dismiss all proposals of transfers or economic support from outside, and one can understand them. The evidence is discouraging. Until now, the industrialized countries' so-called 'aid' has contributed mainly to the economic projects of the poor countries' élites and our own industrial and growth-directed objectives. And as long as our demand that our own wealth continues to grow, and our belief in our own model of culture and growth, remain unshaken, there will still be grounds for scepticism regarding our supposed solidarity. But what we are discussing here is the restructuring that will follow the adoption of the new objectives that are gradually being developed in the rich countries, ones based on new values and opposition to our own industrial growth. Only through this change of course can new and positive support for self-determined development from below become not only possible but necessary. While our growth objectives have till now put us on the side of the poor countries' élites and have in practice contributed to the oppression of their majorities, a new attitude to growth could put us more consistently on the side of the poor. Or, as Gunnar Myrdal says, 'If a change in people's attitude to growth and environment in the rich countries ... should become a reality, and if these rich countries wish to increase their payments to developing countries, then this would undoubtedly make it possible to exercise a quite different influence on their policies than today.'[16]

A restructuring in the direction of reduced consumption, production and imports in the rich countries will do little in the next few years but create problems for the world's poor unless it is combined with direct support for those who suffer its initial effects. The FAO's vice-director, Keith Abercrombie, pointed out in an article addressed to the Norwegian government's Development Aid Organization that it is necessary to acknowledge the poor countries' need to sell their agricultural products to industrialized countries in order to obtain the foreign exchange necessary for the imports on which they are still dependent: 'Reduced consumption in the rich countries scarcely helps them. In all probability, a reduced consumption in the rich countries would only compel them to go over ... to other cash crop products for export.'[21]

At the same time, the production of agricultural products for the rich countries is clearly not acceptable for people who need all the land they have for their own food production. Can there be any solution other than that we, while extricating ourselves from this 'bloodsucker trade', provide compensation in the form of direct transfers to those who are the first to be hit by decline?

In practice, of course, this means far more politically directed transfers to poor countries than there have been previously. It follows from our new objectives that we must *insist* that every such transfer be disposed of locally, by the poor countries' poor themselves, on their terms and in support of local work, education and the meeting of basic needs, thus benefitting development from below. The Third World representatives who oppose such support can surely not be speaking on behalf of the working majorities in Third World countries. It is hard to imagine that, among the oppressed themselves, anyone would oppose unconditional support for liberation from powerlessness and for the realization of their own objectives.

Lecturing in New Zealand in 1974, Nyerere argued that development aid can make a big contribution, if it is given and accepted for what it is – a possible catalyst for local development'.[22] And direct, local aid of this sort need not necessarily wait until political development in the industrialized country in question has been restructured. If the groups in the rich countries who wish to hasten the transformation combine their opposition to globally antisocial growth in consumption with such 'interlocal' transfers, they will be contributing to an understanding of the two-sided politics which, it seems, must come into being: on the one hand, an end to a trade and world order dominated by the industrialized countries; and, on the other, political and economic support for development from below in the Third World.

The idea that there is a contradiction between supporting liberation movements or political change in Third World countries, and a willingness to provide direct, unconditional economic aid towards basic needs, seems again to result from an unnecessary theoretical one-sidedness. In reality, it is reasonable to think that one ought to work to the advantage of the other. Or, in the words of the ILO report:

A basic needs-orientated policy implies the participation of the people in making the decisions which affect them ... . For example, education and good health will facilitate participation, and participation in turn will strengthen the claim for the material basic needs. The satisfaction of an absolute level of basic needs ... should be placed within a broader context – namely, the fulfilment of basic human rights, which are not only ends in themselves but also contribute to the attainment of other goals.[13]

The report also says that 'collective self-reliance is a distinctive feature of basic-needs strategies. This does not, however, rule out the use of external resources in the service of such strategies.'

Development aid theories

Economic aid to underdeveloped countries and peoples is a principle accepted by most people, but opinions vary as to how aid should be provided. Some people prominent in public life maintain that 'aid' should be given in the form of support for the operation of our own businesses in the Third World. This, however, so obviously contributes to development from above that little more will be said about it here. It of course represents support for the development plans of many poor countries' élites, but for precisely this reason it only strengthens the élites' power to perpetuate policies of inequality. It is time that the concept of 'aid' was divorced from this form of support for the increase of our own wealth and that of Third World élites.

Many people in the rich countries regard government transfers to development projects in cooperation with the governments of poor countries as the only, or at least the most important, means of eradicating poverty. The principle of development aid is itself an expression of the broader perspective we are developing. But because in all industrialized countries our own increasing affluence is still given priority over principles of solidarity, the scale of development aid has generally varied according to the industrial countries' own economic growth. Thus, the combined development aid from the Western industrialized countries, measured in real terms, was actually somewhat *lower* in 1972-3 than in 1964.[13] Measured as a percentage of the donor countries' combined gross national product, it fell over the ten years from 0.48 per cent to 0.33 per cent, despite the fact that it was increased in certain countries such as Sweden and Norway. In many cases, aid has also clearly been tied to the donor countries' own economic interests through the requirement that the money must be used to buy goods from the donor country.

The primary demand that the rich countries' own affluence be assured has also diminished the significance of development aid in several ways. For one thing, many rich countries have given aid to patently reactionary regimes, with the obvious intention of securing their cooperation with the donor country's domestic economic interests. When Allende came to power in Chile in 1971 and tried to change his country's development from above for the benefit of the majority, the Inter-American Development Bank, the International Monetary Fund and the World Bank stopped all credits to Chile. When Allende fell and the military junta restarted an oppressive development from above in collaboration with the rich countries' giant concerns, the Inter-American Development Bank approved the biggest loan that had ever been made to Chile.[23]

Certain rich countries, including Norway, have increasingly channelled their development aid towards countries which give priority to the interests of the majority, and have preferred to support projects promoting development in agriculture and rural areas. But even this help does not contribute to the most necessary change – the liberation of the majority of Third World populations, whose growth towards self-determination is held back by élite power. At the same time as supporting development in the few countries where development from below has already started, we also support, through our trade and our business involvement, other Third World regimes where the majority are still very much oppressed. In this way we help to ensure that reactionary Third World regimes (the greater number) continue to dominate the poor countries' collective negotiations with the rich countries over the content of the New International Economic Order. (It is an expression of the dominant position of reactionary Third World regimes that one of their common demands to the rich nations has been increased scope for the export of *foodstuffs* from the hungry world to the overfed world.)

If our development aid is to contribute to liberation and democratically controlled development from below in the Third World, it must start from a much more active willingness to forego economic self-interest than exists today. Aid should chiefly be given to the most disadvantaged, and should be linked to absolute demands for verification that such aid will contribute to development from below by extending practical basic education, employment in locally controlled small-scale industry, agriculture, crafts, and the provision of basic needs as defined by the majority.

There is no doubt that political demands of this sort will uncover conflict between the policies of élite groupings and donor countries, and in many cases such help will probably not be accepted. But these governments will thereby be forced to reveal their anti-social policies, thus strengthening political opposition to their regime in world opinion.

Today this combination of aid with political pressure on élite regimes is unrealistic. And the reason is clear – we are dependent on a good relationship with even the most reactionary regimes (Brazil's is a current example) in order to secure our access to raw materials, our trade and our investments – which we do precisely by collaborating with and thereby supporting the oppressors. It is clear, however, as Gunnar Myrdal says, that giving priority to other values before increasing wealth, alongside increased development aid, 'would undoubtedly make it possible to exercise a quite different influence on their policies than today'.

Development aid need never have the character of charity. 'In one world, as in one state, when I am rich because you are poor, and I am poor because you are rich, the transfer of wealth from the rich to the poor is a matter of right,' says Nyerere. 'It is not an appropriate matter for charity.'[12]

The natural goal would seem to be a progressive taxation of the rich nations, apportioned by an international authority to the benefit of the most impoverished populations. National taxation for development aid is a step towards this goal – at least, if it is provided in accordance with the principles of development from below. But private, local development projects for local, self-determined development in poor countries are also of great importance in promoting an understanding of the principle of solidarity that such transfers of wealth must be based on – as long as they are regarded as a means of furthering a comprehensive national involvement on the part of the rich country, and not as a substitute for it. Within the broadened perspective that we have discussed, the principle of transfers through taxation to disadvantaged groups is obviously as legitimate in relation to poor nations in the Third World as in relation to a rich country's own citizens.

To the extent that the broadened perspective makes it natural to evaluate our production in relation to the unmet needs of the majority, it will presumably seem increasingly senseless to use our production capacity for the manufacture of luxury commodities and trivial throwaway products. It is likely that a redirection of production towards the needs of the poor rather than the greed of the rich will seem natural and necessary.

This question is already an important issue in a number of rich countries with high levels of unemployment, because high levels of production cannot always find outlets on flooded markets. In such countries every possible means is being used to try and find or create new luxury demands that production can be tailored to. And as long as the acquisitiveness of the industrialized countries and their inhabitants remains the main driving force behind development, this is the only possible short-term solution. In the longer term, a solution to the problem might involve the dismantling of highly automated, large-scale industry and its replacement by more labour-intensive, smaller-scale industry, in accordance with ecological theory; but this will take time. If, however, people's basic motivation rested more on a sense of human solidarity, it would be possible to conceive of shorter-term solutions. Then production for the less affluent local market in poor countries, subsidized through taxation as well as traditional development aid, in order to assure these countries of the resources and equipment needed for their self-determination, would no longer seem inconceivable. Again, it is important to make clear that this idea, too, is worthless, or even counter-productive, if it is not based on a clear principle of solidarity. If it were to be promoted as part of the present pattern of objectives, it would only serve to subordinate free development aid to the object of solving our own production problems; the poor countries would thus become the dumping ground for products we cannot sell. Similarly, any aid which is based on self-interest and charity rather than human solidarity will continue to be of little use to the oppressed of the world.

But regardless of what form of direct transfer is chosen, it is unlikely that this alone will be enough to start a process of development from below. As the ILO report emphasizes, aid given to improve health, education and employment will obviously be an important contribution to increased political participation and thus to new social development. But the demolition of the power positions of Third World élites also presupposes political support for liberation movements and democratic revolution – as well as demanding that we gradually free ourselves from industrial growth that depends on the one-sided export of raw materials from the Third World. It also means we must have the will to achieve a fundamental change in the economic world order dominated by the rich countries.

Again, the natural solution seems to be a parallel pursuit of several strategies rather than a dogmatic belief in a single theory to the exclusion of all others.

In discussing the various theories of development and transformation, it is useful to go back to the underlying question concerning 'the purpose of it all'. It is important to avoid conflicts between theories, on the one hand, and people sharing a common ultimate objective, on the other. Conflict should be identified|not|between|the many possible means, but between opposing motives and premises. Actions that are clearly motivated by a respect based on common humanity for the equal rights of others, and that have this as their *primary* objective in a broadened perspective, can scarcely avoid contributing to a general movement in the right direction. No matter how logical and systematic it may be, a theoretical model is not an expression of the empathy that active solidarity must always build on.

In all rich countries there are today countless groups which wish, on the basis of various theories, to support and to cooperate with the world's poor in their efforts to achieve freedom and human rights. To the extent that these groups have human solidarity and fellowship in the broadest sense as their underlying motive, and to the extent that they are willing to strengthen one another by cooperation, they are all members of a broad movement for change which will sooner or later usher in new social systems in both rich and poor countries, and with them, a new economic world order. The driving force of this movement will not be infallibility of theory but the strength of a common motivation and a common attitude to values. Without this motivation and the will to act on its premises, the theories alone are dead and powerless; but in so far as they build on a common motivation, they also point in the direction of the same, decisive change of course in the rich countries. What does this mean in practice?

It should be sufficient to refer again to the motive or moral basis that we have discussed: if human solidarity is put above economic self-interest, it follows that national economic, industrial and personal competition for increased affluence must be replaced by more human objectives. But since many people in our society tend to believe in theories regardless of the motivation behind them, it might be useful to look at what the concrete consequences of the main theories mentioned seem to be for ourselves.

The New International Economic Order theory demands that the rich countries give up certain economic advantages. A fully expanded raw materials fund and the proposed exchange relations adapted to the needs of poor countries will reduce the industrialized countries' possibilities for managing the world economy in their own favour. Similarly, a broad cancellation of Third World debts would mean an expense for the rich countries that is virtually inconceivable today. Third World debts are now so great that, in total, the poor countries are paying about the same amount in interest and in instalments on earlier loans as they are receiving in the form of new funds. The same applies to free access for exports to the rich countries' markets; if this demand is taken seriously, it would obviously mean an expensive, major restructuring of the production that has previously been protected by import duties against competition from countries where prices are low. The domestic refinement of raw materials in poor countries would, moreover, hit major sectors of industry in the rich countries. Similarly, a takeover by the poor countries of the transport of these raw materials would reduce our income from shipping in a manner that would have noticeable effects on the national economy.

If these and other proposed changes in the economic world order are to bring about anything more than verbal support and the usual insignificant concessions – indeed, if the New International Economic Order is to be taken at all seriously in the rich countries – it will probably mean that, even in periods of boom, the industrialized countries will have to accommodate a noticeable drop in national wealth. In practice this would necessitate an active transformation of the system of industrial growth of which all rich countries today are the helpless slaves. Among other things, it would be likely to mean – if the majority accepted a reduced level of prosperity – that the decline must not hit the large groups of the low-paid and pensioners, nor social welfare provisions. The consequence would therefore be an all the more noticeable decline for high-income groups. In other words, a major step in the direction of more or less equal incomes for all – a principle that would be politically impossible under our present system.

The widespread belief that a New International Economic Order can be realized in parallel with the current internal competition for relative economic advantages therefore seems to rest on unrealistic premises. About this, Gunnar Myrdal says, 'The crazy competition between the various income groups in all developed countries, which is one of the forces driving inflation, allows little possibility for greater generosity towards the under-developed countries.' He also points out that 'Governments are dependent on the attitude of their people. The difficulty with all rational planning in a democratic country is that it ultimately boils down to an attempt to pull oneself up by one's own bootstraps.'

The comprehensive transformation that seems necessary in the industrialized countries presupposes, in other words, a willingness to accept a way of life built on other values than economic competition. 'The naked truth,' says Myrdal – and in this he is supported by the Nobel Prize-winner Jan Tinbergen – 'is that without very radical changes in the rich countries' pattern of consumption, all talk of a New International Economic Order will remain pure bluff.'[16]

This statement from two Nobel Prize-winning economists stands in direct contradiction to the view maintained during the 1979 UNCTAD conference, namely that the New International Economic Order depends on renewed growth in the affluence of the industrialized countries. As long as the system of industrial growth carries on unchanged, such increase in wealth can only be created by further encouragement to materialistic competition. And this in itself stands in contradiction to concessions to solidarity. Indeed, even the hope that long-term growth in the industrialized countries, with gradual small concessions, will eventually create greater prosperity in both rich and poor countries, seems unrealistic – because this, too, assumes a perpetuation of the drive to consume among the voters of the industrialized countries which conflicts with a willingness to make concessions to the demands of international solidarity on the way. In practice, there is also little to suggest that increased wealth contributes to an increased willingness to renounce material advantages as long as differences of income and the rat-race mentality are maintained.

Among the most extreme adherents of the one-sided revolutionary theory, there are also many who reject the idea that effective support for liberation in developing countries presupposes less materialism on the part of working people in industrialized countries. Their reasoning is often that it is only the industrialized countries' rich investors and the owners of the multinationals who stand to lose from revolution in the Third World.

Let us take a brief look at the likely consequences of the necessary revolutionary upheavals in the Third World, if they should eventually involve the poor majority in the manner that we have taken as our premise. As has been said, there is every reason to think that this would, and must, bring about far more changes than the takeover by the people of foreign-owned companies and plantations. In the interests of the general population, foreign and élite-controlled companies would need to move from export production to production for local use and perhaps for export to more equal partners in other poor countries. As a result, the plantations that have produced, for example, virtually all our coffee, tea, cocoa and a large part of the sugar, tropical fruit, tobacco, cotton, rubber and copra we use, will be divided up by land reforms. They will be taken over by smallholders who will use the land, before anything else, to grow their own food.

Many of those in the Third World whose cheap labour has supplied us with minerals and important raw materials for our industry, and has held down the prices on goods imported from poor countries, will demand higher wages, thus raising the price of these products. Moreover, they will prefer to export their goods to other Third World countries, and they will probably go over from export industry to local, small-scale industry geared to their own needs. This will affect all areas of our consumption that rely on raw materials from the Third World. According to the UN statistics for 1970, the Western industrialized countries were then dependent on importing from poor countries 65 per cent of all their bauxite, almost 85 per cent of all tin, chrome and manganese, almost half of all copper and over half their oil, to give only a few examples. The moment these supplies are stopped, prices will rocket for all goods containing constituents such as these, and many others besides. The consequences of such a change will grow with the increasing level of consumption. According to the National Materials Policy Commission, even the USA, which twenty-five years ago was virtually self-sufficient in all the most important raw materials needed for its industrial production, will be dependent on importing 80 per cent of these commodities before the year 2000.[24]

In other words, the revolutionary takeover by the peoples of developing countries of their own raw materials will inevitably result in far-reaching changes in the rich countries. Either we must stop using these raw materials which today are essential elements in our consumption, or we must produce them ourselves. The latter option would be considerably more expensive – otherwise, we would scarcely be importing them today – and such production would have to displace more advanced consumer production. In addition, national tax revenues from our investments in the Third World would be lost and the relevant public expenditure would have to be met by an increase in ordinary taxation.

To imagine that all this can happen without powerful effects on the standard of living of ordinary citizens in our own countries must be described as wishful thinking. If those who work to propagate theories of this sort do not at the same time oppose the current materialism, the goal of growth and the expectation of continually increasing wealth, they will sooner or later contribute to a conflict between our own popular objectives and wishes and the just demands of the liberated peoples of the poor world.

The ecological theory intrinsically builds on reduced materialism and reduced consumption in the rich countries, because it assumes a decline in both our imports from the Third World and in our own large-scale industrial production.

It is similarly self-evident that the theory of development aid – if it means that national taxation and transfer of wealth is to give basic human rights to all – must noticeably reduce the level of affluence in the rich countries. It ought to be sufficient to mention the cost of even the simplest aids to basic education for illiterate people whose numbers exceed the total population of school age in all the rich countries. Or the expense that would necessarily be involved in providing tools for several hundred million unemployed, and health care and accommodation for the developing countries' growing army of slum-dwellers. In President Nyerere's words:

> Without hesitating or apology I assert that if the wealthy nations – and I include Britain, Australia, Canada and New Zealand in that category – still have an ambition for material growth and greater consumption, then they need to ask themselves whether they are serious in their desire to reduce the gap between rich and poor countries and eradicate poverty from the earth. The objective must be the eradication of poverty, and the establishment of a minimum standard of living for all people. This will involve its converse – a ceiling on wealth for individuals and nations, as well as deliberate action to transfer resources from the rich to the poor within and across national boundaries. The leaders of the rich countries must have the courage to tell their people that they are rich enough.[11]

Here, Nyerere is a spokesman for the future – for the broadened perspective that is still only acknowledged theoretically, and then only by sections of the electorate in the rich countries on whom a change will ultimately depend.

Regardless of the theory or the model for change on which we base a solution to the global majority's problems, it seems difficult to avoid a common conclusion: *If everyone's right to freedom, and other fundamental human rights, are to be respected, the rich countries must replace increasing wealth with a new goal.*

Whether these countries' *production* can be, or should be, reduced in the short term must be discussed on the premise of the same values. At all events, it seems clear that production must be restructured according to an evaluation of needs before purchasing power.

It looks as though this change of course will be difficult or impossible as long as materialism overshadows the idea of solidarity among the majority of voters in the industrial countries. And if other values were to be given priority by these populations, it would clearly tear the foundations from under the entire system of industrial growth and point towards something new and essentially different. Without wanting to suggest that it is possible or desirable to predict how this new society will be organized, it should at least be possible to look for an answer to the following question: what changes in the system must be achieved for it to be possible to abolish the need for growth?

5. What Is the System's Driving Force?

As we have seen, the human objective for the global majority stands in opposition to the industrial countries' policies of economic growth. Merely halting growth, however, is obviously of little help. The crises that have hindered or stopped growth in the rich countries have aggravated rather than improved the situation of developing countries. What stands in the way of change and improvement in the Third World is clearly the *objective* itself – the purpose and the goal of our economic policy – and this remains unshaken: the greatest possible production for the highest possible level of consumption is the industrial nations' paramount objective and their remedy for all problems, regardless of whether the economy is in crisis or booming.

There is much to indicate that this narrow goal of national growth is an integral element inherent to the economic systems of the industrial countries, whether state-capitalist, private-capitalist or based on a mixed economy. The modern industrial system is constantly faced with the choice of growth or death. Despite an increasing understanding of the negative aspects of increasing wealth, and despite what politicians may say about needing to emphasize *other* values, no government in a rich country has yet dared to take as its target a permanent end to growth. It is generally accepted by the governments of industrial countries that growth in demand and consumption is a precondition for avoiding unemployment and economic problems. Indeed, 'economic problems' have actually become synonymous with a stable, non-growing level of consumption and production.

Two press clippings from 1975 illustrate the point: 'Spend money! That was the government's plea to the ordinary American after President Ford told them they will get 12 per cent of their income tax for last year paid back to them. Economic experts are almost convinced that this injection of money will give new impetus to stagnating production, provided that Americans "do their duty" and spend this unexpected gift from the government, preferably all at once and on something as expensive as the down payment on a new car.'

The same invitation to consume more was used as a means of counteracting tendencies towards crisis in Sweden during Palme's social-democratic government. Clearly, the promotion of a sense of human solidarity and other values before competition for status symbols such as new cars, fashions and luxuries stands in direct contradiction to what the system of industrial growth demands of the individual. In West Germany, too, 'Chancellor Schmidt recently made it clear that ... the urge to save is a hindrance to an economic upswing and he earnestly appealed to West Germans to spend more.'[25]

If we accept the conclusion our basic values and our global responsibility have led us to, we must therefore face this question: what changes in our economic system are necessary to put globally responsible development in place of increasing affluence?

This in turn raises another question – is it the system which creates the scramble to consume, or is it the scramble to consume which creates the system? Or is it, as socialists often claim, certain power groupings and other forces within the system that prevent change? First, however, let us look briefly at the system itself. What factors in industrial society make constant growth and competition for material self-interest necessary, thereby hindering development in the direction of other values? Let us try to find an unbiased answer to this question by looking first at economic liberalism, as it is described by its adherents, then at Marx's analysis of the system, and finally by evaluating both views in the light of the object and outlook of this book.

Economic liberalism

Economic liberalism lays great emphasis on the concept of liberty. It 'conceives of society as the sum of the individuals who compose it ... and conceives of the individual as the bearer of a human nature that is not to be formed, but merely allowed to develop freely by the removal of hindrances in its way ... By attending to his or her own interest, the individual also acts in the interest of the whole.'[26] Economic liberalism sees private trade and the right of ownership as the principal basis of a harmonious society, though modern neo-liberalism has acknowledged, to an increasing extent, that intervention and regulation are in fact needed to ensure everyone a basic minimum of economic and social security.

In an isolated society with a multitude of more or less equal producers and consumers and no great inequality of income or purchasing power, a liberal economy would perhaps be able to satisfy the population's *material* needs and freedom of choice better than any other existing system. In theory, production would be guided by consumers determining, through their demand, what is to be produced and in what quantities. The competition among many equal producers for consumer favour would ensure the lowest possible prices and the highest possible degree of quality and renewal. The producers' free competition would also ensure that the less efficient were weeded out while those who develop the most efficient means and methods of production, and thus contribute most to the prosperity of their society, would always lead development. The firms and managements best able to adapt themselves to the wishes of the consumers would also be those to emerge victorious from the competition. The advantage of the individual producer would also be that of the individual consumer, and vice versa.

Despite all the economic modifications, encroachments and checks that have been brought in, it is still the main principle of liberalism – competition for consumer demand and the producers' right to invest their profit in new production equipment – that is the basis of Western economic development, whether under conservative, liberal or social-democratic governments.

In arguing for the maintenance of this liberal market economy, comparison is often made with the state-capitalist countries of the Eastern bloc where there is clearly a far poorer correlation between production and need, where industrial advances do not seem so dynamic, and where distribution often fails to get the goods out to the buyers.

According to the theory of liberalism, the balance between the free forces in society is crucial. Two main problems in particular, according to the advocates of the system, diminish its benefits. Firstly, when the state disrupts free competition by interfering in other ways than as a necessary adjusting mechanism. Secondly, when the balance of forces is upset – either by the emergence of cartels and monopolies which ignore the rules of competition, or as a result of organized workers making wage demands that prevent producers from investing in equipment necessary for the increase of production that is supposed to benefit society as a whole.

Liberalism's interpretation of the concept of liberty is a central point in the debate over the justice of the system, and this will be taken up below. The important question here is the extent to which the system is able to satisfy the conditions we have posited: the equalization and stabilization of national consumption at a globally defensible level, and the development of the values of fellowship and solidarity which make this possible.

Admittedly, it is not usual to hear advocates of liberalism defend this system as being well suited to a reduced and stable national consumption. On the contrary, the argument is usually that economic liberalism is the surest way to increased affluence. It is also self-evident that a purely liberal economy can scarcely stop growing, since its most fundamental principle is that only through competition will the most productive enterprises and the most sought-after goods be free to develop. As long as there are accessible resources and new possibilities for promoting demand, such a system will be expansive.

Could a liberal economy function within a nationally established framework for a stable national consumption of resources? Any such restriction of competition would of course be impossible for a country with open foreign trade in the international market economy (unless the other industrial countries were to adopt equivalent restrictions), but what if the national economy was largely self-sufficient? It is possible that liberal competition for profits might turn out to be a very effective means of exploiting and recycling alternative and renewable resources. But what happens when these opportunities for expansion are also exhausted? Is there, in a system based on competition between privately owned enterprises, an inbuilt growth dynamic which *cannot* be combined with a stable consumption of resources?

In seeking to answer this question, it might be useful to examine briefly Marx's analysis of capitalism as a system – not least because his analysis includes an examination of the reasons for the growth of capital. (And even if Marx's conclusions are not applicable to the present situation, his method of analysis may provide a basis for further discussion of this question.) Moreover, many of Marx's concepts and analytical tools will prove useful in other contexts in later chapters.

Because opposing attitudes to Marx are so strongly and often passionately held, it should be made clear that the account which follows is not based on any dogmatic belief in or rejection of Marx. It is primarily an attempt to present the main points in Marx's analysis as Marx himself put them – wherever possible by means of direct quotations from *Capital* – so that we can then judge the relevance of his analysis to our society.

For those who are not familiar with Marx's principal work, a brief outline may be necessary; to discuss a revolutionary transformation of our society without taking Marx into consideration would not only be meaningless, it would also make more difficult an open dialogue between freethinkers among Marxists and non-Marxists, who are often closer to one another than they realize.

Marx and Capital

The core of *Capital* is a description of the historical reasons for and the consequences of the fact that a limited section of the population own the means of production in industrial society – or, to put it another way, that most workers are deprived of the right to own the machines and tools they need in order to be able to produce for industrial society.

Since the first volume of *Capital* was published in 1867, the concept of 'Marxism' (a term Marx himself disavowed) has had a central position in discussion of social relations and economics. It is important to understand, however, that much of the opposition to what is seen as Marxism is due to a mixture of Marx's analysis and Lenin's extensive interpretation and augmentation of it. Thus reference is often made to the consequences of Leninism, especially in the Soviet Union.

Marx's concrete directions for the future are, as has been said, few and vague, and they give rise to no end of interpretations and suppositions. One of the post-Marxists of our time, André Glucksmann, to whom we have referred previously,[3] criticizes Marx for this. In *The Master Thinkers* he shows how, at the few places where Marx discusses the transition to and the carrying through of the future social form, he falls into loose and incomplete speculation. The question is whether Glucksmann is not here attacking Marx on the wrong premises – and contrary to his own 'anti-élitist' ideas.

Marx's ideas have perhaps survived so successfully precisely because he contented himself with a general analysis of capitalism's basic principles and developmental tendencies, and only suggested the main features of the future society that in his opinion was a historical necessity, otherwise leaving the way open for a free development of views as to how these principles might be organized.

In the *Communist Manifesto*,[19] Marx and Engels do outline some general proposals which might 'be pretty generally applicable' in the most advanced countries, such as the expropriation of privately owned land, progressive taxation, the abolition of the right of inheritance, a national bank with a monopoly, public transport, etc. But these steps towards the future society were proposals, not dogmas. In their preface to the 1872 edition of the *Manifesto,* the authors were already saying that they regarded these proposals as out of date and that they would 'in many respects, be very differently worded today'.

There is reason to believe that Marx, unlike many of today's dogmatists, did not think that the society of the future would be built over a prefabricated framework. Within the limits of historical circumstances, the future was to be formed by the mass of people who participated in the process of transformation. In his 1888 preface to the *Manifesto,* Engels says that Marx did not wish to tie development to a preconceived model. The programme of the International Working Men's Association had to be approved by the many different groups within it. He says that 'Marx, who drew up this programme to the satisfaction of all parties, entirely trusted to the intellectual development of the working class, which was sure to result from combined action and mutual discussion.'

It is important to make this clear, so as to help free our thinking from the straitjacket of narrow Marxist theory. Marx himself seems to have had a greater sense of an undogmatic 'development from below' towards a future society, which would find its form on the way through the general development of consciousness, rather than tying development to preconceived élite models.

Marx calls his method *dialectical.* This concept is so central to any discussion of Marx that a little more should be said about it. The word has been given various meanings in the history of philosophy, but it always concerns an interaction between forces and conditions affecting development.

In Kant's philosophy, the dialectic is a logical method for resolving the apparent contradictions that arise in our thinking because of an incomplete understanding of reality, which is always free of contradictions, or because our thinking is not based on real experience. Hegel's dialectic takes Kant's idea further with a wide-ranging doctrine concerning the manner in which our consciousness develops towards objective reason by understanding and thinking through the contradictions in the reality we perceive. Hegel is not concerned with any other reality than that which can be perceived at given time. History is for him an expression of the necessary development of the human spirit's increasing insight and consciousness of itself and its relation to the environment. The power driving this development is the creative struggle between perceived contradictions (theses and antitheses) which constantly leads us on to new syntheses – the next step towards a higher consciousness and development. For Hegel, it is therefore the development of the idea or the spirit and its interaction with the reality in which it is contained which shapes history.

Marx takes as his point of departure Hegel's view of historical development resulting from a struggle between contradictions. But he sees the process from another angle. In the Preface to *Capital* he says:

> My dialectical method is, in its foundations, not only different from the Hegelian, but exactly opposite to it. For Hegel, the process of thinking, which he even transforms into an independent subject, under the name of 'the Idea', is the creator of the real world, and the real world is only the external appearance of the idea. With me the reverse is true: the

ideal is nothing but the material world reflected in the mind of man, and translated into forms of thought.

This view is based on the principle that in Marxism is called *historical materialism*. According to this principle, human historical development is determined by the objective material conditions on which people are dependent and the conflicts of interest which arise through the use of the tools and opportunities that are derived from them. The principal changes occur through revolutionary upheavals when the contradictions have become sufficiently acute. This need not necessarily be seen as absolute determinism. Marx's analysis can also be understood as an attempt to systematize the principal features in historical development which provide a framework for social struggle.

Marx, then, sees social development as a process in several stages, in which the relations of production are always the determining factor. In the original, primitive stage, production was based on the extended family's work to satisfy its own needs: hunting, fishing, gathering from nature and the earliest agriculture. There was a certain exchange of goods, but this too was geared to meeting immediate needs – not to the accumulation of wealth.

The first contradictions that changed this situation probably arose with the transition to settled agriculture and the resulting need to protect territory. Through warfare and the capture of slaves the strongest groups consolidated their power and security, and the first great kingdoms came into being. In the next stage – antiquity – social relations were dominated by a ruling class of land- and slave-owners and production was based largely on slave labour. Production by the slaves created wealth for an élite who still did not regard wealth as an end in itself, but as a requirement for a free life. In ancient Athens, so greatly celebrated, it is thought that each free household had an average of three or four slaves.[27] The free smallholders still produced for their own use but the large slave class existed solely as the tools of their owners.

Later the conflict over the right of land ownership resulted in the emergence of the feudal mode of production in Europe. Gradually, the big landowners forcibly appropriated the property of free smallholders and control over the administration of the state. The peasants became serfs – with the right to produce for their own needs on the strip of land allotted to them, but with the duty to put their labour at the disposal of the landowner according to his wishes. The nature of a landowner's relations with his serfs varied from a certain paternalistic care to exploitation bordering on pure slavery. Power through wealth had now become an end in itself, though the individual estates were still largely self-sufficient and stable. The élite's main concern was to preserve the status quo. The desire to profit by expansion was not a major motivating factor. This was also true of the free craft production which still existed in a peasant society, often organized into independent guilds.

The new contradiction arose with the industrial revolution. Both the old ruling class of landowners and the organized artisans wanted to protect their positions by means of restrictions on trade and production that would obstruct the development of the free trade on which the new class of industrial capitalists was dependent. The power of the capitalists grew, however, with industrial development; and the capitalist system, based on the economic liberalism of the theories of Adam Smith, and later Ricardo and Malthus, secured a foothold.

The great change inherent in the capitalist epoch was the accumulation of capital in the form of industrial means of production which made possible more efficient production on a larger scale. Artisans and smallholders could in no way compete with this. Instead of selling their production, they now had to sell their labour-power. There came into existence a growing proletariat of 'free' labourers who had lost the right to own their own implements or means of production and who therefore had to put their labour at the disposal of the owners of industry.

This wage labour created the conditions for the rapid accumulation of capital in an ever-growing production apparatus controlled by the capitalists. In Marx's words: 'So-called primitive accumulation, therefore, is nothing else than the historical process of divorcing the producer from the means of production.'[6]

Nature does not produce on the one hand owners of money or commodities, and on the other hand men possessing nothing but their own labour-power ... It is clearly the result of a past historical development, the product of many economic revolutions ... [Capital] arises only when the owner of the means of production and subsistence finds the free worker available, on the market, as the seller of his own labour-power. And this one historical pre-condition comprises a world's history.

Marx's now formulates his doctrine of *surplus-value*. Unlike earlier economists who regarded the commodity as the real measure of value and saw profit as a 'mysterious' and not readily explicable increase in value with purchase and sale, Marx claimed that the only tenable measure of a commodity's value is the labour that is needed for its production.* When commodities are exchanged, this labour acquires its standard social value through its quality as 'average social labour'. 'Price is the money-name of the labour objectified in a commodity.' And profit, says Marx, can be rationally explained only by the fact that the employer pays the worker for only *part* of the labour-time he puts into the product.

If the money that is invested in the production of commodities through the purchase of labour corresponded to the full value of that labour, then the value of the labour and other inputs (materials, etc.) used would be exactly

---

*More recent economic theories, concerning 'marginal utility', etc., have sought to correct Marx in this respect by pointing out that variations in the relationship of demand and scarcity can give different prices to commodities representing the same amount of labour. Eco-Marxists have also criticized this theory of labour-value because it takes no account of the fact that natural resources are finite and must therefore be ascribed a value of their own.

equal to the value of the finished product. The circuit money-commodity-money (M–C–M) would start and finish each round at the same level. No profit would come into existence. 'The complete form of this process,' says Marx, 'is therefore M–C–M′, where $M = M + \Delta M$, i.e. the original sum advanced plus an increment. This increment or excess over the original value I call "surplus-value".'

Surplus-value cannot arise as a result of the seller being able to sell his commodity at a higher price than its value, for each seller is in turn a buyer and *vice versa*. The sale or exchange of goods in itself creates no additional value. The only thing the capitalist can buy 'cut price' is labour-power, and he can do this precisely because, on the one hand, the workers are free to 'negotiate' the price of their labour-power for a limited time and, on the other hand, because they depend on the capitalist's means of production and must therefore generally accept what he offers them. (The changes which have occurred since Marx's time in these relations are discussed later.)

In other words, the worker creates surplus-value for the capitalist by granting him a certain number of hours' free labour. For example, he puts eight hours' work into the product but is paid for six. The value of these two hours' additional work is the basis of the surplus-value or profit that the capital owner makes on the sale of the product.

What, then, according to Marx, constitutes the value of labour-power? This corresponds to what the average worker requires for subsistence, an amount that is determined partly by 'the climatic and other physical peculiarities of his country', and partly by custom: 'the habits and expectations with which the class of free workers has been formed'. 'His means of subsistence must be sufficient to maintain him in his normal state as a working individual.'

The value that the worker puts in *in excess of this* is therefore the additional value that the capital owner takes and can invest in the constant renewal of production equipment, and in renewed purchases of raw materials and the labour needed to make use of it. In Marx's terminology, in other words, the exploitation of labour creates the constant increase of capital which in turn makes possible unstoppable industrial growth.

The creation of capital is in this respect merely the accumulation of unpaid labour. If one accepts that labour is a value-creating factor – indeed, if one in any way accepts that labour has a certain value – then the consequence is that if the capitalist really paid this value, there could not be capital and his money would not be transformed into capital. 'Accumulation requires the transformation of a portion of the surplus product into capital.'[6]

Surplus-value and capital growth can be increased in two ways. In capitalism's infancy it was done by further increasing the length of the working day beyond the time that was paid for (absolute surplus-value). When legislation to restrict working hours was brought in, it was done by increasing the proportion of surplus labour in an unchanged working day (relative surplus-value). This is made possible by increased productivity which reduces the price of the provisions – and consequently the wage – the worker needs, and presupposes an increase in the intensity of labour.

The objective of the development of the productivity of labour within the context of capitalist production is the shortening of that part of the working day in which the worker must work for himself, and the lengthening, thereby, of the other part of the day, in which he is free to work for nothing for the capitalist.

From the moment that it was made impossible once and for all to increase the production of surplus-value by prolonging the working day, capital threw itself with all its might, and in full awareness of the situation, into the production of relative surplus-value, by speeding up the development of the machine system ... It imposes on the worker an increased expenditure of labour ... to a degree which can only be attained within the limits of the shortened working day ... In addition to the measure of its 'extensive magnitude', labour-time now acquires a measure of its intensity, or degree of density.

The characteristic feature of this process, says Marx, is the purchase and sale of labour-power as a commodity, which implies that there exists a class of free workers who have nothing to sell but their own labour-power. From the worker's point of view, the productive use of his labour-power only becomes possible from the moment that it is associated with the means of production, which are owned by others. The owner of the labour thus encounters the means of production as alien property. And in this lies the worker's entire dependence and incapacity to influence development at this early stage of capitalism: 'Once the capitalist mode of production takes hold, it annihilates all forms of commodity production which depend either on the producer's independent labour or on the sale of produce that is left over in a subsistence economy'.

In order to create the financial, commercial and legislative conditions for the development of capitalism, the state must, to an increasing degree, perform as an instrument of the capital owners. The state, in the capitalist system, is a necessary precondition of the social structure which capitalism needs. In Marx's work, in other words, the state is not, as it is often represented today, an obstruction to the freedom of capitalism, even if it creates certain restrictions for the individual capitalist. The main function of the state is, on the contrary, to secure the legislation and the systems of finance and distribution that are necessary for capitalism's growth.

Capital, particularly the first volume, describes the social background to Marx's condemnation of the nineteenth-century capitalist system and its backers. His account of child labour, starvation wages and working conditions which shortened working people's lives to less than half those of the upper class, the capitalists' protests against the Factory Acts and against the legal limitation of working hours which often amounted to twelve hours per day or more – all this must be seen as the background to his theory of inevitable, violent revolution.

Since the worker spends the greater part of his life in the production process, the conditions of this process are to a great extent ... his conditions of life, and economy in these conditions of life is a method of increasing the profit rate ... This economy extends to crowding workers into confined and unhealthy premises, a practice which in capitalist parlance is called saving on buildings; squeezing dangerous machines into the same premises and dispensing with means of protection against these dangers ... Not to speak of the absence of all provisions that would make the production process humane, comfortable or simply bearable for the worker. From the standpoint of the capitalist this would be a senseless waste.[28]

Compulsory work for the capitalist usurped the place, not only of children's play, but also of independent labour at home, within customary limits, for the family itself.[6]

With the development of social liberalism in our century, and the increasing interest in social reforms for the contribution that they too can make to the growth of capitalism, much of the immediate, material need was gradually alleviated. By then, however, the possibility of a decent life and personal development had already been lost for several generations of workers in our culture, in the same way as is happening today in other parts of the world. But Marx does not justify the necessity of revolution with moral arguments. Sooner or later, in one form or another, it will come as the result of the contradictions which, in his view, are constantly made more acute with the development of capitalism.

The source of these contradictions was, according to Marx, the steady growth of capital and industrial means of production in fewer and fewer hands. The capital equipment which is created with the aid of the unpaid part of the workers' own effort gradually takes over more and more of their work, leaving them unemployed. Past labour, in the form of means of production, plays a part in their labour process, says Marx: '... it is their own previous unpaid work which now does service.' 'Since the working class, through its own labour, produces the constantly increasing capital, it therefore generates on an ever-increasing scale the means which make it superfluous.'[6]

At the same time, however, this development means that workers who were previously isolated in small enterprises are increasingly brought together through the need to organize labour in larger units. This gives the working class new opportunities for cooperation, organization and power: 'With the number of workers the accumulated capital puts into action, grows their resistance and, with it, also the pressure the capitalist exerts in order to overcome this resistance.' In Marxist terminology, then, the dialectical contradictions between the classes grow through an interplay of mutually reinforcing circumstances which ultimately bring about the change. This, in parallel with the deterioration in conditions of life which, according to Marx, capitalism must cause, will finally create the necessary conditions for revolution:

Along with the constant decrease in the number of capitalist magnates, who usurp and monopolize all the advantages of this process of transformation, the mass of misery, oppression, slavery, degradation and exploitation grows; but with this there also grows the revolt of the working class, a class constantly increasing in numbers, and trained, united and organized by the very mechanism of the capitalist process of production. The monopoly of capital becomes a fetter upon the mode of production which has flourished alongside and under it. The centralization of the means of production and the socialization of labour reach a point at which they become incompatible with their capitalist integument. This integument is burst asunder. The knell of capitalist private property sounds. The expropriators are expropriated ... capitalist production begets, with the inexorability of a natural process, its own negation. This ... does not re-establish private property, but it does indeed establish individual property on the basis of the achievements of the capitalist era: namely cooperation and the possession in common of the land and the means of production produced by labour itself.

An important element in this development is what Marx calls the *tendential fall in the rate of profit:* competition to invest in ever more labour-saving equipment means that the sum of invested capital grows faster than the number of workers employed. This means that the capital which must later be invested in new equipment increases in relation to the labour that is needed to serve this equipment. But since it is only the labour employed that creates surplus-value, the total capital needed also becomes greater in proportion to the surplus-value it creates. This ratio of surplus-value to total investment capital forms, in Marx's view, the basis of the profit rate, which must therefore fall with the centralization of capital. If the overall profit is to grow in spite of this, as capitalism demands, then capital, i.e. the production apparatus, must grow quicker. 'This two-fold effect ... can be expressed only in a growth in the total capital that takes place more rapidly than the fall in the rate of profit ... It follows from this that the more the capitalist mode of production is developed, the more an ever greater amount of capital is needed to employ the same amount of labour-power ... The rising productivity of labour thus necessarily gives rise, on the capitalist basis, to a permanent apparent surplus working population' – i.e. unemployment.

Since the rate of profit is the spur to capitalist production, 'a fall in this rate slows down the formation of new, independent capitals and thus appears as a threat to the development of the capitalist production process; it promotes overproduction, speculation and crises, and leads to the existence of excess capital alongside a surplus population.'[28]

Yet 'the mass of profit certainly does grow, even at a smaller rate of profit, as the capital laid out increases. But this brings about a simultaneous concentration of capital, since the conditions of production now require the use of capital on a massive scale. It also leads to the centralization of this capital, i.e. the swallowing-up of small capitalists by big, and their decapitalization.' This concentration of capital in fewer and fewer hands, the internationalization of business activity and the increasing significance of regulation by the state are characteristic of capitalism's second phase of development, monopoly capitalism.

In this late phase of capitalism, imperialism has an increasing role, as Lenin, Rosa Luxemburg and others were to show. But Marx already describes the beginning of such a process in *Capital:*

> By constantly turning workers into 'supernumaries', large-scale industry, in all countries where it has taken root, spurs on rapid increases in emigration and the colonization of foreign lands, which are thereby converted into settlements for growing the raw material of the mother country ... A new and international division of labour springs up, one suited to the requirements of the main industrial countries, and it converts one part of the globe into a chiefly agricultural field of production for supplying the other part, which remains a pre-eminently industrial field.[6]

This period also sees the amplification of the constantly recurring crises which, according to Marx's *crisis theory,* are a necessary element in the development of capitalism. The crises always start in a period of boom in which the growth of capital makes possible such rapid industrialization that even the need for labour increases. This leads to competition among capitalists for the purchase of labour, and wages rise. In other words, the workers are paid for a greater part of their established working hours, and the proportion of unpaid surplus labour declines accordingly. 'But as soon as this diminution touches the point at which the surplus labour that nourishes capital is no longer supplied in normal quantity, a reaction sets in: a smaller part of revenue is capitalized, accumulation slows down, and the rising movement of wages comes up against an obstacle.'[6] At the same time, the reduced supply of capital means that industrial expansion stops again and the need for labour declines. In addition to reduced wages, comes unemployment.

The combination of increasing capital power for a diminishing number of proprietors, the constant proletarianization of new sectors of the population and the effects of the crises on the working class which is meanwhile being brought together in growing numbers, inevitably intensifies the class struggle which ultimately results in the revolution of the proletariat. The working class takes over state power and the ownership of the means of production. The dictatorship of the proletariat is introduced to prevent the old capitalist class from carrying out a counter-revolution, but only as a transitional stage towards the free and classless communist society.

Thus Marx analyzed the capitalist system and its expected development and collapse. What has happened in practice?

The development of industrial society after Marx

Given the social conditions Marx experienced, the development he outlined towards a decisive revolution no doubt appeared natural and necessary. And indeed revolution *came* half a century later. But it came in Russia and not, as predicted, in a highly industrialized society.

A central point in Marx's analysis is that the capitalist form of production must have reached its full development before conditions are right for revolution. With the Russian revolution of 1917 this was far from being the case. Agriculture was still dominant in relation to industry, the peasantry was still the biggest social class and the industrial workers had not reached the stage of class-consciousness and organization that Marx had seen as a necessary condition. The Russian revolution therefore had to be directed 'from above' in quite a different dictatorial manner from that which Marx had presumably envisaged, by the assumption of absolute power and leadership over the working class by Lenin and his party cadre. This élite power was taken further, as we know too well, with Stalin's mass elimination of opponents, and it continues to exist. The revolutions that have been carried out since have also all occurred in non-industrialized developing countries – and under the direction of the same sort of revolutionary élite, which always seems equally difficult to get rid of once it has established itself. What was it that prevented the revolution *in industrial society* which Marx's analysis predicted?

For one thing, it looks as though the more or less capitalist system of industrial growth, once it is introduced, has a far greater capacity to adapt and survive than Marx realized. For example, the contradictions between the growth of capital and the working class's *material* interests, which for Marx was the decisive force driving the revolution, have been blunted by the introduction of new principles of business management.

About the turn of the century, Frederick W. Taylor's theories came into widespread use. The principle behind 'Taylorism' was to increase workers' efficiency with the aid of scientific work studies, specialization and economic rewards. Work was clearly divided between leadership functions and various areas of manual activity, and manual workers' interests were taken as being narrowly and individually materialistic. Interposed into the simple antagonism between the capitalist and the wage labourer came a new and significant group with its own interests – foremen and supervisors at various levels.

The next important step in the attempt to neutralize the contradictions of the capitalist system emerged in the USA during the twenties and thirties. Business managers realized that the workers' interests were not only individual and that their attitude and their behaviour towards the company and their work could to a considerable extent be understood as social group reactions. The new school, which was given the name *human relations,* was therefore an answer to Marx's thesis that the organization of labour in larger units would bring workers together in groups whose interests would come into increasing conflict with the proprietors' demands for profit. By emphasizing that management was interested in the conditions of these groups of workers, by neutralizing protests from group leaders and individuals and by listening to their problems, management could reduce social unrest and increase productivity: 'A happy workforce is a productive workforce.'[27]

But Taylorism's stress on the technical aspects of the work itself remained a factor which provoked resistance. Reaction against the monotony and inhumanity of work in big modern industries, which Marx had foreseen, was countered with socio-technological management. In order to achieve optimum production, it was found that both technological and social considerations had to be balanced. Workers had to be made to feel both that there was consideration for them socially and that they were taking part in decision making as regards the planning of their own inputs within a framework drawn up by management. What was lost as a result of less efficient specialization could thus be regained through increased effort and interest in work. To a certain extent, specialized functions were combined into more comprehensive work tasks, often within small 'self-managing groups' with a limited responsibility of their own.

These steps in the development of management theory have generally been based on purely economic criteria affecting profit. In order to maximize profit, the resistance expressed through workers' trade-union organizations must be neutralized. The aim was to give the workforce a sense of common interest in the progress of the enterprise. As a result, the conflict of economic interest between owners and employees, which Marx presupposed, became not a battle between opposing interests, but, to a considerable extent, a matter of amicable negotiation over the division of the economic result. The employees' representatives would have an interest in an adequate proportion of the profit being invested in expansion to secure the growth and competitiveness of the company, and management, for its part, had an interest in preventing the purchasing power and demand of ordinary workers from stagnating.

There was, nevertheless, right up to the time of the Second World War, much that confirmed Marx's account of capitalism's road to collapse. The economic depression and the unemployment and poverty which hit large sections of the industrial countries' working class during the thirties seemed to demonstrate Marx's crisis theory. But even for this disease, remedies were found – not the least of which was a change in the role of the state.

In 1936, the English economist John Maynard Keynes published *The General Theory of Employment, Interest and Money,* which showed how the state can influence a given society's economic development through active economic and employment policies. Keynes's principles and their extension, which today characterize the economic policies of most industrial countries, have not been able to eradicate the fluctuations and crises of the international economy, but they have softened the consequences for the rich countries to such a degree that the Marxist conditions for the final collapse of capitalism are no longer present. Keynes's theories prevented the Marxist revolution by giving capitalism artificial respiration.

The heightened economic contradictions that were to arise as the result of the crises have also been diminished by the transfers of income and the social security provisions which were enforced through the increasing social influence of the labour movement and the majority of the electorate.

Keynes's theories take economic competition as a necessary driving force, but call for such regulation of economic development that major conflicts of interest are avoided. Competition thus becomes a force driving the growth of the industrial system not only at the level of economic management, but also for the ordinary worker. Keynes thought that this competition for individual and collective gain would eventually take industrial society forward to such a level of general affluence that new and more social attitudes could take root. However, as he said in 1930: 'For at least another hundred years we must pretend to ourselves and to everyone that fair is foul and foul is fair; for foul is useful and fair is not. Avarice and usury and precaution must be our gods for a little longer still. For only they can lead us out of the tunnel of economic necessity into daylight.'[30]

What has occurred in the industrial countries since Keynes's death in 1946 indicates, however, that his expectations of an affluence that will eventually satisfy everyone cannot be fulfilled by the growth of wealth alone. One of the reasons seems to be that the general competition for economic advantage, which lies behind every effort in our growth system, presupposes distinct differences of income. Once the basic natural heeds have been satisfied, it is consequently no longer merely the commodities themselves which motivate individuals and groups, but just as much what they signal and symbolize with regard to the individual's position on the economic ladder.

This has been confirmed by studies of the sense of satisfaction of various income groups with their situation, undertaken a number of countries. In particular, Richard A. Easterlin's 1974 study on the relationship between economic growth and quality of life suggests that people's sense of contentment depends not on their absolute but on their *relative* level of affluence. Correlation of interview replies from nineteen countries at various economic levels shows generally that the proportion of the population that is satisfied with its situation does not increase with the country's wealth, but depends everywhere on the individual's position on the national income scale. The great increase in wealth in the USA between 1946 and 1970 has thus not contributed to any increase worth mentioning in the proportion of Americans who describe themselves as 'very happy' or 'fairly happy'.

The equalization of incomes at a reasonable level of affluence ought therefore to help create a more widespread sense of tranquillity and satisfaction. But this general sense of satisfaction would obviously also remove the motivation for extra effort and industrial growth which our society must clearly have if it is to avoid economic crises.

This brings us back to the basic question: what is it in the society of industrial growth which seems to make a necessity of economic inequality, and thus of competition for income and growth in consumption contrary to the objective that is indicated by our posited fundamental values?

Can Marx's analysis tell us anything about the growth dynamic?

In Marx's time, and for several generations afterwards, a general national increase in wealth was clearly necessary. Marx's main concern was the unequal distribution of the right of disposal over combined property and income. As long as society's total wealth was still seen as being too limited to be able to assure prosperity for everyone through equal distribution, growth in industry and production was a natural goal in itself. For Marx, capital's steady accumulation of labour-saving machinery was a necessary evil in order to reach the stage at which the working class could take over the advanced production equipment created by the toil it would now free them from. Similarly, the capitalist himself is, in Marx's eyes, a temporarily necessary evil:

> He is fanatically intent on the valorization of value; consequently he ruthlessly forces the human race to produce for production's sake. In this way he spurs on the development of society's productive forces, and the creation of those material conditions of production which alone can form the real basis of a higher form of society, a society in which the full and free development of every individual forms the ruling principle.[6]

While Marx discusses the earlier artisans' and peasants' individual production as a condition for their original freedom, which they lost under capitalism, he regards this original mode of production as an impediment to the necessary and desirable large-scale enterprise which the working class is to take over:

> This [previous] mode of production presupposes the fragmention of holdings, and the dispersal of the other means of production. As it excludes the concentration of these means of production, so it also excludes cooperation, division of labour within each separate process of production, the social control and regulation of the forces of nature, and the free development of the productive forces of society. It is compatible only with a system of production and a society moving within narrow limits which are of natural origin. To perpetuate it would be ... 'to decree universal mediocrity'.

Here it seems clear that Marx's capacity to foresee the future weakness of industrial society failed him, perhaps because he could scarcely imagine that capitalism could survive long enough for *superabundance* to become a general problem affecting society and resources. In the nineteenth century it would also have been difficult to foresee that automated technology would itself reach such an advanced and complex stage that it could only be controlled and guided by a new élite of experts, more or less independent of property relations. In Marx's time it had still not become clear that technology in itself can enslave and oppress the majority.

It might nevertheless be instructive to look briefly at Marx's own account of the forces which bring about unstoppable industrial growth and the over-exploitation of resources in capitalist industrial society. Even though it will later become apparent that his conclusions are not tenable or applicable in today's situation, his analysis may stimulate further examination of this problem.

According to Marx, the real motive for technological growth did not lie with the individual capitalist. The force driving development originated in the fact that there existed a class which provided not to consume but to accumulate capital in the form of an expanding production apparatus. If we imagine that the capitalist class itself consumes the entire surplus-value instead of investing it in the expansion of the means of production, 'we destroy the very basis of the capitalist mode of production.' Indeed, this

would be to 'preclude both capitalist production and the capitalist himself.'[28]
Even if the majority of capitalists *wanted* to halt growth, it would in practice
be impossible to do so, because of the vulnerability of the big companies.
'Every capitalist requires a constantly growing reserve in order to be able to
meet price fluctuations and to be ready for favourable economic conditions.'
If the business is to survive, its owner must constantly accumulate capital in
order to increase the volume of production and appropriate for himself the
result of the technological development.

But any general wish on the part of owners to halt this development is
actually unthinkable in a traditional capitalist society, Marx claims, because
the system itself is built through competition among individual capitalists.
Once this competition is established, it presents every proprietor with a
choice of growth or ruin. In order to maintain this imperative, it is enough
that *some* capitalists, wanting short-term individual gains, are always
introducing more efficient forms of technology and production. Those who
bring in improved methods of production, of course, appropriate a larger
proportion of the working day as surplus labour than do other capitalists in
the same sector. But this additional surplus-value disappears as soon as the
new method of production becomes common – so, according to Marx,
constant technological growth and renewal becomes necessary in order to
satisfy the profit motive: 'The law of the determination of value by labour-
time makes itself felt to the individual capitalist who applies the new method
of production by compelling him to sell his goods under their social value;
this same law, acting as a coercive law of competition, forces his
competitors to adopt the new method.'[6] Or in other words, to invest in the
same automation, the same advantages of producing on a larger scale, and
the same growth in production as other competitors.

The urge to self-enrichment on the part of the owners which Marx
discusses, and which only need be present in *some* of the capitalists for all to
be compelled to participate in the process of growth, is not expressed in the
desire for wealth for private use and consumption. It is rather a matter of the
wish to reinforce the position and the power which the ownership of the
means of production confers.

'One must therefore never treat the capitalist production process as
though its immediate purpose was to satisfy the capitalist's personal needs.
One would then be ignoring the distinctive feature of this mode of
production, ignoring everything which forms its inner kernel.'[29] 'The
driving motive and determining purpose of capitalist production is the self-
valorization of capital to the greatest possible extent, i.e. the greatest
possible production of surplus-value ... '[6]

But for many capitalists, perhaps ultimately the majority, it is simply a
question of obeying the game's rules of growth in order to survive. The
capitalist's 'urge to self-enrichment' therefore does not even need to be a
personal motive; it is above all

the effect of a social mechanism in which he is merely a cog. Morever,
the capitalist production makes it necessary constantly to increase the
amount of capital laid out in a given industrial undertaking, and
competition subordinates every individual capitalist to the immanent

laws of capitalist production, as external and coercive laws. It compels him to keep extending his capital, so as to preserve it, and he can only extend it by means of progressive accumulation.'[6]

Marx's view is therefore this. *Growth,* through the constant accumulation of surplus-value in the form of capital or means of production, is the fundamental and necessary condition of production in a capitalist society. And the precondition for this is the existence of one class with no means of production which is obliged to sell its labour in order to obtain an income, and another class which, by having the means of production at its disposal, can demand that some of the value of the labour is invested in the growth of these means of production. In a nation or a world in which the capitalist market economy dominates, competition will force every firm into the growth race, regardless of individual intention or form of management.

What we have covered so far therefore seems to bring us to the following conclusions:

1) The capitalist system in the individual industrial countries is still being driven, even where it is regulated by Keynesian state intervention and modified by trade-union organization, by inbuilt 'laws of growth' bound up with the special position of a minority in society. In accordance with the moral premises mentioned previously, it therefore seems necessary to aim for a change of this system and its division of power.

2) The contradictions which according to Marx should bring about the collapse of the system have, however, clearly been weakened more than strengthened over the last century. The economic contradictions which still exist obviously do not provide the majority with sufficient motivation for change. These economic contradictions are – in modern industrial society – exploited as a source of power for maintaining the system and growth. If this conclusion is valid, then other contradictions and motives than economic ones on the part of the majority must drive the transformation through.

3) What may be relevant today in Marx's analysis is his account of the principal reasons for this growth, namely:

   Firstly, the fact that a minority in society have decisive influence over the means of production and can only secure their position through competition for industrial growth, regardless of their own or others' natural needs.

   Secondly, the fact that the majority do not themselves control the means of production and therefore cannot determine the extent and nature of production in accordance with common needs, but must put their labour at the disposal of the minority who can and must use it for growth for growth's sake. The competitive economy that is thereby created compels every individual enterprise within the system to obey the laws of competition for growth.

4) It therefore seems that the necessary change must occur 'from below', through the majority being able to decide what is done with the results of their labour and through society freeing itself from its dependence on competition for growth in the international market economy.

A transformation of this sort will obviously run into conflicts of interest. The question is, however, whether the social classes and their conflicts follow the same lines as in Marx's time. Which groups in particular can today be expected to oppose this sort of 'change from below', in order to protect their own positions?

6. What Are the Forces Obstructing Change?

The American economist John Kenneth Galbraith is among those who have most clearly demonstrated the shifts of power that have occurred since Marx's time. Because of Galbraith's undisputed knowledge about economic relations in the society of industrial growth, and because his views are internationally respected by many on both Left and Right, it might be useful to look briefly at his analysis of the forces which today seem to govern the industrial countries' economic development, and international economic development generally.

According to Galbraith, the ordinary employee is indeed still without significant influence on the means of production and social development, but his or her former adversary, the traditional capitalist, no longer represents the decisive power factor.

Here, it is important to distinguish between the right of ownership and the right of management and control. When Marx speaks of the right to own the means of production as the basis of social power, it is actually the importance of ordinary workers being able to develop and use the means of production on their own basic terms that he is discussing. In a society with a more surveyable structure, such as the one Marx knew, this sort of control could perhaps have been achieved by the majority through common ownership. In the vastly complicated industrial society of today, with its networks of connections between advanced technology and research, multifarious national and international economic relationships, thousands of distribution channels and communications lines, and the almost incomprehensible legislation and bureaucracy needed to make it function, ownership is no longer synonymous with control. In relation to this system, everyone is powerless unless they have the specialist training needed to understand at least a *sector* of the whole. For this reason, advanced education and professional leadership have to an increasing degree become the power factors, more or less independently of property relations. As long as this complex technosystem, with its need for specialized planning, is maintained, takeover by the majority of ownership of the means of production will change little in the relations of control. What may be changed is the distribution of the results of production. But what is perhaps the main problem for most people in such a society – powerlessness in relation to the constant upheavals in their conditions of life, consumer needs, and living and working environments following the onward march of technology – all this will probably remain unchanged. In this respect it looks as though there is little difference between so-called communist and capitalist industrialized countries; modern technological society every-where obeys its own laws, supported by the social groups which have secured their social position through being the only people who understand how the different parts of the system function.

This also accounts for the reduced power of the traditional capitalist class in Western industrial countries. Capital today must, on the whole, obey the rules that the professional leadership draws up. Since this is still not acknowledged by many more dogmatic Marxists, it is worth looking a little more closely at Galbraith's account of modern society as presented in *The New Industrial State*[31] from which quotations are taken in the rest of this section.

Galbraith's point of departure is the USA, the multinational companies' principal homeland, but the development he outlines is, to a greater or less degree, applicable to all industrial countries, not least in the matter of the international relations between the power groups which weave the economies of the industrial countries and the rest of the world into an interacting whole.

In the earlier capitalist system which Marx analyses, the proprietors had real power and were also able to influence the state to their own advantage. Galbraith calls the final phase of this system the 'entrepreneurial' system. The big proprietors of entrepreneurial corporations could largely take law and order into their own hands. They still supervised their enterprises and their relation to society, and they therefore still had power. We are now leaving this system for another which demands group decisions of enormous complexity. This new system has put power in the hands of specialist-educated, professional and interlinked groups of leaders, working at various levels in the bureaucracy and in business.

What gives this new multiform power group its special position and influence are the conditions which result from the size and complexity of the modern corporation. By the beginning of the 1960s the 500 biggest industrial corporations already had over two-thirds of the USA's productive capital; and 384 corporations each employing more than 5,000 workers accounted for 85 per cent of the total expenditure on industrial research and development while 260,000 firms with fewer than 1,000 employees covered only 7 per cent, according to the studies cited by Galbraith.

At the same time, the giant format which is increasingly necessary to bear the capital obligations of modern technology makes the big corporation vulnerable to fluctuating price and market conditions against which it must protect itself. The specialization of industrial society makes these enterprises dependent on a specific type of demand – for the only things they are able to produce. A failure in this demand or in the supply of the necessary raw materials will create economic catastrophe on an enormous scale. Modern corporate planning is therefore largely directed at 'getting rid of market uncertainty,' says Galbraith. The bigger the concern, the more important it is to eliminate risk in respect of raw materials, labour and demand – but at the same time the greater are the possibilities of controlling these factors through systematic planning. This occurs particularly in four areas:

1) To secure themselves against fluctuations in price or inadequate supplies of the relevant raw materials, the planners take over the sources of supply: the aluminium company takes over the sources of bauxite, the

steel company the sources of iron ore; the big fruit, tea and coffee producers buy up the plantation land that is needed in order to plan on the basis of secure raw materials. To a great extent, of course, purchase of this sort occurs in the Third World, where the price of labour, too, can be controlled by the company's planners. Uncontrolled bargaining is replaced by internal decision making.

2) In the same way, the big concern is able to control its many sub-contractors and the firms which buy its products. General Motors' decisions whether to buy or not can mean life or death for its suppliers. GM has control because it can always procure a material or a component for itself. And no individual firm buying GM's products can force any change by withdrawing its custom – the dominance of the market by a few big firms reduces the purchasers' choice. Competition between these big firms is eliminated by their common interest in stable prices as the basis of secure planning. Market fluctuations, too, are replaced by planning, with contracts between seller and buyer to remove market uncertainty for both parties, says Galbraith.

3) Control over the pay and incentives of the workforce is also vital to large-scale corporate planning. This is achieved through cultivating the employees' identification with the firm, so that the Marxist conflict between labour and management ceases, as discussed earlier: 'The way is open for the worker to accept the goals of the organization ... The worker being more identified with the firm, the union has less enmity to arouse.' The aim is achieved when the individual begins to see himself as an 'IBM-man or a Sears-man'. With this sort of identification, and the workers linking their personal goals with those of the firm, monetary incentives, at least above a certain pay level, become less significant and planning on the basis of controlled pay becomes possible.

This control of work motivation and incentive is exercised even more directly, if on another level, in relation to those working for multinational concerns in poor countries. For example, enterprises established in developing countries can make their workers into obedient tools by inducing in them a dependence on modern clothing or other products which presuppose incomes where people previously got by on what was mainly a subsistence economy.

4) Management of demand is also a decisive precondition for the fourth and most important form of control exercised by the big modern company – control of the consumer market. This control has rendered liberalism's ideal model wholly redundant, says Galbraith. 'The initiative in deciding what is to be produced comes not from the sovereign consumer who, through the market, issues the instructions that bend the productive mechanism to his ultimate will. Rather it comes from the great producing organization which reaches forward to control the markets that it is presumed to serve and, beyond, to bend the customer to its needs. And, in so doing, it deeply influences his values and belief ... '

The large scale makes it possible to control what is to be sold through advertising, a well-tended sales organization, and careful product supervision, assuring the necessary customer response. The models do not reflect the fashions of the day, says Galbraith, they *are* the fashions of the day. People's idea of the right shape for a car is what the car designers say it is going to be.

In the absence of the massive and artful persuasion that accompanies the management of demand, increasing abundance might well have reduced the interest of people in acquiring more goods. The consequence – a lower and less reliable propensity to consume – would have been awkward for the industrial system. Advertising and its related arts thus help develop the kind of man the goals of the industrial system require – one that reliably spends his income and who works reliably because he is always in need of more.

Planning is the distinguishing feature of our age's industrial society, says Galbraith. Those with power are therefore the specialists with the qualifications to perform this planning function. And planning must bring *all* human relations under its control. Complete demand management was the last step in this development.

The power of the technostructure

Complete planning and control of all variable factors, which is not only possible but necessary in big modern corporations, demands a new form of management, a new power élite. The capitalist, the formal economic owner, the shareholder, does not have the specialized knowledge required for this planning. Even control of the surplus-value that is needed to ensure investment and growth is taken over by the firm's internal management and professional planning groups. 'Savings,' says Galbraith, 'are supplied by the large industrial enterprise to itself as part of its planning.' The big corporation secures its sovereign position and its independence from owners, capitalists and financiers by obtaining its own capital from its own savings, i.e. capital that is no longer under the owner's control, but that of the internal management.

Galbraith also quotes Professor Ben B. Seligman, a specialist on the new power élite's control over access to capital: 'The new managerial class discovered that with an adequate supply of funds stemming from accumulated profits they could get along quite well without Wall Street tutelage ... Today, it is the paid professional who governs the corporation' (from *The American Corporation: Ideology and Reality,* 1964). The goal of professional management is therefore no longer to maximise the owner's profit, which is determined as one element of internal planning. The goal is industrial growth: 'Size is the general servant of technology, not the special servant of profits.'

Power goes to the factor which is most difficult to replace – and that, in modern industrial society, is the professional expertise without which no firm can survive. What is demanded from outside is no longer capital but 'the modern scholar of science, mathematics, information systems or communications theory [who] is ever more in demand to guide the mature corporation through its besetting problems of science, technology and

computerization.' The demands of technology and planning have greatly
increased industry's need for specialist talent and organization, and *this* the
big corporation cannot generate internally. Groups possessing this
knowledge therefore represent the decisive power factor and hold decisive
influence over industrial society's development, while the shareholder
becomes more and more a background figure, fighting for vestiges of past
power.

The shareholder does not even have any real influence on the selection of
management: 'The men who now run the large corporations ... are selected
not by stockholders but, in the commonsense, by a Board of Directors which
narcissistically they selected themselves,' says Galbraith. He also describes
with great humour the ceremonial theatrics that management put on at
company general meetings in order to give the many shareholders the
impression that the firm's future activity depends on their decisions. In
reality everything has been planned and decided long ago by the internal
professionals whose dispositions the general meeting has not the slightest
means of understanding or influencing. The power of professional
management is also strengthened by the tendency to spread shares between
many holders. Galbraith refers to studies which, several decades ago when
the concentration of capital was greater, showed that the majority of shares
were held by blocs owning less than 1 per cent of the total capital: 'This
means that to change control, more stock-holders must be persuaded,
against the advice of management, to vote their stock for someone whom, in
the nature of the case, they do not know and will not be disposed to trust.
The effort must also contend with the tendency of the indifferent to give
proxies to the management.' The shareholder can of course vote, says
Galbraith, but the vote is worthless. The corporation's need for long-term,
careful planning simply does not allow any interference from outside and
incompletely informed sources. Both the shareholders and the bureaucracy
of the state must cooperate on the lines laid down by the internal experts.
Those who are not active in management have less and less information
about what is happening and less reason to ask. Important planning is strictly
confined to the circle of leading experts – all the more so, the more the
firm's size and complexity increase the need for specialist knowledge as the
basis for any intelligent decision-making. And even if the takeover of power
by professionals is not complete, the principle has general validity.

But this new power is not embodied in individuals. No single manager can
command the ocean of specialist knowledge that lies behind the big modern
corporation's multifaceted planning and management. 'Decision in the
modern business enterprise is the product not of individuals, but of groups ...
this is how men act successfully on matters where no single one, however
exalted or intelligent, has more than a fraction of the necessary knowledge.
It is what makes modern business possible and in other contexts it is what
makes modern governments possible.'

Galbraith is here talking about specialist engineers, chemists and
physicists, computer experts, psychologists, economists and marketing
specialists, designers, administrators, economic and political negotiators,
sales planners, production and work managers at many levels. This is not

however a system that fosters a new and rare source of talent – as its defenders often maintain. 'This is pure vanity. Were it so, there would be few such achievements. The real accomplishment of modern science and technology consists in taking ordinary men, informing them narrowly and deeply and then, through appropriate organization, arranging to have their knowledge combined with that of other specialized but equally ordinary men.'

This new multiform élite which to an increasing degree is taking over the capitalists' old position of power, Galbraith calls the *technostructure*. It has enormous influence over us all, but not in the same way as the old capitalists: the technostructure supplies not capital but specialized talent and organization 'so there is no longer, *a priori,* reason to believe that profit maximization will be the goal of the technostructure ... the first goal of the technostructure is its own growth.'

One would expect that this shift (from capital to organized intelligence) would be reflected in the deployment of power in the society at large. This has, indeed, occurred. There has been a shift of power as between the factors of production which matches that which occurred from land to capital in the advanced countries beginning two centuries ago. It is an occurrence of the last fifty years and is still going on.

The shift in power has been disguised because power has not gone to another of the established factors as they are celebrated in conventional economic pedagogy. It has not passed to labour. Labour has won limited authority over its pay and working conditions but none over the enterprise.

Galbraith emphasizes mainly the social power held by the technostructure's élites in the giant private and state companies, particularly of the USA and the Soviet Union. The planning power of the multinationals reaches not only to Third World countries, where they control access to raw materials, but also far into the other highly industrialized countries. One doesn't have to fish long in the economic waters of our own businesses to bring up the tentacles of a giant squid whose head is in a corporation on the other side of the Atlantic.

As the big corporations widen their market, so their need for international market control grows. One of the most interesting examples of this is the international development of the advertising agencies. It has been known for many years that Madison Avenue, the old main street of American advertising, is dominated by the big corporations whose accounts mean life or death for the individual agency. During the sixties and seventies, these multinational companies insisted that the control they exercised over American advertising agencies be extended to overseas markets. In order to keep their principal clients, the American agencies, which are themselves often as large as a major European company, have had to gain control of influence on the market in a whole series of industrial countries in Europe and elsewhere. In order to combine overall market planning with knowledge of the local market, this has often been achieved through buying a majority control of shares in foreign agencies. In Norway today, only a minority of big advertising agencies are now not in some way dependent on foreign agency capital, and thus under the indirect control of the multinationals, contributing in return to their global planning and 'demand production' for world-famous trademarks.

This might give rise to a misleading picture of international power relations. The opposite of power is powerlessness; the suppression of one's own interests and goals. But the links which exist between the techno-structures of the big countries' giant concerns and the corresponding planning élites in smaller countries give no expression to such conflicting interests. When Colgate and Ford sell in Norway, Tandberg in the USA, Coca-Cola in the Soviet Union and Toyota in Britain, there is, admittedly, competition for markets. But it is in the interest of planning élites in all these countries that this competition continues, to the benefit of complex industrial growth on a global scale and the leadership this requires. This again must not be reduced to a question of good or bad will on the part of individuals. For one thing, there are hardly any individual factors in this complex interplay whose purpose is to break all the rules without being put out of the game. The advantages achieved by *one* enterprise when it adopts a more efficient method of production, management or influence, compel others to follow its lead. This is not really a question of thinking consciously of individual power advantages at the expense of the many the system makes powerless. It is rather the common human tendency to regard the system to which one owes one's power and authority as something one obviously wants to defend. It is not easy to see that one's lifelong education, knowledge and activity contribute to maintaining a system that oppresses the freedom and self-determination of the majority, and that, in accordance with the values in which one perhaps believes in one's heart of hearts, ought to be transformed. There are nevertheless an increasing number, even among those who have power and influence within this élite system, who see its destructive effects in a wider perspective and try to resist. In practice, there is little they can do without jumping off the merry-go-round. Some people who have done exactly this – especially young people after an education supporting the system – choose to use their knowledge to oppose it. But the real conflict of interest in the colossal apparatus of control from above is between the few who control and the many who are controlled. It is among the latter that the motivation and power to create change is growing, and it is they that defectors from the élite system must support if a development towards freedom for the majority is to be possible.

The role of the state

What, then, is the position of the state in this new power scheme?

In the old liberal economy with competing individual proprietors the role played by the state was to maintain the system of finance, distribution and legislation that safeguarded free capitalist development and competition. Beyond this, however, the state was not to interfere in the market mechanism.

The task of the state is still to secure working conditions for the most important power grouping in society, which is now the technostructure of collaborating planners, professional managers and specialists in the firms which control the market. Whether these are based on state or private capital is less important. The goal is the same in both cases, and this is not in fact determined either by the state or by the owners of capital, but by the technostructure itself. The object is to protect the position of the expert élite by securing the development of the technology, planning and market control which are the conditions of its existence.

In this process, the state is not, generally speaking, an independent power factor with its own objectives. Regardless of the official ideology, the state is compelled to obey the technostructure's own laws. And for this reason only minor changes occur in the evolution of the society of industrial growth when power is transferred from a conservative to a social-democratic regime, or vice versa. If the state attempts to interfere in the system with an *ideological* intention, an imbalance is created in the planning system and the politicians in power are accused of 'mixing politics with business'. But in the state apparatus of modern industrial society, 'ideological' politicians have very little influence in comparison with the professionals who understand and accept the rules of the game – whether they are democratically elected or employed by the state. In industrial society, therefore, the important power in the governing and state apparatus lies not with those who want to comply with the governing party's political ideals – whether conservative social-democratic or state capitalist – but with the same type of highly trained specialists and planners as are found in the internal apparatus of the big companies. Indeed, they actually belong to the same technostructure: they are recruited from the same educational milieu, they have the same terminology and the same way of thinking professionally, they generally belong to the same cultural and income groups, and they have, to a great extent, a common view of the significance of technology, planning and social control. In other words, the interplay between the power élites of the state and those of big business is no longer a cooperative interaction between two different social groups; the two groups are now actually one. And economic planning is the generally accepted principle, whether society's formal power is attributed to the state or to big corporations.

The widely held belief that the managements of 'private' firms are usually opponents of economic planning rests on a complete misunderstanding, says Galbraith. Economic planning is the very basis of their own operations. Consequently, 'the fully planned economy, so far from being unpopular, is warmly regarded by those who know it best,' he says. This seems to be confirmed, moreover, by the surprising number of private business executives who, by their own account, would have no objection to serving as the managers of equivalent state enterprises.

The individual proprietors and 'capitalists' of whom there are still many, although their numbers and power are declining – do not always understand that their interests are opposed to those of the big corporations. These survivors from an earlier age often seem to imagine it is still the 'free market forces' of liberalism that ensure the further development of technology and the economy. On the basis of an ideology that has long been abandoned by those with real power, they protest against 'the planned economy and state interference and control'. They are living in the last century. As Galbraith writes,

> The industrial system, in fact, is inextricably associated with the state. In notable respects the mature corporation is an arm of the state. And the state, in important matters, is an instrument of the industrial system.
>
> The mature corporation depends ... on the state for trained manpower, the regulation of aggregate demand, and, though less explicitly, for stability in wages and prices ... Its influence on the state is, in fact, incomparably much greater than that of the entrepreneurial corporation.
>
> When planning replaces the market, and identification and adaptation supplement pecuniary compensation, matters are very different. No sharp line separates government from the private firm; the line becomes very indistinct and even imaginary.

According to Galbraith, therefore, both those who regard the state as the enemy of modern business and those who look for *capital's* power over the state are stuck in the post. The technostructure is the power factor which ties state and business together into a unit and 'the myth of separation helps to suppress any suggestion that the mature corporation in its public business is, in principle, a part of the larger public bureaucracy.' The state and the corporations participate in the technostructure's scheme regardless of whether the industrial society in question is 'capitalist' or 'communist'.

> In the Soviet Union and the Soviet-type economies, prices are extensively managed by the state. Production is not in response to market demand but given by the overall plan. In the Western economies, markets are dominated by the great firms ...
>
> The technostructure's power will not be peculiar to what in the cadenzas of ideology is called the free enterprise or capitalist system. If the intervention of private authority, in the form of owners, must be prevented in the private firm, so must the intervention of public authority in the public firm. As a further consequence, puzzlement over capitalism without control by the capitalist will be matched by puzzlement over socialism without control by the society.

Galbraith quotes C.A.R. Crosland [*The Corporation in Modern Society*], who says: 'In Britain, the public corporation has not up to the present been in any real sense accountable to Parliament whose function has been limited to fitful, fragmentary, and largely ineffective *ex post facto* criticism.' Galbraith adds: 'The technical complexity, planning and associated scale of operations that took power from the capitalist entrepreneur and lodged it with the technostructure, removed it also from the reach of social control ... The choice being between success without social control and social control without success, democratic socialism no longer seems worth the struggle.'

The role of the trade-union movement

What, then, is the role of the trade-union movement in the system of industrial growth? In terms of power, does it represent opposition to the technostructure?

Between the *fundamental* interests of the technostructure and those of the workers there is still a clear conflict, which we shall come back to. But the interests which are expressed in trade-union politics are on the whole compatible with the objectives of the big corporations and the whole technostructure. The priority given by the trade-union movement to economic improvement for all income groups – at the expense of demands for changes in the social structure itself, in the content of production and in economists' developmental goals, at the expense of an active interest in the process by which technology deprives the majority of power, at the expense of a redistribution of income, power and control, and, last but not least, of other important values – this one-sided and outdated politics accords extremely well with the planning of the new power élite. In this way the trade-union movement actually contributes to the development of the technology and the surplus production on which the power of the technostructure is based. As Galbraith points out, the trade-union movement works to the advantage of the technostructure and the society of growth by helping to guide demand, by providing support for the professional planner's desire for constantly increasing production (e.g. by seeing growth as a defence against unemployment) and, more important, standardizing 'wage costs between different industrial firms and to ensure that changes in wages will occur at approximately the same time. This greatly assists price control by the industry. And it also greatly facilitates the public regulation of prices and wages.'

The trade-union movement's leaders officially base their politics on the old idea that the struggle is simply between the workers' right to the surplus-value they produce and the capitalists' profit objectives. But for the new power élite, whose salaries are high but regulated, it is not the capitalist's profit to which everything is subordinated, but technological development and the securing of their own position.

> The first goal of the technostructure is its own security. Profits, provided they are above the minimum necessary for security, are secondary to growth ... This means that the technostructure may readily trade profits for protection against such an undirected event with such an unpredictable outcome as a strike. Once again there is the important fact that those who make the decisions during union negotiations do not themselves have to pay. But no reduction in profits may be required from yielding to the union. Since the mature firm does not maximize profits, it can maintain income by increasing its prices.

> The most important thing for the technostructure is to secure the greatest possible demand – the real requirement for its progress. For this reason a regular increase in real wages to ensure a higher level of consumption,

increased materialism and therefore increased effort at all income levels, are all very much in the interest of the new power groups. To contribute to this, both active marketing and the trade unions' role in increasing pay and consumption are equally necessary. And as long as equalization between diferent income groups always comes second for the labour movement, group competition will be maintained, ensuring that no group, not even the most highly paid, is ever content with its situation. Group competition for economic and material status makes everyone into obedient slaves of the planners' professional demand production – and credit, loans and hire-purchase arrangements make people even more dependent. 'Advertising and salesmanship – the management of consumer demand – are vital for planning in the industrial system. At the same time, the wants so created ensure the services of the worker. Ideally his wants are kept slightly in excess of his income. Compelling inducements are then provided for him to go into debt. The pressure of the resulting debt adds to his reliability as a worker.'

Another circumstance which serves to neutralize the power of the labour movement is the social prestige, arising from higher education and specialist knowledge, which the technostructure's position contributes to. More and more people want to move from the role of ordinary worker to specialist status, and are consequently willing to move away from associating themselves with the labour movement and regard themselves as members of the technostructure, thus identifying with its objectives. It is in industrial society's interest to increase the number of white-collar workers because 'they tend to identify themselves with the goals of the technostructure with which they are fused'.

The takeover of workers' functions by machines has a similar effect. Education reinforces the technostructure by replacing blue-collar workers with machines on an ever-increasing scale: 'Modern technology opens the way for a massive shift from workers who are within the reach of unions to those who are not.'

An important factor in evaluating the place of the trade-union movement in the new industrial society is the fact that a growing section of the union leadership, especially at the top level, has begun to associate itself with this society's planning élite and its objectives. Increasingly, therefore, union leaders will coordinate their politics with the state's, which coincide in turn with those of the big corporations. This is perhaps given clearest expression in the senior union leadership's more or less consistent opposition to popular protests against rule by experts and their plans. The competition which still continues between the leaders of the employers' organizations and those of the trade unions should mislead no one into believing that what is being expressed here is a fundamental conflict. Its purpose clearly seems to be to avoid upsets in the balance of power between the two groups on which the society of growth is dependent. Both leading castes belong to the highly paid and highly placed planning élite which wants above all to avoid changes in the social system on which its position is based. Nor should one take much notice of the different ideological languages of the two groups of leaders.

Verbally, one party defends the ideology of economic liberalism while the other is inclined to talk of the struggle against economic oppression in the old Marxist sense. But what they both seem to be defending are their own leading positions in the power of the existing system and its pyramidal structure. The senior leadership in the labour movement is, in other words, more and more frequently a part of the same, total planning élite which dominates the state apparatus and big industry.

Let it be said immediately, however, that there are of course individuals in every group of leaders, including those in the labour movement, who are working for fundamental change on the basis of a consistent opposition to the prevailing world view. They represent the real revolutionaries in the modern labour movement. These were the words of Arthur Svensson, president of the Norwegian Union of Industrial Chemical Workers, speaking at a conference in Oslo in 1978:

> Have we become so saturated by the consumer ideology of the capitalist system that we put continued increase in our own wealth before and above working to abolish want and poverty in the world – global solidarity? Unfortunately, I think we must affirm that this generally is the case ... For far too long the trade-union movement has concentrated one-sidedly on economic growth and higher material standards ... An important basis for increased global solidarity is a greater equalization – a fairer distribution in our own society ... Have we perhaps got too many who are privileged and highly paid in our own movement, so that there is no basis for doing anything about it? The group that is privileged has perhaps become so big and holds such positions of economic and political power that it isn't possible to redirect development towards a fairer distribution ... The tension that exists in the party [the Norwegian Labour Party] concerning the balance between human values and growth in production will, I think, turn to the advantage of human values in public opinion.[32]

The view Svensson speaks for here stands in marked opposition to the usual official positions and politics of the senior union leadership, which were expressed in a 1975 interview with the vice-president of the Norwegian Confederation of Trade Unions, in which he was asked whether from considerations of solidarity he saw any reason to halt growth in consumption in the foreseeable future. The vice-president replied, 'No, I consider that neither possible nor desirable'![33]

Whether this view, which in practice implies a commitment to the system of industrial growth, its lack of solidarity and its materialist competitive principle, is in accord with the wishes of the trade-union movement's ordinary members, is a question that has scarcely been raised. At all events, the leadership has never confronted them with the fundamental choice indicated by the conflict of values we have discussed.

Élite control in East and West

Taking Marxism's power analysis as a basis, and accepting liberalism's demand for personal freedom as a right for the *majority,* a picture emerges, in Galbraith's account among other places, of a world which seems increasingly to be consolidating new, élite positions of power at the expense of that majority's freedom and influence.

The old conceptions – which were based, on the one hand, on the conflict between economic liberalism and communist dictatorship, and, on the other, on the conflict between the power of capital and the power of labour – seem more and more artificial and inapplicable in relation to the forces which now guide the world economy. Under all forms of government, élite groups of the same type seem to plan and control development – but outdated ideas often prevent both sides of the political spectrum from seeing the injustice the new constellation of power is contributing to in every industrial society.

One side sees the problem of oppression resulting from centralized state power, but not that resulting from the planning power and manipulations of big business. The other side sees the danger of global control by the big corporations, but is reluctant to discuss the élite control and the disempowering of people which occurs in the name of the community.

There is much to suggest that this blindness in both right and the left eye prevents today's reality being seen. One of the conclusions following from Galbraith's analysis in *The New Industrial State* is that

> there is a broad convergence between industrial systems. The imperatives of technology and organization, not the images of ideology, are what determines the shape of economic society.
>
> The modern large corporation and the modern apparatus of socialist planning are variant accommodations to the same need.
>
> Since technology and planning are what accord power to the technostructure, the latter will have power wherever these are a feature of the productive process.

In the Soviet system corporate planning is undertaken by the state, but – and here Galbraith quotes Ely Devons [*Listener, 29 August 1957*]:

> The Russians have learnt by experience that you cannot have responsible and efficient action at the level of the firm with continuous intervention and instruction from numerous outside authorities ... Every argument for delegation, decentralization and devolution used in discussions about business administration in the West is echoed, although in a different jargon, in Russia.

In his book *Russian Close Contact*[34] Jahn Otto Johansen shows how the ordinary person is affected by this in the same way in both types of society. Exactly like the citizen in the West, the ordinary Soviet citizen is powerless in relation to the effects of industrial growth on the environment, traditions and values, culture and living conditions.

As a result of society subjecting itself to the technostructure's demand for economic growth, and consequently technological development, as the supreme objective, the planning élite's power is consolidated in all types of society. Progressive technology means status, promotion and power for

technologists and management groups everywhere. But in the traditional
political war of words there is no place for these new oppositions; there are
still only the traditional divisions – right/left, East/West.

Of course a very visible power struggle is in progress between Eastern
and Western industrial countries, one form of which is the arms race and
military-economic blocs on both sides. But if one looks for the real interests
behind this development a new picture seems to emerge, not of competing
but of common élite interests. According to this view, the circles which are
ultimately in control of development have the same *supreme* objective: to
further technological and economic development according to the same
basic pattern as today's. Competition between the ideological groupings
does not, for any of these parties, point in the direction of change on the
majority's terms, but towards preventing shifts of power among the various
countries' ruling groups.

Seen in this way, it is no more than natural that élite-ruled communist
China, to achieve its new targets for industrial growth, should be
cooperating with the fascist junta in Chile, that social-democratic Norway
should want 'good economic links' with the military rulers of Brazil, or that
the USA should enter into friendly trade talks with the USSR. Behind all
these *ideologically* incomprehensible capers is the same desire to protect the
system of industrial growth, ruled from above, and the groups the system
gives power to.

The arms race also has its natural place in this scheme, according to
Galbraith: 'Modern military and related procurement and policy are, in
fact, extensively adapted to the needs of the industrial system. It seems very
probable that this is a tendency of all planning, communist, socialist or non-
socialist, however denoted.'[31]

In 1974, the resources being used for military purposes already amounted
to more than the total annual income of the entire populations of South and
East Asia and Africa, and this expenditure is doubling every fifteen years.
There are few areas where economic realities are more clearly in conflict
with ideal objectives. During the first twenty-five years of the United
Nations, the General Assembly passed a total of 116 disarmament
resolutions. During the same period, the global arms bill was tripled.[36]

If the interest of the populations is to be the decisive factor, the danger of
wiping out the human race through continuing the insanity of the arms race
outweighs the risk accompanying a *limited first step towards disarmament* by one
side. It is interesting (though not particularly realistic) to imagine a
multinational referendum to find out whether the populations in question
are willing to accept this very limited risk in order to turn the armament
process in a new direction. Even though this would to some extent 'disturb
the balance of armaments', considering that each side would still have a
retaliatory capacity allowing annihilation of the opposing side many times
over, there is every reason to think that the result of such a referendum
would reveal a clear conflict between the inhabitants of industrial societies
and their ruling groups. But then people have never been confronted with
this choice. It seems to be in the interests of the technostructure to present
the problem as though the alternative, even to negotiated disarmament, is

guaranteed occupation and subjection to the opponent's dictatorship. Galbraith, who can scarcely be accused of running errands for the Soviet Union, says regarding this:

> That the risks of agreed disarmament are greater than those of a continuing and unresolved weapons competition is ... remarkably unproven. It is not clear why agreements can be negotiated in good faith with the communists on all subjects except disarmament. To eliminate civilized life for all time in response to a short-run calculation that liberty might otherwise, be endangered is also irrational ... It is extremely important in itself to know that our imagery is, in part, derived from the needs of the industrial system. This leads to introspection and scrutiny that would not, otherwise be forthcoming. For the same reason it helps us to know that part of our view of the world and its politics originates not in our minds but in the needs of the industrial system.[31]

And these needs are always formulated *for* us – from above.

Irrespective of one's view of Marx in other respects, his emphasis on the significance of conflicting interests in the process of change may be useful. It also seems reasonable to think that the goals and forces which stand in the clearest opposition to established power, and its objectives and privileges, are also the forces that are likely to create change.

Galbraith's analysis has led to the view that the industrial system's international planning élite represents the principal power maintaining this system. But as opposition to this élite – and as the most important power for change – Galbraith proposes a new élite group: the *educational and scientific estate*. His hope is that this 'estate' or caste will develop a consciousness of other values than those of the industrial system, and bring this new perspective into the technostructure it will educate.

Without doubt there are many within these groups who represent such a hope, but Galbraith's general conclusions ignore the conflict that the principle of expert and élite control has created in relation to the general population in the highly industrialized countries. And on this point Galbraith's view conflicts with interesting pespectives held by a number of other writers who have concerned themselves with the question of conflicts in modern society and who have perhaps got closer to the core of this problem.

7. Where Are the Conflicts of Interest?

Herbert Marcuse, Paolo Freire, E.F. Schumacher, Ivan Illich and André Glucksmann are among the many writers who have described in various ways how our complex industrial society, or its élites, in practice deprive most people of power. They belong to a growing group of free-thinking people who, even though themselves part of an intellectual élite, want ordinary people to have the freedom and rights they are lacking today under the élite rule of both capitalism and socialism, in both poor and rich countries: the right to responsibility for the goal and the meaning of one's own work; the right to determine social development through meaningful work and personal judgement.

Of course this human objective does not provide – and nor should it – any single answer to the question of precisely what type of social organization would allow room for such freedom. What does seem clear is that a fundamental change is required of the industrial system we have today. It points towards a new form of production, a simplification and a decentralization of the technological apparatus that can only be understood and controlled by élite groups.

This does not mean a regression to the toil of the past, nor that we scrap every type of technology that can lighten people's work. But if technology is to be consistent with the values we have taken as our point of departure, it must be an aid to the creative work of individuals, and of people working cooperatively – as opposed to the machinery of power which forces the majority into mass effort towards goals that are not their own.

The conflict of interest over social change will therefore be between those who want to experience a development towards such a society as a liberation, and those who want to oppose it in order to protect their privileged position.

In Marx's classical model society could still generally be portrayed as a pyramid of power, with monopoly capital representing the narrow summit under which came the state and the church, then a broader layer of smaller capitalists, in turn lying above a rather bigger layer of supervisors. Below them came the remaining artisans and smallholders, and then, in the lowest and broadest layer, the majority, the industrial proletariat who were ultimately to turn the pyramid upside down.

The power structure of modern industrial society can hardly be drawn as single pyramid of this sort. It would be more illuminating to draw it as a series of interlinked power pyramids, each influencing one another.

Between the pyramid summits representing the 'technostructure' of the state, big business, associated research and other institutions, there is, as a rule, systematic cooperation combined with limited competition. A stronger mixture of competition and cooperation exists between those pyramid summits which wish by this means to strengthen their own position without causing any significant structural changes in the relations of power. This seems to be the basis for negotiations and power struggles between the trade unions and the employers' associations, between the top levels of consumer and producer alliances and business leaders, and between leading groups in many types of special interest organizations.

But into this scheme, which is largely an illustration of Galbraith's analysis, some other power pyramids should be brought which are not so clearly acknowledged. There are pyramids of ideology and opinion representing the various population groups' views of social and political questions. At the top of these pyramids are those that André Glucksmann calls the 'master thinkers': those who formulate ready-made ideology and 'single and final solutions'; those who rally people around the total belief systems and leadership plans that are theoretically much too complicated for most people to understand, let alone question; those who are constantly luring people in under their banners by claiming that their thought structures have been created 'for the people', but who never, never accept that the solutions have to be developed *by* the people themselves. It is they who cling to their theories, developing and discussing them within their own closed circle in an élite language which itself expresses contempt for ordinary people's forms of thought and expression. In this way, they shape their exclusive ideas in discussion with people who share the same ideological knowledge, while what they address to the people is given the form of primitive propaganda for ideology as ideology, without any suggestion of a more profound basis: 'The majority in society today are the object of an altogether fantastic, "learned" contempt. This contempt has its source in the élite and is directed against everything that stands outside itself'.[3]

Between the tops of these pyramids, competing to suppress public opinion, a verbal battle for power over people is also in progress. The total theories which are their property and their means to power may be revolutionary or conservative, they may be based on economics, religion or social science. But in one important respect the master thinkers have a common interest: they want to preserve the leading position of intellectuals, of better-knowing theoreticians at the pyramid tops, whether they see themselves there as revolutionary leaders of the people, as proprietors or as planners. And this is evidently the characteristic feature common to those with power today. The significant class divisions run not only between those with property and those without, between capital and labour, nor even between the technostructure's planners and those who are controlled by them. The general difference of class and power seems today to be between those who, by virtue of education and supposedly superior knowledge, determine social objectives, and the many who by the same criteria are excluded. Whether they want to preserve or to change society is less important in this respect; what is important is that what they are aiming at is still a pyramidal society. Even the most revolutionary among them lack the majority's motive for the *decisive* change – the elimination of the pyramid principle itself, because they themselves do not suffer by this principle. The rewards for the new class include 'exemption from manual work; escape from boredom and confining and severe routine; the chance to spend one's life in clean and physically comfortable surrounding. ... Overwhelmingly, the qualification is education,' says Galbraith in his book *The Affluent Society*.[37] And this class division is noticed first and foremost by those who suffer from it. 'In the USA suspicion and rancour is no longer directed against the capitalists or those who are merely rich. It is the intellectuals – the effete snobs – who are eyed with misgiving and alarm ... This reflects the relevant class distinction in our time.' Previously it was having money and economic power that justified contempt for those who had nothing. 'In recent times education has become the difference that divides,' says Galbraith. It 'doesn't serve to paper over the conflict. It is visible in almost every community.'[31]

Of course this does not apply to all intellectuals. The characteristic of this conflict is not knowledge in itself, but the manner in which it is too often used – as a means to power and the suppression of opinion. The oppressive power is 'master thinking', the conviction that theoretical knowledge and understanding is so superior to popular understanding that it justifies leadership and terrorism of thought. 'The master thinkers have given expression to the will to power which, on a smaller scale and more secretly, spurred on the commanders and the aspiring commanders of disciplinarian society,' says Glucksmann.[3]

Why should so much significance be attached to this broader concept of power? If society needs to be transformed, is it not a good thing that someone takes on the task of leadership and of formulating a *complete* ideology concerning the transformation process and the goal?

The answer has two aspects. In the first place, experience shows that the invalidation of popular opinion, which the master thinkers' monopoly of thought leads to under an élite-controlled revolution, in virtually all known instances has created a society ruled from above. The élite which convinced people that it knew best how the revolution should be led, is inclined to claim that it also knows best how the new society should be organized. The revolutionary élite maintains its power by virtue of a population that is used to responding to the signals given by ideological leaders.

It is this perspective of the intellectual class concerning the difference between those who have 'understanding' and the primitive masses who understand nothing, which lies behind Leninist revolutionary theory, based on an ideology which, according to Lenin, must come to the proletariat from above. Claims that such theories arise from the interests of common people always sound equally convincing – until one begins to listen to the superior knowledge which lies, on behalf of the unknowing, behind the words – as, for example, in Georg Lukács's book about Lenin's revolutionary theory in which he says: 'the stringency of the demands made on party members is only a way of making clear to the whole proletariat (and all strata exploited by capitalism) where their true interests lie ... '[38]

Or, as Lenin himself said of centralized leadership after the revolution: 'Marxists will in no sense accept the principle of federation or decentralization. A big centralized state represents a huge historical advance on the way from medieval fragmentation to the socialist unity of the future ... '3

Here there is a clear division between Lenin's demand for the party's monopoly of both discussion and leadership, and Marx's confidence in 'the intellectual development of the working class, which was sure to result from combined action and mutual discussion.'[19] Marx and Engels also wrote in the *Communist Manifesto* that the revolution's advocates 'do not set up any sectarian principles of their own, by which to shape and mould the proletarian movement.' 'The proletarian movement is the self-conscious, independent movement of the immense majority, in the interest of the immense majority.'

Leadership by a socially oriented élite *may* of course be the quickest route to improvement in an underdeveloped country. But élite power has a tendency to corrupt, whether it is capitalist, bureaucratic or 'revolutionary'. And even a truly socially oriented élite leadership would always be unstable where the population were accustomed to being deprived of power by rule from above. A coup d'état bringing in a more reactionary government is both tempting and easily achieved for those who know that popular opposition will cease as soon as a new leadership is established. Jan Bredsdorff who, after many years working in China, wrote *China: Return Ticket to Revolution,*[20] says of the shift in power in China, which immediately obtained popular approval for new objectives and political directions:

> China's new leaders were not selected by the Chinese people. It is very possible that, as the propaganda surrounding them says, they are at one with the people and intend to serve nothing but the interests of the people. This is not the principal issue in this context. The essential point is that, through a coup, China's population of a thousand million got a new leader whom they had previously known little about, and had had no opportunity to consider, where only time and the new leaders' actions will show whether they are the best solution for the people. As I have said, I do not believe that a fascist coup of any sort has occurred, but if one imagined that it had, it would already be too late to mount any opposition to it ... A great deal is said about freedom to express criticism in China, but if one investigates this in more detail, it turns out that this freedom is in many respects limited to a freedom to express dissatisfaction with what *has* been, in particular, of course, the 'Gang of Four' and its activities.

The implication of the fact that the Gang of Four are now denounced as fascists, says Bredsdorff, is that the Chinese people allowed themselves to be led for ten years by what they today regard as a fascist government. And no one dared to protest.*

---

*Here it should perhaps be said that Mao Zedong's thinking seems to have been far less élitist. At all events, he said in his speech at the Chinese Communist Party's national conference on propaganda work in 1957 that 'Truth develops through debate between different views... This is development through the struggle of opposites, development conforming to dialectics... It will solve no problems simply to issue administrative orders forbidding people to have any contact with ... erroneous ideas.'[39] But even Mao's prestige was evidently not great enough to prevent more power-hungry leaders from taking over the government of a people who were unused to making up their own minds.

Countless revolutions superseded by counter-revolutions, which always suggest power struggles confined to the uppermost levels, also appear to confirm that hopes for democratic government and democratic freedom after an élite revolution are not very realistic. Master thinking, therefore, seems in itself to contribute to another type of society than that we should be aiming for.

The other problem with élitist theories is that they clearly obstruct the very process of transformation in an affluent society.

In a poor country, where unequal distribution is the population's main problem, the majority may naturally and demonstrably allow themselves to be led by a revolutionary élite promising them what they lack. This is not the case in an affluent society where the system itself constantly increases the material standard of living of the proletariat. There it seems unlikely, to say the least, that a revolution for material objectives would be worth the trouble for the majority. Probably not even Marx would have believed in a revolution in such circumstances, because 'the ultimate reason for all real crises always remains the poverty and restricted consumption of the masses in the face of the drive of capitalist production to develop the productive forces as if only the absolute consumption capacity of society set a limit to them.'[28] In other words, the preconditions would be that economic need and powerlessness represented the decisive antagonism to the power of the ruling class. But in our society, as has been said, the main opposition seems to be between the groups possessing oppressive power by virtue of their positions as intellectual élites, and those who feel themselves rendered powerless by such 'superior thinkers' and decision makers in all areas. If this has any validity, it seems unthinkable that leadership on the basis of élitist theory could win the majority to the side of change. The time now seems to be right to redefine the concepts of power and antagonism for our own time, so that respect for popular opinion and common sense can be revived and ordinary people can be inspired to take independent standpoints in relation to the society we now have and the society we can create.

There are of course still economic conflicts of interest in the rich countries and there is obviously still real exploitation and poverty. But this is not to say that power today is *only* the ownership of capital and the control of production, or that powerlessness is *only* economic oppression. The significant force for change must be a more general opposition; something the majority experience as a problem of powerlessness.

According to Gudmund Hernes, author of *Power and Powerlessness*,[40] any analysis of powerlessness should pay attention, among other things, to 'those who are without interest and to interests that are not expressed politically'. And among several factors that can diminish a person's power, he says that 'an individual's power may be reduced to the extent that he is prevented from participating in the decision-making process.' Hernes also refers to Bertrand Russell's maxim; 'Power means bringing about desired effects.' This is precisely the position of the ordinary person in relation to the *entire* élite which plans, governs, judges and knows on behalf of those who are considered to have no consciousness of their own goals and are generally viewed as the objects of 'consciousness raising' and instruction from above.

Our political system, with its nomination of candidates after sophisticated political discussions for the initiated; the whole party apparatus which confronts people with a choice between a handful of 'theoretical packages' of ready-made élite wisdom; all the political literature and the media debate which always concerns difficult details and almost never the simple overall view – all this is tailor-made for élite participation. It ensures the intellectual minority the sole right to the power 'to bring about desired effects' and creates a corresponding powerlessness among the majority of people by diminishing their opportunity to 'express politically' their views, and by hampering or preventing their participation in the decision-making process.

We have grown so used to thinking that social groups have power as long as there exists an organization whose leadership has the job of looking after their interests. In reality it is often their own élite position that such leaders are mainly protecting. It emerged from an opinion survey concerning attitudes to power relations in Norway,[41] published in 1979, that the institution which the highest percentage of people considered 'too powerful' was the confederation of trade unions. This was also the opinion of 22 per cent of the confederation's own members. But what is interesting is that the question suggested by the response of these 22 per cent was not actually raised in the survey – whether the many members of these various organizations felt that they themselves had too little power in relation to their own leaders and whether they felt that they could make their own views heard. The fact that this question is, as a rule, very seldom raised may well be due to the fact that the questioners themselves take the pyramidal structure for granted or as something they would be reluctant to see altered. At all events, it is a fact that for the most part in the organizational life of modern society, only a small fraction of people feel they can take part in the processes leading to decisions.

In politics, organizational life and labour relations, the pyramidal model sets the pattern: at the top, a small group which discusses, evaluates and decides 'on behalf of' the broad base. And the division which exists in almost every case between the top and the base is formed by education, intellectual forms of thought and expression, and ideological knowledge.

In *The Master Thinkers*[3] Glucksmann refers to the power that has always been reserved for those with the knowledge and information the masses lack, and generally underlay the first aristocracy, the dominion of the elders, priests and soothsayers, the brahmins, druids and augurs, and every aristocracy founded on knowledge. 'As though it were as clear as day, the master thinkers present their own image of a popular mass which cannot rise to its own fate unless it allows itself to be led theoretically. Glucksmann's attack on both bourgeois and revolutionary élitism is merciless. The leading group's ideological text is always the 'law' giving the leaders power over the common people:

The law thus convinces those subject to it of their hopeless ignorance; the law, in being completely incomprehensible, serves as living proof of their inferiority: *Lenin's collected works in forty volumes represent the subjugation of the masses.* I mean this literally, for today the masses have neither time nor cause to tackle such a field of knowledge for intellectuals ... A sure sign that these texts are the property of power: they become incomprehensibly effective for those who will not understand that they are making themselves effectively incomprehensible ... The secret is to know how to make others ignorant and oneself incomprehensible.

Intellectual master thinking, expressed through ideologies in master language and always formulated *for* the masses by those who have raised themselves above them – it is in this, according to Glucksmann, that oppressive power lies, and this power is exercised by both revolutionary and conservative ideologues: 'Reactionary or progressive, aristocratic, bourgeois or "proletarian" thinkers scarcely dissent from one another except in the details that they use to embellish the essential fact that those who maintain the law stand "outside" the rest of society ... Russian, American, Chinese – they are now so numerous, the variations of master-thinking doctrine. But in their practical consequences they resemble one another.'

This class division, with multifarious groups each defining both the discussion's premises and the ideology's answers for the broad public, this distinction which so effectively makes ordinary people passive and which contemptuously rejects all direction from below – why is it so little acknowledged? Why is it not a central theme in political debate? Could it be because those who mainly discuss the concept of power, the revolutionary theoreticians, themselves represent the summit of one of the power pyramids? Could the reason be that those who never cease drawing the masses' attention to capital's position of power as the only form of power, wish to camouflage the fact that they also regard themselves as a superior class with a special right to lead 'the people' to the future society they have conceived? Is there not an intolerable arrogance in the attitude to people these dogmaticians reveal when they permit themselves to define the majority of people solely by the term 'workers', without personal characteristics – not as individuals with different feelings and aims, but always only by the place they occupy in the theoretical Marxist social model? And in presenting 'the worker' in this way, as a person who is so spiritually crippled under the yoke of capitalism that he or she does not even have the *possibility* of taking the initiative towards a goal-directed change without ideological leadership, are the revolutionary theoreticians not strengthening their own position of power at the expense of popular self-confidence and participation?

'All this corresponds both to the most hideously banal employer's strategy and to what Marx predicted about it,' says Glucksmann. 'But to say that it therefore corresponds with reality, that is to deceive oneself.' Yet this image 'is not intended to correspond with reality, the aim is to make reality correspond with the image while worker resistance is reduced to nothing.'

The 'scientific' definition of ordinary people as pawns with no possibility of playing any other role than that which the system has allotted them can easily become self-confirming – because it makes all listening to the people's own voice uninteresting, something that can only be interpreted in relation to the élite's theory, and because it confines the debate to the master thinkers' clichés. What has been obliterated during this 'barren frost of science [are] the multitude of faces defying the chains and not speaking the same language. The multitude is there, however, and history is never anything other than what happens to them.' But master thinking makes a transformation *from below* unthinkable and effectively blocks the way to it.

Glucksmann exposes in his book the self-contradictory element in the revolutionary élite's 'freedom for the people'. 'Fight for freedom!' is the slogan. 'Be free!' But freedom must never encompass doubt or opposition to the ideologues' account of how it is to be organized and won. 'The ambition to stage the revolution is common to all master thinkers,' says Glucksmann. But the theory and objectives of the revolution are too complicated to be developed outside an exclusive circle that has even evolved its own language – with a terminology that every revolutionary master thinker must command in order to be taken seriously. Colloquial speech is removed from the language of all élite groups, 'but the only secret this involves is the fact that they are eliminating and invalidating the common, popular way of expressing oneself.'

Now revolutionary dogmatists are obviously by no means the only master thinkers in modern society. They simply represent a principle that our entire system is based on. A principle that assumes that problems are always attributable to forces outside people themselves, and must be discussed as though the people in question need to be 'led' out of them through institutional solutions, suitable commodities, or 'treatment'. But dogmatic Marxism does nothing at all to weaken this tendency; it is in practice based on the same principle. By dismissing scornfully everything that smacks of personal responsibility for any difficulty the poor stereotypical individual, 'oppressed by the system', may run into, and by attributing all power over the person to 'structures', the way is left open for the master thinkers' leadership. Don't on any account believe that you yourself can do anything about your situation or the difficulties you are facing. You are a miserable victim of circumstances you cannot influence – only *we* know how society, or your problem, needs to be dealt with. We have the prescription. Listen to us, and don't on any account think that you yourself are responsible!

Élite authority penetrates all society, says Ivan Illich in *The Right to Useful Unemployment and its Professional Enemies*.[42] One effect of what he calls 'modernized poverty' is 'that people are helpless to recognize evidence unless it has been certified by a professional – be he a television weather commentator or an educator; organic discomfort becomes intolerably threatening unless it has been medicalized into dependence on a therapist...'

And all this treatment and institutional planning for the majority is more than oppressive, claims Illich; for most people, it magnifies the problems they have to solve and the result is 'time-consuming acceleration, sick-making health care, stupefying education.'

In innumerable ways, capitalist growth society counteracts the objectives it claims to further. This is also the case with its supposed reduction of working hours and easing of work, says Dag Osterberg in his book *A Preface to Capital*:[43]

> Economic growth does not necessarily reduce the pace of work or shorten working hours. On the contrary, the pace of work increases and it is doubtful whether working hours have become significantly shorter since the eight-hour day was introduced over fifty years ago, considering all the disguised forms of extra work, and the fact that travelling time to and from the workplace has increased greatly for many people, constituting a great additional burden ... And last but not least, the time that goes on individual shopping has increased greatly ... In short: our forms of growth economy brings about an increasing scarcity of *time* – the stuff of life, according to Lincoln.

A particularly good illustration of the 'inverse effects' of growth thinking on the general public is Illich's well-known example of how modern society's solution to the traffic problem compels people to spend *more* time than before to travel over a given distance. Putting together all the time the average American spends earning money for a car, driving it, maintaining it, parking it and walking to and from it, and dividing the total time by the total distance covered, one arrives at an average speed roughly equivalent to a normal walking pace. With a bicycle, the effective speed would be greater, but the individual has been deprived of the freedom to choose this far freer and better means of transport by the traffic planners who have imposed their 'solution' to the traffic problem in the form of mass motoring. By this means, people are also distanced from one another, the distances they must cover every day become greater, their freedom less. Illich says he cannot fail to 'observe the decline of freedom in societies in which rights are shaped by expertise.'

Constant expert planning and professional solutions have not only deprived people of the belief that they can do something themselves to improve their situation, they have removed people's confidence that they can determine their own desires and goals. Illich calls the last twenty-five years 'the Age of Professions'.[42]

> The Age of Professions will be remembered as the time when politics withered, when voters guided by professors entrusted to technocrats the power to legislate needs, the authority to decide who needs what and a monopoly over the means by which these needs shall be met. It will be remembered as the Age of Schooling, when people for one-third of their lives were trained how to accumulate on prescription and for the other two-thirds were clients of prestigious pushers who managed habits. It will be remembered as the age when ... intimacy meant training by Masters and Johnson; when formed opinion was a replay of last night's talk show, and voting an endorsement to a salesman for more of the same. ...
>
> Let us first face the fact that the bodies of specialists that now dominate the creation, adjudication and satisfaction of needs are a new kind of cartel. And this must be recognized to outflank their developing

defences ... Educators and doctors and social workers today ... gain
legal power to create the need that, by law, they alone will be allowed
to serve ...

What counts is the professional's authority to define a person as
client, to determine that person's need and to hand that person a
description which defines this new social role ...

Government by a congress that bases its decisions on the expert
opinions of such professions might be government for, but never by, the
people.

Not surprisingly, Illich has been attacked for his views of our age's new
power and class divisions, not least by the groups which discuss the concept
of power without themselves being willing to give up their position as the
guardians of the majority.

When I propose the analysis of professional power as the key to social
reconstruction, I am usually told that it is a dangerous error to select
this phenomenon as the crux for recovery from the industrial system. Is
not the shape of the educational, medical, and planning establishments
actually the reflection of the distribution of power and privilege of a
capitalist élite? Is it not irresponsible to undermine the trust of the man
in the street in his scientifically trained teacher, physician, or
economist precisely at the moment when the poor need these trained
protectors to gain access to classroom, clinic, and expert? Ought not
the industrial system's indictment expose the income of stockholders in
drug firms? ... Why spoil the mutual dependence of clients and
professional providers, especially when increasingly – as in Cuba or
the United States – both tend to come from the same social class? Is it
not perverse to denigrate the very people who have painfully acquired
the knowledge to recognize and service our needs for welfare? In fact,
should not the radically socialist professional leaders be singled out as
the most apt leaders in the ongoing task of defining and meeting
people's 'real' needs in an egalitarian society?

The arguments that are implicit in these questions are frequently
advanced to disrupt and discredit public analysis of the disabling effects
of industrial welfare systems which focus on services. Such effects are
essentially identical and clearly inevitable, no matter what the political
flag under which they are placed. They incapacitate people's autonomy
through forcing them – via legal, environmental and social changes –
to become consumers of care. These rhetorical questions represent a
frantic defense of privilege on the part of those élites who might lose
income, but would certainly gain status and power if, in a new form of
a market-intensive economy, dependence on their services were
rendered more equitable.

Even when the need to transform the centralized, resource-wasting
society of big enterprises begins to be recognized, there are new, highly
educated élite groups wanting to define and solve the problems 'from
above':

The brightest of the new professionals see clearly that growing scarcity pushes controls over needs ever upward. The central planning of output-optimum decentralization has become the most prestigious job of the late seventies. But what is not yet recognized is that this new illusory salvation by professionally decreed limits confuses liberties and rights ...

Consciousness raisers roam through local communities inciting people to meet the decentralized production goals that have been assigned to them.

Even working for change, if it is based on the disqualification of the majority and revolutionary master thinking, can undermine popular, imaginative power and the majority initiative that is needed if a transformation is to be realized. If all the élite groups working for a change in the system continue to make the general public passive by denying their free participation and independent understanding, by restricting social debate to incomprehensible and dogmatic theories, and if all ideas concerning social change continue to come from above and to be formulated for and not by ordinary people – then the only result will be to strengthen the forces that *preserve* our system of industrial growth. The power that these forces have over people is due precisely to the fact that there is virtually nothing that inspires the majority of people to feel responsibility for their actions, to develop a personal scepticism and resistance, to ask questions, or to come to their own conclusions on the basis of a consciousness of what they actually stand for.

Who can expect people who always have their problems and solutions predefined for them by others to be able to liberate themselves from the influence of the system in order to take an active part in a process of change?

Built into the modern industrial system, there is already an immeasurably influential force making people passive and preserving the system, especially in three areas where this influence may ultimately become irresistible if a general resistance is not liberated in time: in the areas of leisure, working life and consumption.

In all industrial countries free time seems to be becoming dominated more and more by television, at least as far as the great 'silent' majority is concerned. In Europe, this tendency has to some extent been limited by the state monopolies, but with the widespread and always self-fulfilling superstition that 'you can't stop progress', it is reasonable to assume that sooner or later both video-cassette television and satellite transmissions from many countries will become a reality. According to the latest reports in this field, it is already technically possible to offer viewers virtually unlimited transmission time and a choice of up to 300 channels. This suggests that the place television has gained in the daily life of Americans may be far exceeded in other countries as well.

In 1977, an average American spent four hours of every day in front of a television – more time than on any other leisure activity. A study conducted in 1976-7 showed that more than a third of American families had no other shared activity than this.[44] But the danger lies in the lack of resistance to *further* technological development. If technical progress continues to be seen

as inevitable we will all come to experience the new possibilities that are
being developed – such as the projection of the television picture in video
format on the walls of one's living room, combined, naturally, with stereo
sound. The effects of this kind of almost complete substitution of reality,
occupying perhaps most of people's free time, could be catastrophic. It could
mean that millions become almost completely reduced to the reality
presented by a state- or business-dominated élite. The illusion of having
opinions, which in reality would almost inevitably be shaped by the social
perspectives of the élites, could very easily put a *passive* majority into the
hands of those with power to an extent one can scarcely imagine today.

An attempt to maintain the status quo in working life has long been under
development by the major world companies. One aspect of 'socio-technical'
business management, which, according to Galbraith is an important feature
of employees' 'identification' with their firm, is 'job motivation'. This is
being strengthened by increasingly advanced and manifold means – and
always with the result of distracting the workers' attention from the actual
social process they are involved in. The systematic 'understanding and
treatment' of social problems which otherwise might have created a new
consciousness of these problems' deeper social causes, is only one aspect of
this form of management. More technical means of stimulation have also
proved effective. For example, muzak – scientifically designed and tested
music for the workplace – can demonstrably affect attitudes to work and
thus input. Similarly, the effect of colours and lighting on the contentment
of employees is the subject of deliberate research. Much of this is as yet only
used to a limited extent, but competition for growth and efficiency will
naturally make such methods necessary for more and more firms, once some
have begun to use them. And here the thesis that 'you can't stop progress'
indicates that increasingly advanced means of influence will be developed –
and used. Inspiring film shows and lectures projecting the management's
view of their firm's beneficial activity in the development of the growth-
and consumer-based society are only the more transparent forms of
manipulation.

The danger of all this, of course, is not that it improves working
conditions, but that the planned and stupefying 'harmonization' of workers'
goals with those of the business turns their interest towards internal
adaption at the expense of attentiveness to the social consequences. If
employees have been rendered powerless in advance by being deprived of
confidence in their own judgement, it will be easier to manipulate them into
participating in what is perhaps a destructive development, socially or in
terms of production, based on the planning élite's premises.

The third area where frightening possibilities of manipulation may be
under development – the manufacture of needs and demands – has been
debated for a long time, but again mainly as a problem that is inherent in
'inevitable' progress. In a system that seems to be helplessly dependent on
increasing demand, and where consumption may in the course of a few
decades reach absurd heights, a more efficient and scientific development of
needs may simply become a necessity. It is difficult to predict what forms
this manipulation will take, but at the moment it looks as though the more

direct forms, lying outside the traditional advertising media, are offering the greatest scope. For example, there seem to be greater opportunities for the systematic exploitation of the need to belong socially than have been made use of hitherto. Key figures in pop culture were given new products to use at the launching of the films *The Great Gatsby* and *Grease;* and the collaboration that occurred between the film industry and the producers and retailers of mass-produced fashion pointed towards new possibilities. The opportunities the big and increasingly advanced sales outlets have for systematizing such influence at the point of sale should also be mentioned – making it 'a place to be' with forms of service, lighting, colours and muzak that have been carefully tested for their psychological effects.

This account may seem one-sidedly negative today – and of course it is. But it cannot be denied that the possibilities which have been mentioned, and which already exist, may very easily be realized if no resistance is mobilized. The combination of the system's active adaptation of individuals to the established course of development, and the master thinkers' destruction of people's self-confidence and personal judgement, serves precisely to weaken opposition to élite planning and management from above.

It is therefore vitally important that ordinary people's belief in their own judgement and own choice of action be reinforced. There are many indications that conflict is growing around this whole issue and that resistance from below may develop in protest against increasing pressure from above.

The new class divisions

The intellectual ruling class has a tendency to be marked by mental inbreeding. Only rarely has this milieu been opened to popular forms of thought and expression. It is no doubt recognized theoretically that there exist two different cultures with very little mutual contact – the popular and the intellectual – but in the closed circles of the élite it is seldom understood that these can represent equally valid and mutually enriching versions of reality. The intellectual contempt that is almost consistently shown for readers of the popular press – who in fact account for 90 per cent of the population – is a characteristic expression of this élitist arrogance in relation to the popular. Moreover, the master thinkers who are most eager to talk about the liberation of the proletariat or the people tend to attach greater importance to the respect they inspire in élite circles by writing in sophisticated theoretical terms *about* the people than to writing for the people themselves. Rather than communicating with the majority of people through the papers and magazines which reach them, they prefer to split ideological hairs in the periodicals read by the little élite group that they themselves belong to. In response to the argument that the mass circulation publications exclude socially critical viewpoints, it should be asked whether any attempt has ever been made to formulate such views in the terms of reference of the readers of the popular press. Even if there are good reasons for criticizing much of the content of the popular press, this is no justification for writing off the form.

Behind this lies a negative evaluation not only of the content of the popular press, but also of its presentation, which actually represents the ordinary, popular means of approaching people: the personalizing of issues and problems. It has become such a hardened dogma that personalizing is an unacceptable form of presentation that it can scarcely be challenged by anyone who wants to retain a minimum of intellectual respect. But to reject this form of communication is to exclude the overwhelming majority of the population from the social debate which concerns above all them.

Of course, there are really no grounds for thinking that it is impossible to present issues in a personalized form. An excellent example was provided by *Holocaust,* the television series about the Nazi extermination of the Jews. By personalizing the issues involved and this ensuring that the films reached the majority, the makers succeeded in making entire populations *feel* and understand for the first time the dangers of racial discrimination. But the film was criticized by a number of élite groups precisely because it appealed to common, personal understanding rather than presenting the problem in intellectual terms, which probably would have confined its range to the élite itself.

Alex Haley encountered a similar reaction to his book *Roots,*[45] from various élite quarters. By personalizing the problems of American blacks and their history, he created, with this single book, more understanding and a more profound change than the thousands of academic works on the subject had ever done. But for many intellectuals the book was not good enough. It could scarcely be criticized for the effect it actually had on public opinion, but they complained that it was 'unscholarly'.

The differences between élite forms of expression and those of the majority are so great that even those attempts that have been made by various intellectuals to give an account of the proletariat's problems 'for the people' rarely reach the general public.

What seems to be most important, in many areas of political and intellectual life, is to demonstrate to one's comrades that one has mastered the group's terminology, that one is a stalwart verbal warrior for the correct ideology. Rarely is the issue to present problems and possible alternatives for action in such a way that ordinary people can make up their own minds. The main concern is to describe people or to instruct them on the basis of theory and ideology. The fact that this approach seems to be totally ineffectual in promoting change is evidently no particular cause for concern.

This must not be taken to mean that the élite is not interested in the popular, the proletariat, the working class. On the contrary, never have so many theoretical interpretations of ordinary people been written. The 'ordinary worker' has in fact become so interesting for the intellectual that he has virtually been put on a pedestal to be studied under a magnifying glass and described with diagrams on graph paper. The immense enchantment that overcomes intellectuals when they venture into the life of the sacred ordinary worker and perceive that he actually bears a certain resemblance to a human being is not unlike the fascination one sees among spectators in front of the gorilla cage at the zoo. It is an interest in something that is different from oneself, something on the other side of the bars, the other side of the class division; something one is incapable of understanding experientially and must therefore describe in terms of theory.

The lack of contact across the intellectual class barrier is probably largely due to the particular manner of experiencing reality that is developed through theoretical studies. In most fields of study, higher education involves accustoming oneself to objectification and thinking in terms of models, the popular counterpart of which is personification and personal experience. Theoretical methods of approach are useful and necessary for systematic thinking, but it is important to realize that they can alienate the highly educated from more commonplace human modes of understanding and experience which represent an important corrective. And since the élite groups have been so successful in holding up *their* way of seeing as being real and correct, it may be necessary to point out that their way has its shortcomings and that intellectuals ought to be able to learn from the popular perspective that they have distanced themselves from.

'Objectification' arises from the necessary process of accustoming oneself not to allow one's personal feelings and values to enter into scientific analysis. One result of this may be, however, to forget the fundamental choice of values which provided the premise for the analysis itself. This was presumably what happened to the scientists who developed the atomic bomb, and it may be what is happening to those who are today developing methods for controlling human genes and hereditary characteristics. Another result may be that this consistent impartiality, which is necessary in the context of research, weakens the capacity to identify with and understand other people's feelings and circumstances of life. The tendency to dismiss popular personification based on exactly this sort of sympathetic insight is another expression of this. The less 'educated' have a clear advantage here. The human fellowship and solidarity that a better society must be founded on cannot *exchange* sympathetic, experiential understanding for objective, theoretical understanding. If the natural ability to share feelings with others is weakened, so too is the capacity for cooperation and fellowship, the ability to listen to others and to accept their views and their legitimacy.

Thinking in terms of 'models' is necessary in analyzing problems; in order to describe a part of reality, it must be simplified to a model in which the known facts are placed in a systematic relationship with one another. But again, thinking in terms of models can restrict free thought to the extent that the model acquires a value of its own. For the academic, the model may become more real than reality itself, and it may get in the way of an under-standing of the multiplicity of alternative possibilities and contexts that the model excludes. Dogmatic belief in the model's validity can prevent the model thinker from seeing people and things in any other way than as the model describes them. The tendency to want to instruct others as to the effects of the model that, for the intellectual, has replaced reality is often an expression of the limitation of consciousness that can result from overly theoretical training.

The model can thus become a hindrance to fresh thinking – as has happened with power models which exclude all forms of oppression apart from those described in Marx's model; or as happens when the idea of giving direct help to people in need is written off because a dogmatic revolutionary model allows only one type of action in solidarity.

It is well known that defending a lifetime's model can become a matter of power and prestige. This is what happened with the scientists and churchmen whose positions rested on teaching people that the earth was at the centre of the universe, when Copernicus wanted to pull that model to pieces. And this is the case today, every time anyone raises challenging questions about accepted models of society or revolution.

Here too, the unschooled person may have certain advantages inasmuch as his or her ideas are not confined by the narrow framework of the model, perhaps especially when human relations are at issue.

While the theoretician tends to see people as the stereotypes of models and structures, most people see the structures only in terms of living human beings. For this reason it can be useful to admit the popular doubt that is rooted in feelings and experiences which contradict a model's neat and cosy simplicity. All in all, there is an increasing need for a popular revolt against the principal sickness of our age: the superstition that theoretical concepts are reality. We should be very aware of any conflict that arises between theorizing, which often makes describing reality into an end in itself, and the *experience* of the same reality, which has a far greater capacity to motivate action and change.

Many people who see themselves as intellectuals may react against this account of the dangers of intellectualism. My intention is not to condemn all intellectuals or to dismiss the importance of intellectual activity, but to counteract the opposite tendency: the devaluation of ordinary, popular experience and ordinary ways of thinking. Intellectualism has sufficient prestige; it is a belief in the wisdom of ordinary people that is lacking, and it is always this that the freedom of the majority must be based on. There is no harm, therefore, if free-thinking intellectuals relinquish a little of their prestige in order to contribute to the self-confidence and the participation of the majority of people.

There is no future in maintaining an absolute division between the intellectual and the popular. On the contrary, equality and cooperation between the two sides may be mutually beneficial. It is between the master thinkers and those whose thoughts and opinions are suppressed that the dividing line runs – and the more intellectuals who go over to the side of the majority the better.

If the division between the many groups of master thinkers and the general public represents a general antagonism in our society, governed, as it is, from above, then, if Marx was right, it should be the experience of the increasing pressure of this antagonism that brings about a transformation. And this is what is happening.

Manifestations of popular revolt

A rebellion is already in progress – visible to anyone willing to see it. It is a popular revolt for new values and human objectives – and against all the master thinkers who want to channel this into their narrow ideological pigeonholes in order to strengthen their own élite positions and their claims of absolute superior knowledge. This protest has not yet roused the majority to open action, but its penetrative power is growing. The revolt has many aspects. Its multiformity makes it difficult to survey in totality. Let us therefore take some of the countless forms in which it is being manifested and then try to find a common denominator.

The protest that *workers* are beginning to make against the development they are being drawn into has perhaps found its clearest expression in the action initiated at the Lucas Aerospace factories in Britain (which manufacture among other things advanced equipment for aircraft production) and which has since spread to a number of other countries.

According to the report from a symposium held in November 1978, Mike Cooley,[46] one of the Lucas action's most prominent spokespeople, described the workers' initiative as being based on the 'embryonic realization of the social and economic costs of the "efficient factory" in terms of structural unemployment, frantic energy consumption, the loss of job satisfaction and the squandering of society's most precious asset, which is the skill, ingenuity, creativity and enthusiasm of ordinary people.' In industrial society our usual planning methods, says Cooley, are 'such as to seek to reduce human beings to a mechanistic appendage to the machine, and thereby [fail] to recognize and accept that the human being is the dialectical opposite of the machine.' Instead of

designing equipment and organizing productive and social processes to enhance the creativity of the human being and give full vent to his or her tacit knowledge, we seek through advanced technology to do the opposite. Thus the forms of technology we decide society should have will inevitably have profound effects upon wider issues such as industrial democracy and freedom of choice.

Faced with these massive contradictions, there are now growing and encouraging signs that industrial workers are increasingly questioning what it is they make, how they make it, why they make it and in whose interest.

The Lucas action arose in response to the threatened introduction of rationalization programmes that could make thousands of workers redundant. The Lucas employees organized a combine committee that was unique in the British trade-union movement in that it united highly trained technicians and workers on the shop floor. And the situation compelled them all to raise questions, concerning not only the company's organization and goals, but also the whole economic system that was incapable of using the labour power that existed to the benefit of the many unmet needs of our time. 'It seemed absurd to us,' says Cooley, 'that we had all this skill and knowledge and facilities, that society urgently needed equipment and services which we could provide, and yet the market economy seemed incapable of linking these two. What happened ... provides an important object lesson for those who wish to analyze how society can be changed.'

As examples of the system's shortcomings, Cooley refers, among other things, to the fact that there are an estimated 180,000 unemployed building workers in Britain at the same time as the statistics show that 7 million people are living in semi-slum areas; that thousands of electricians are being robbed of the right to work at the same time as there is an urgent need for heating systems which they could help to make more available.

To find out what the company's own threatened workers might produce, the combine committee at Lucas drew up 180 letters with details of the employees' skills and the company's plant which they sent to prominent authorities among those who had written and spoken of the need for the humanization of technology, requesting suggestions for alternative production. They received a total of four replies. It was a lesson for the Lucas workers. 'We did then what we should have done in the first instance. We asked our own [trade-union] members what they thought they should be making.' And the questions were put in such a way that they allowed an evaluation of vocational skills and the company's potential in relation to social needs. In the course of a few weeks, 150 ideas came in for socially useful production which could provide work for all those threatened with redundancy. These were eventually collected into a report consisting of six volumes, each of 200 pages.

Cooley mentions five examples: Lucas could produce kidney machines, and when the combine committee researched the country's needs for these, 'we were horrified to learn that 3,000 people die each year because they can't get one. ... We regard it as outrageous that the skilled workers who design and make this equipment face the prospect of the dole queue'. 'Having foregone wage increases in order that we could expand the services to the community at large, we should have the opportunity of producing medical equipment which they require.' Cooley also mentions that the workers' own ideas resulted in a vehicle for handicapped children who had previously had to crawl on the floor. There was a demand for the model from several quarters, but the Lucas management opposed production because 'it was incompatible with their product range.'

Other examples of workers' proposals for new production included a build-it-yourself solar energy house and various products which could make the people of poor countries more independent of the West's complex technology and energy supplies, including a power source which could be driven with the aid of marsh gas and a simple combination of train and bus which leaves the rails on steep gradients, saving tunnels, cuttings and bridges and thus reducing installation costs to about one-fiftieth. In cooperation with North-East London Polytechnic, the Lucas workers have also been able to help local communities to set up 'non-hierarchical cooperative workshops which will help them to produce products which they require locally.'

The Lucas workers' action is an excellent example of the wave of initiative and fresh thinking that is now building up among pioneering groups of workers in various places, often against strong opposition from established managers and planners in society – a revolt against the role the capitalist system forces upon the worker as Marx described it in *Capital*:[6] 'It is in the nature of wage labour, when it is subordinated to capital, that the character of the work is unimportant to the worker. He is willing to let himself be used in accordance with the needs of capital ... '

In the early seventies, the famous 'Green Bans' movement developed in Australia, where the construction workers' trade union refused to destroy the environment through development that was solely in the interest of property speculators. There have been similar instances, inspired by the Lucas plan and the Green Bans, growing out of local circumstances, in Italy, France, Norway, Sweden, Denmark, Britain, the USA, the Netherlands, West Germany and Belgium.

All this shows very clearly, says Cooley, 'that ordinary people not only have the capability, but also are showing the determination needed, to insist on their right to have a say how their industries are run, what products they make and in whose interests. At an industrial level it means a challenge to management's right to manage. As a worker in Lucas Aerospace put it: "We have discovered that management is not a skill or a craft or a profession but a command relationship ... "'

Characteristically, however, traditional leading group have dismissed ideas of this sort – both business management and, in Norway, the senior levels of the Norwegian trade-union confederation, as has been shown, for example, by the Swede, Matts Heijbell, in his book on alternative production.[47]

There is a clear community of ideas between, on the one hand, the many initiatives being developed by workers wanting influence over the social effects of production and, on the other, the countless popular environmental movements. The reaction of traditional planners to these is predictable.

In all industrialized countries, environmental movements are sprouting like wildfire in the wastelands of organized big business managed from above. They take the form of national or international movements for a social development which puts natural, biological balance and people's responsibility for their environment and for each other before the demand for growth in technology, the economy and planning. They take the form of local campaigns against environmental destruction through hydroelectric development, new motorways, the establishment of big businesses in small communities, the decline of agricultural land, nuclear power installations, and the pollution of water, air and land with industrial waste and poison sprays. And everywhere the simple, popular attitudes and values underlying this are ridiculed by professional wisdom with the same arguments: people 'don't understand' that all this is *necessary* in order to secure the prosperity 'we all want', to help the weak, to create the means of repairing the damage that this growth in prosperity is itself causing, to provide energy for jobs – in short, to maintain our economic system.

What these professionals do not understand is that this protest is a more or less conscious reaction against the very system that *demands* such developments – that it puts other values higher than artificial, material affluence, that it wants to provide security for the disadvantaged by distributing wealth rather than by increasing it, and that the protesters, if they were able to choose, would probably *pay* the price of ensuring employment by means of less energy-intensive, polluting, freedom-robbing, automated and 'profitable' production methods.

It is not a matter of popular ignorance versus the experts' deeper understanding. Two attitudes to people and values are in collision: the immediate but profound feeling that industrial society and its solutions to problems are trampling on the values one most needs, versus the 'objective' analysis which takes this system and its values for granted. There is a collision of interests between the freedom of the majority to decide their own value priorities, and the right of élites to maintain a society based on growth and planning which assures the planners of their own social position.

The broad environmental movement has grown innumerable side shoots. A mass of different groups are working for a more ecologically balanced, a simpler and more controllable and decentralized technology – liberation from mass motoring in the interests of more vulnerable road users and the safety of children, for the use of bicycles and collective transport – all against persistent opposition from those who want to reduce the problems of motor transport with growth-society's costly repairs.

An autonomous popular movement, based on similar values, is expressing the smallholders' protest against the depopulation of peripheral areas by big business, centralization, and urban civilization's violence against local culture and individual development. In Norway this has broad support among young people who want more and more to get away from a sterile city life to meaningful activity in country districts. The same basic wish to protect traditional, popular values lies behind the flourishing interest in folk dancing, music and ballads – a tendency that would have been unthinkable a couple of decades ago. The same desire for contact with the natural values industrial society denies lies behind the thousands of small allotments people grow their own food on, behind the growing number of berry, mushroom and herb gatherers, and behind the new movement for a more organic agriculture which is more responsible in terms of resources and which avoids the use of artificial fertilizers and poison sprays – again, in the face of scornful opposition from professional wisdom.

The revolt against the centralizing forces of growth is also manifested in increasing protest against the global centres of power, against the multinational companies, against the organizations protecting the interests of the industrialized countries such as the EEC and the International Energy Agency, and against the insanity of the superpowers' arms race and their conflict over sources of raw materials. And it often finds expression in a demand for national liberation from these bonds through increased self-sufficiency and independence.

The women's movement is yet another expression of protest against the existing order – perhaps potentially the most powerful of all if it mobilizes around the fundamental values which seem to be its source. The suppression of supple, common humanity, which women have traditionally struggled for against men's individualistic and oppressive self-assertion and competition, has created a demand for equality for women, women's values and women's culture which may prove extremely explosive in industrial society. The women's movement seems to have gained a really major political significance through its powerful position in the peace movement, where it has made clear demands for alternatives to male ideas concerning the prestige of power and the right of might.

The rebellion of youth is an equivalent force. Even if it no longer attracts the attention of the media to the extent it did during the hippy period and the violent outbreaks of the sixties, it has continued to grow quietly. In a form that is perhaps more consistent, its growing strength is being manifested in the increasing numbers of young people who are refusing to accept the fashions and values of the time, refusing to take the jobs they have been trained for, raising and challenging questions concerning the purpose and meaning of the development they have been asked to take part in. The 'underground culture' is part of this, as is the new interest in oriental mysticism, meditation and spiritual consciousness in opposition to materialism and technical efficiency.

Pointing in the same direction are the many initiatives for new and more human schools, in which cooperation, direct experience of life, individual responsibility and personality development will replace competition and training for the demands of industry. In Norway, *folkehyskoler* (peoples' colleges) with more and more courses in environmental and rural studies and global consciousness, the 'mobile colleges', the experimental schools and the Rudolf Steiner schools all give more or less direct expression to protest against development.

Yet another group consists of the growing numbers of socially conscious Christians who are working in various ways on the basis of the Christian message, which is actually revolutionary, for a social evolution based on greater human solidarity. In combatting dogmatic theology's passive acceptance of existing economic conditions, they are working against the growth system's materialism, privileges and self-interest, and for a social system based on human fellowship, equality and shared responsibility.

The many groups advocating alternative lifestyles and liberation from the demands of consumerism, market manipulation and the throw-away mentality, are another sign of the popular demand for change. Among these groups there are many people trying to get away from the influence of consumer society by developing new ways of living communally and cooperatively.

These groups have gained a surprising degree of support in many countries. In the USA alone there are said to be about 6 million individuals and over 5,000 groups who are protesting, through personal practice, against the consumer role society tries to force on them – amid a chorus of derisive laughter from the planning élites.

The same condescending, professional contempt meets the greatly increased interest in alternative medicine as a means to preserving one's own health with diet and herbal remedies, which the weekly magazines are full of. This too is evidence of an awakening scepticism in relation to the experts: orthodox medicine and the disenfranchizing effects of the institutions' monopoly of 'treatment' for every human problem.

A vast number of local organizations and campaigns for world solidarity, for direct contact with local communities in developing countries, against racism, and in support of development projects and liberation movements in the Third World, must also be regarded as part of the popular movement – against a society based principally on competition for material gain.

Behind all this lies a widespread wish to take responsibility – for others and for oneself, to liberate oneself from the forces of control which always 'know best'. This is manifested in a general antipathy to any control from above, to the takeover by institutions of human responsibility and participation, to expert judgement and master thinking, to the competitive élitism of politicians and their monopoly of opinion, and to the political pigeonholing of all new thinking.

A powerful illustration of the interest that exists in a rebellion against established positions and dividing lines was the reception given in Scandinavia to the book *Revolt from the Centre*[48] – a far from lightweight book about liberation from the dogmas of both Right and Left, and a real alternative to the system of industrial growth, which quickly sold out an edition of almost 150,000.

Another instance of rebellion against control from above – one that is not readily conceded by the dogmatic Left – is to be found in aspects of the wave of right-wing revivalism that is now running through Europe. In socialist quarters this has been interpreted as a victory for economic egotism – and no doubt it is to some extent. But the many opinion surveys indicating that people in general are giving higher priority to personal and political goals other than increased affluence suggest that this cannot be the whole explanation. We should ask whether this too is not largely an expression of antipathy to the mentality of control itself, and to the guardianship and the expert planning exercised by the state and the bureaucracy. The swing to the right, which includes a considerable section of the labour movement, *may* be part of a popular rebellion against oppression by the master thinkers, a sympathetic response to slogans about individual freedom and responsibility – even though the new leaders are likely to show that their change merely shifts control to other power groups. There is in any case little in the programmes of conservative politicians to suggest that freedom is ever to encompass the right of the majority to determine their own work or to escape from the technostructure's planning and demand production. Nonetheless, it is far from inconceivable that it is verbal appeals for 'freedom from government' that have tilted the balance. Indeed, even the reaction to high levels of taxation may be an aspect of this. The greatest possible consumption is not necessarily the primary motive behind protest against taxation. It *may* simply be an expression of antipathy to the fact that a centralized state administration, with no particular understanding for the problems of local communities, is using large parts of people's income to further its own power and control from above, in defiance of the general desire for responsibility and participation.

At all events, the swing to the right is being interpreted and exploited on the élite's premises on both political fronts. It may be an expression of popular revolt against control from above, but it has effectively been neutralized as a political phenomenon by being put into *one* of the traditional political camps – in the same way that a subsequent swing to the left will probably be interpreted and exploited to the advantage of planning and control by other master thinkers.

The popular revolt's distinctive features and its opponents

What is it, then, that links – or could link – the manifold and fragmented popular protest movements against the main features of industrial society? What is the common characteristic that could be a uniting force in the direction of the change we need?

One unifying factor has already been mentioned: the demand for participation and influence, for the right to take decisions in opposition to experts and suppressors of opinion. The acknowledgement that one is being controlled is itself vital if there is to be change: 'It is possible that people need to believe that they are unmanaged if they are to be managed effectively,' says Galbraith. 'Were it to be recognized that [our personal choice] is subject to management, we might be at pains to assert our independence. Thus we would become less manageable.'[31] Many things have happened in the last ten years to show that a change is under way. In particular, the antagonisms have been clarified for ordinary people. Illich writes:

> In 1968, for example, it was still quite easy to dismiss organized lay resistance to professional dominance as nothing more than a throwback to romantic, obscurantist or élitist fantasies. The grass-roots, common-sense assessment of technological systems which I then outlined, seemed childish or retrograde to the political leaders of citizen activism and to the 'radical' professionals who laid claim to the tutorship of the poor by means of their special knowledge. The reorganization of late industrial society around professionally defined needs, problems, and solutions was still the commonly accepted value ... Today, lay confidence in public policies based upon the expert's opinion is tenuous indeed. Now thousands reach their own judgements and, at great cost, engage in citizen action without any professional tutorship; through personal, independent effort, they gain the scientific information they need ... They know, for example, that the quality and amount of technical advice sufficiently conclusive to oppose atomic power plants ... is simple and clear enough for the layman to grasp and utilize.

But opposition to change from below is strong and multifaceted, and 'crises', in the Marxist sense, do not seem to advance such change. 'Crisis, understood in this way, is always good for executives and commissars. And they are often an excuse to yell "Driver, step on the gas". But crisis need not have this meaning. It need not imply a headlong rush for the escalation of management. Instead, it can mean the instant of choice, that marvellous moment when people suddenly become aware of ... the possibility of a different life. And *this* is the crisis, that, as a choice, confronts both the United States and the world today.'

Ordinary people are now raising the fundamental questions about 'the purpose of it all' which the experts have shoved aside. While professional leaders dismiss the entire protest as 'emotional argument', the new grass-roots movements demand influence over the simple, fundamental choices of values and directions.

However, the antagonisms and the class arrogance of the élites are also expressed within the protest groups that are springing up everywhere. Those who cannot give up their belief that development towards a free, democratic society must be directed by ideological leaders are battling for positions of power in these new movements. They have yet to understand that the very means of control they want to use to take people forward to participation and a sense of responsibility *obstruct* the active personal responsibility that such a society depends on. They do not understand that the right of ideological leadership which they assume is itself the antithesis of the movement! Whenever they nevertheless succeed in usurping leading positions and force their narrow ideology on participants, all they do is to sap the movement's power and potential for growth. A movement which was itself a protest against pyramid structures has itself become a pyramid structure. A revolt against the superior knowledge of the experts has itself been subordinated to expert leadership.

The combined power of the countless popular action groups campaigning for change would probably be enough to get the process of change under way if the dogmatists had not split the movement in an élitist conflict for ideological power positions. Practically all grassroots movements are exposed to the same élitist demand that they define themselves in ideological terms, and the meaning is always the same – that leadership should be handed over to those in possession of the most advanced theoretical knowledge of the single correct ideology.

Nonetheless, the new social movement is becoming aware of the need to fight this internal opposition, at least according to the post-Marxist sociologist Alain Touraine,[40] one of those who have put their specialist knowledge freely at the disposal of activists and campaigners. Protest groups refuse to have their needs defined by others, he says; they want the right of self-determination, the right to act independently, to develop skills, to create new organizational forms and to influence the apparatus of power. They refuse to enter existing parties or state bodies. New social movements cannot start from within the parties, says Touraine; their task is to renew social thought and practice.

Those fighting for influence in the workplace, in the women's movement, in environmental protection groups or in national separatist movements are not in themselves the bearers of the central conflict, but through them the central social movement of our time can evolve. What is at issue, according to Touraine, is the *direction* social development is to take, and how much say the individual is to have over his or her own life.

It is clear, however, that a revolt from below, even if it constitutes a combined protest against all forms of élite control and master thinking, is not necessarily a *one-way* force for change. There may be – and there are without doubt – conflicting interests and motives behind various parts of the overall grassroots movement. What all the campaigning groups seem to have in common is a desire for a more or less thoroughgoing transformation of society and its effects on people's lives. The fact that groups vary in how profound a change they are demanding does not, in itself, imply weakness; in confronting the obstacles our present society puts in the way of their efforts, they will undergo a natural process of consciousness-raising. Any problem of weakness arises from the fact that the need for change may point in conflicting directions, and may rest on conflicting attitudes to values and human nature. Since what we need is a transformation of industrial growth society, we must therefore ask: What fundamental values are characteristic of this society's development? What values are the necessary precondition of its existence and development? And what is the antithesis of these values – what, in fact, would have a *counteractive* effect on the society that must be transformed?

8. Counteraction

In 1971 the sociologist and criminologist, Thomas Mathiesen, published a book which deserves to be better known than it is among those discussing social change. The book is entitled *The Unfinished: A Contribution to the Theory of Political Action*.[50] (Quotations given below are from this work.) Two of the main principles in Mathiesen's undogmatic analysis help us to get to grips with the questions we are now confronting, especially as they greatly facilitate a free and unmanaged development from below.

Mathiesen starts from his experience of working for penal reform, but his views are valid for all campaigning groups working towards 'the alternative society'. His main thesis will be dealt with later. First, let us look at a simple point on which Mathiesen is in agreement with Marx, namely that a new idea, or a choice of action, if it is to contribute to fundamental change, must have a 'counteractive' or 'competing' effect on what is fundamental in the existing system. He argues convincingly that a socially transforming idea must not be woven into what exists but must be 'alien to the system'. The most important thing is to avoid ideas and actions that can be absorbed by the system, such as reforms without any effect whatsoever on the basic structure or the course of development that is to be changed: 'It has been claimed that one can enter the old system, work for short-term improvements on the system's premises and maintain, at the same time, the long-term, revolutionary objectives ... This overlooks the absorption that occurs through such practice ... In practice, it leads to a turning away from the long-term objectives.' One is initiated into the system's laws and the limited proposals for reform that are actually realized are only those that can be accommodated within the laws of the existing development.

> With piecemeal reforms, the main structure remains that of the time; changes occur in detail ... In other words, working for such reforms can serve directly to strengthen and to consolidate the existing order. Whether *all* minor reforms have this effect is an open question, but it does sometimes seem so, and in any case the defenders of continuous, piecemeal reform as a means to fundamental structural change have no clear proof to the contrary ...

However, says Mathiesen,

> I think it is possible to go a long way and to avoid the psychological fixations ... associated with normal reformist policies. These fixations exist to the extent that the revolutionary objectives are merely very long-term objectives which it is thought to achieve through a series of cumulative partial reforms. It is in this process of piecemeal reform that we turn away from the long-term objective. These fixations can be avoided when demolition of present structures is not only the

overall, long-term goal, but also always the immediate target – if only
in a very limited field ... Counteraction must be the constant and
immediate aim in the field one has chosen to work in ... as an element in
the long-term policy.

It is crucial that short-term undertakings 'on the way towards the long-
term, counteractive objective *must be of a very definite type, and they must be
consistently counteractive. Only in this way – by sticking stubbornly to the counteractive principle even in the immediate context – does one have a chance of resolving the
conflict between short-term and long-term objectives.'*

This argument points to a principle in developing a *realistic* strategy for
change. It is not a matter of defining accepted courses of action on the basis
of a narrow ideology. It eschews the 'safe' reforms that can be swallowed up
and exploited by the system one wants to transform. It also suggests
something far closer to reality than the revolutionary romanticism whose
adherents carry on with their theory, entirely without effect, in the
expectation of the one big revolution that will change everything at a single
stroke.

At the same time, establishing a counteractive principle does not mean
tying down the process for the participants. 'Wanting counteraction'
merely means that one wants something essentially different from what the
system's development is leading towards and is based on. If this will is not
present, there is no basis for cooperation — participants would share neither
the same value basis nor the same plans for action. But if every move, every
action great or small, is based on the same counteractive principle, it will be
an element in a realistic revolution with room for everyone sharing the same
basic outlook.

What, then, is the counteractive principle that is so alien to the system
that it cannot be accommodated or exploited by the status quo, but ensures
that every step becomes a link in the process of fundamental change?
Mathiesen provides no answer. So let us judge the question on the basis of
what we have established so far.

As we have seen, material and economic antagonisms no longer contribute
to changing the system. An increased effort by the majority to achieve a
higher material standard of living has no counteractive effect, because an
interest in highest possible consumption is woven into the system and only
serves to preserve its basic structure. People's economic self-interest is no
longer 'alien to the system'. The capital accumulation necessary for growth
under the planners' control is assured precisely by the fact that economic and
material goals are central for everyone. 'The individual serves the industrial
system, not by supplying it with savings and the resulting capital; he serves it
by consuming its products,' as Galbraith has demonstrated.

Now the economic demands of wage earners can of course be pushed so
high that both the shareholders' profit and the managements' investments
are curbed. Such demands, and a high level of consumption without saving,
can drain capital in accordance with Marxist-Leninist strategy. As has been
said, this would be difficult to bring about on a mass scale, as it would also

threaten the cosy position occupied by the trade-union leadership in the existing growth system. But *if* it happens, it would inevitably result in economic crises, the closing down of businesses as a result of decreased competitiveness on the export market, unemployment and consequently increased public expenditure by the state and increased income taxes, with a general reduction in consumption as a necessary result. And *because the motivation of the majority and the driving force behind it would consist of narrow economic and material objectives,* the growth-system's planners would then win the majority over to back their demands for a new acceleration of growth. Step on the gas, increase consumption and effort, but confine your demands within the limits that can help us reinstate the permanent growth in prosperity that you want!

In other words, general materialism seems today to be a *requirement* of the system, rather than a counteractive motive. On the other hand, it is clear that an antimaterialism which expresses itself in modest wage demands solely from the desire for a more relaxed way of life will not in itself contribute to change either. In the short term, it would increase business management's share of surplus-value and thus increase the potential for export and investment in new areas of 'demand production', perhaps particularly the leisure sector.

In other words, neither materialism nor antimaterialism seems *in itself* to be a counteractive force in the modern industrial system. And, as we have learnt, nor are the many campaigns for 'control from below' necessarily counteractive in their effect; they may conflict with one another if they lack a common, unifying power and direction, and without doubt many of them can very easily be accommodated within existing growth development.

What motive is there, then, that *cannot* be accommodated within the system we want to change, or must change, which could be the starting point for counteractive activity?

As we have seen, the system's prime requirement is that the majority of individuals and groups actively compete for positions on the economic ladder, and that this competition be manifested in the highest possible consumption as the all-pervading aim for individuals. In this way the ruling élite obtains the power to preserve the system and its own position. The potential for transforming property relations, or control over the means of production, in favour of the majority's freedom, therefore depends on the breakdown of this requirement – through the perception of its antithesis in counteractive action.

It therefore seems clear that counteraction entails the liberation of ordinary people's solidarity – their willingness to replace competition for economic gain with active work for equality, fellowship and cooperation. That is to say, not merely passive anti-materialism, but antimaterialism combined with active solidarity!

If this motive is not found, or cannot be expressed as a new and fundamental driving force, there is probably no basis for transforming the system. Then we have the system that conforms to our wishes. But if, on the other hand, an increasing number of campaigns and actions based on this motive develop in society, they will inevitably dissolve the basis of the existing system and, at the same time, pave the way for a new one. I.e. they will have a counteractive effect.

There is also much to suggest that the conflict of values inherent in the counteractive principle is parallelled by the power antagonism we have discussed between élite authority and the majority. The values that are suppressed by control from above, and which the majority are clearly feeling the lack of to an increasing degree, are precisely the values of fellowship, the capacity and the opportunity for communal life and shared experience, something to live for beyond narrow economic egotism.

Can this idea of what is needed for a counteractive effect be applied in practice? Is it true that an action is counteractive or socially transforming when it replaces competition for economic gain with active work for equality, fellowship and cooperation?

Henceforth, the concept of 'counteraction' will be used in this sense, and existing movements and alternatives will be considered in the light of this key concept.

The meaning of the counteractive principle in practice

Loneliness and feelings of emptiness and meaninglessness seem to lie behind many of the most serious problems in our society. Attempts to find an escape in alcohol, narcotics, stimulants, mental illness and suicide are all marked by sharply rising curves. And people's inner conflict and sense of purposelessness are expressed in increasing violence, aggression, marriage breakdowns and conflicts between generations.

But because we all *allow ourselves to be manipulated* into putting what the system demands – competition for consumption and status – before the counteractive solidarity that we want and lack in the most profound way, we become ensnared in the system and help to make things worse for ourselves and others. By accepting the master thinkers' image of us as irresponsible subjects of treatment, we blind ourselves to the choice of values that is facing us. Even if the choice of values is severely limited by the compelling power of the system, we still do not see the possibilities we actually have for allowing solidarity to be expressed in an initial counter-active action. The result of allowing ourselves to be rendered powerless in the matter of these fundamental value choices is that the dialectical interplay between action based on solidarity and political change, which seems to be the only way to a new and better society, is obstructed.

By allowing ourselves to be manipulated into taking part in the economic competition between individuals and groups on the growth planners' premises, we become incapable of accepting the equalization of income which could destroy the rat-race mentality and pull the foundations from under the entire system of industrial growth. By accepting society's need for growth in consumption as a personal goal, even though tens of thousands of our fellow citizens could use this growth better than we can ourselves, our attitude to others remains as the system demands it: they become objects of comparison for our own material success; they become competitors instead of companions. Or, as the German sociologist Dieter Duhm puts it in his book *Commodity Structure and the Destruction of Human Interaction*,[51] in a commodity society where no values are sacred any longer but where everything is made the object of purchase and sale, 'companions become opponents' whose disasters are my strengths. Wariness, envy and fear thus become the dominant features in human relations.

And it always seems to be the disempowering of ordinary people, the constant dismissal of their attempts to assume responsibility, which prevents them from expressing the fellowship which is there, displaced and unredeemed. And thus it is that the counteractive activity which could, or rather which *can,* arise from the conflict of values which most people are experiencing ever more acutely in our inhuman society, is not given expression.

To accept this fundamental antagonism, and to make room for its popular expression, is not, however, in the interests of the revolutionary master thinkers, because it also challenges them and their positions. Ordinary people, on the other hand, have little to lose and everything to gain from liberating themselves:

From the private materialism that is destroying their lives in countless ways;

from the consumer existence which puts money worries, fashionable furniture and clothes and institutional solutions before the companionship of family and friends, and care for children and the old;

from the isolation of the nuclear family and the focus on the materialism and the entertainment which growth society offers it as a substitute for externally directed activity and communal life;

and from the passive acceptance of the one-sided economic rewards which the technostructure offers as a substitute for influence over one's own work and its results.

A trade-union representative at the Chrysler factories in Britain, Jim Shutt,[52] described, in an interview, a worker's experience of the need to revolt against the forces manipulating him into participating in destructive growth:

> When you spend eight hours a day standing by an assembly line making cars;
> And then, after work, you have to walk quarter of a mile past 200,000 unsold cars to your own car;
> And you sit in a traffic jam for an hour on the way home to where you live, which is by a noisy motorway in an environment poisoned with exhaust fumes;
> All this so you can pay the instalments on the car and buy consumer goods;
> Which make it possible for you to forget what a hellish job you have;
> Then it isn't really so strange, is it, if sooner or later you react against the insanity of it all?

And react was precisely what the Chrysler workers did, by making contact with the workers at Lucas Aerospace in order to discuss a campaign for alternative production based on a socially conscious outlook.

But an understanding that participation in blind growth of production and consumption ruins life for oneself and others is not confined to a handful of 'campaigners'. A nation-wide opinion survey conducted in 1975 by a Norwegian gallup poll on the initiative of The Future in Our Hands[53] showed that over 80 per cent of the Norwegian population foresaw the following results from further growth in general production and consumption: more competition for things and more unnecessary luxury; stress and damage to health in the workplace from measures to increase efficiency; pollution; more unpleasant and inhuman towns.

What all this seems to show is that replacing economic self-interest with common responsibility and solidarity is not only counteractive but also realistic, because it is, in the most profound sense, in the interest of the majority, even in the short term. It therefore seems vitally important to awaken a more active consciousness of the counteractive values and to strengthen confidence that *it is worthwhile* to let these values be expressed – in the areas which the various campaigning groups and individuals themselves feel to be important.

Let us examine briefly how the counteractive principle we have arrived at – active solidarity in place of competition for economic gain and materialism – appears in relation to the many grassroots campaigns for change from below that have been mentioned. Why has the counteractive effect of these campaigns been somewhat limited? Could they have achieved more if they had linked their protest more to the conflict between the motive of material self-interest and active solidarity?

What prevented the Lucas workers from realizing their plans on a larger scale?

Their view is that unemployment need not occur as long as millions of poor, sick and helpless people are suffering the lack of things the unused capacity for production could provide. But they run into the problem that those who need their products, in poor or rich countries, do not themselves have the purchasing power to buy them. Society may pay unemployment benefit to the unemployed, but who is to pay for the raw materials, energy and depreciation of capital? The Lucas management's antipathy is revealing of the resistance to change that exists at the top of the pyramids, but even without this obstruction the workers involved in the Lucas plan would have lacked the economic means to carry out their projects.

In the final analysis, everything runs aground on the lack of consciousness in the rest of society that what is needed to get socially useful production under way is solidarity – the common will of society as a whole to pay for those lacking the necessary purchasing capacity. Moreover, if this willingness to put solidarity before personal gain is not awakened in the public, the Lucas workers will be forced to accept the rules of play of the market economy; and alternative production will become a question of developing unnecessary new products for those with the money to buy them.

All the indications suggest, however, that the will to solidarity already exists in the public. But it is suppressed by those, on both political wings, who reduce both the preservation of society and social change to a battle for material self-interest.

What might have happened if the Lucas workers had combined their action with a campaign to win the public over to active solidarity with the unemployed and the disadvantaged, for whom the company could have produced? There are many possible forms for such action. For example, a special tax on higher incomes could have been proposed, to provide the means of restructuring and operating such production. Or the labour movement could itself have set up a solidarity fund, financed by high-income groups, to make it possible for workers in threatened enterprises to take them over and carry out their plans. The president of the Norwegian Union of Industrial Chemical Workers is among those who have proposed this type of income equalization and solidarity fund as new tasks for the labour movement.[32] What is important, however, is not whether these specific proposals are realistic or relevant for those concerned in this instance. What matters is that such questions are raised – that the counter-active principle of solidarity is brought into the debate and presented as a possibility in which ordinary workers can participate.

What, then, of the environmental movement? Why has it been absorbed to such a degree into the system which creates the problems it is struggling against? How has it been possible for environmentalism to be exploited by politicians and planners who use 'conservation' as a slogan in their programmes of growth? Why does resource-wasting industrial growth continue inexorably in parallel with a growing interest in the environment? Why has this interest not had a counteractive effect on the system? The reason may be that the environmental movement, too, has not been consistent enough in linking its message to the counteractive value choices and activities in which the general public can participate. Information put out by the many campaigning groups often lacks at least one aspect of the counteractive principle: reference to the need for a consistent anti-materialism, or to the connection between this and economic solidarity.

As long as the majority's dependence on consumption remains unchanged, every environmental victory in one area will be a defeat in another. The energy lost when a water system is saved from hydroelectric development must be made up with a corresponding increase in the use of oil or nuclear power – or in the production, by major industries, of alternative energy equipment. And every action against industrial pollution becomes an argument for *increased* growth in order to cover the cost of anti-pollution measures which allow consumption to continue unaffected.

It is common, of course, to link information about the environment to political demands for a levelling off of growth. But in terms of popular participation, this can easily be confined to irresponsible indictments of those who have power and want no change.

Even if increasing numbers of people are acknowledging the connection between environmental problems and the growth in consumption, large sections of the environmental movement have only attached a limited importance to convincing people that what they are saying requires the public to liberate itself from consumer control – a liberation which many people clearly want support for. By representing the common responsibility of ordinary people as a matter of political 'solutions from above', the necessary change from below is excluded, and the majority remain the malleable instruments of the technostructure's demand control.

This brings us to the other aspect of counteraction: the need to link liberation from consumption with active economic solidarity and the principle of economic equality. The omission of this makes it easy for the system's defenders to show that economic levelling off will 'harm the disadvantaged in our society', increase unemployment and reduce demand for the poor countries' raw materials. Similarly, if the alternative values are not stressed, it is impossible to answer the charge that 'economic equality will remove all incentive to work'.

Linking the proposals for economic equalization and reduced consumption with the idea of using funds released to support action in solidarity, makes it possible to counter the usual arguments of the opposition. One can imagine cooperating with and providing economic support for Lucas-type projects on a national scale – or creating solidarity funds to provide support for action in peripheral areas in one's own country or in developing countries.

In the same way, the one-sided political campaigns in support of liberation movements would probably contribute more powerfully to counteractive change if they cooperated with groups working to provide direct economic support for development on the terms of the local population in poor countries. Their political activities would then be doubly counteractive: by increasing the ability of new groups in poor countries to participate in the work of liberation, and by contributing to the liberation of the inhabitants of rich countries from the consumer system under which the Third World also suffers.

The movements for alternative ways of life will similarly only be a counteractive force when the reduction in consumption they are working for becomes more than a question of personal liberation. If this is not linked to the need to *redistribute* the means made available by new ways of life, their opponents will in fact be correct – both those who claim that reduced consumption and hence reduced wage demands increase the share of capital available to business management for reinvestment, and the conservatives who claim that a reduction in consumption hurts both poor and rich countries by producing unemployment and a reduced trade in raw materials. Only when a reduction in consumption is seen as a *means* of acting in solidarity will it be a real contribution to more human and more globally responsible social development, and an element in the process of counteraction.

The women's movement, too, can easily become a factor supporting existing development if it is not consciously linked to counteractive value choices and activities. This is perhaps one of the most explosive issues to deal with, because the question of women's liberation has become so bound up with fixed and dogmatic positions for both Right and Left. But precisely because the counteractive values – equality, mutual support and shared humanity in opposition to individual self-interest and competition – are so strong in the women's movement, there ought to be room for a less dogmatic examination of the implications of these values.

On the Right, it is often claimed that woman's place is in the home, and that children need their mother's care above all else. As a result men easily fall into their traditional role – and their lives become bound up with often inhuman work, separated from close, shared human responsibility, care and fellowship. And because their position gives them privilege in relation to their partner, in terms of both family economy and social contact, it is usually their attitudes, values and power which reign in the family, as in society. And women remain oppressed and isolated, without influence on a development which conflicts fundamentally with the human values they wish to defend.

On the Left, many claim, often just as one-sidedly, that the liberation of women means that social institutions must take over responsibility for children during working hours in order to give women equality in employment. Again, this solution seems to be tailored to the structure of industrial-growth society, to the advantage of the existing power structure and value system and to the obstruction of social change.

When both parents are encouraged to work full-time, the clear need of children for greater contact with their parents is neglected. And the family, in increasing its income, becomes an instrument of growth society's demand for consumption. The result can well be that children grow accustomed to consumption and to substitute values in place of the communal life they are lacking. This is often aggravated by the fact that parents in full-time work have little time left for children when all domestic work has to be done in 'free' time. In this way dependence on industrial society's solutions is once again increased, with cars, bought recreation and more and more automated aids and processed goods allowing no room for personal creativity.

In many respects, institutional childcare represents a liberation for women in patriarchal society. But the lack of contact and concern with children that has characterized the male role now begins to affect women too, while the position of men, and their attitudes, remain largely unchanged.

Institutional childcare also suits perfectly the technostructure's desire for the control and institutionalization of all human activities and concerns, as Illich has strongly pointed out. Caring becomes a profession and raising children a matter for experts. Individual parents are deprived of power even in the role that is closest to them. Children are moulded en masse according to current expert wisdom, inevitably with less of the personal insight, physical contact and love that is expressed in voluntary nurturing – and that is needed more than anything if a positive social transformation is to take place. In this way, too, children are moulded at an early age to fit the institutional control and management they must later subject themselves to in the system.

The claim that this is a 'radical' solution, in the sense of having a counter-active effect on the existing social structure, is almost incomprehensible. This assertion is, nevertheless, such a solid part of conventional, radical-élitist theory that the many people who think differently scarcely dare open their mouths. But there are some who dare, and they are among the most radical. Jörn Svensson, for example, representative for the Swedish Left (Communist) party in the Riksdag, says in his book *Take Leadership and Power:*[54] 'The natural solution for someone who wants to avoid all parental duties is not the complete institutionalization of caring work, but to avoid having children. As long as children have a need for personal and intimate relationships with special individuals, unpaid caring work will continue to exist.' In the socialist society Svensson is working for, there will, he says, 'be legislation making both parents equally responsible for the work of caring.'

Why should it be reactionary to seek solutions of this sort, given a desire for profound social change through counteractive action? Let us examine briefly the direction indicated by the values of counteraction in this important area. If the starting point is solidarity and equality, it goes without saying that women's and men's access to social and occupational roles must be on equal terms. But it follows equally that solidarity must apply to the weakest party – the child. No expert wisdom is needed to know that children have a natural need for parental contact. This may, admittedly, decline with age, but up to school age it far exceeds the time that parents working full-time can give them.

It is also clear that children need to be with others of their own age. And it is particularly important that it should be accepted that parents – perhaps men especially – need to develop the capacity for understanding and companionship which comes from looking after children. How can these demands be reconciled? The obvious answer is that, alongside the institutional childcare which will remain necessary for many single parents, society should arrange things to allow for part-time work, making it possible for both parents of young children to *share* work in the home and outside – alternating for example, every other week, month, or possibly every other year.

At the same time, the child and the parent whose turn it is to be at home could be given opportunities for contact with others in the same situation. It ought to be possible, through local initiatives, to find or to build places where work and play can be combined, where different generations can together bake, pickle, sew, mend, paint and do carpentry, and where grand-parents can also take part, able to feel useful and to have some of the contact which both they and their grandchildren so often miss. And single people would be able to take an active part in the larger community from which they are otherwise excluded in modern society.

A solution of this sort would not only take account of everyone's equal rights. It would also give children and adults access to the form of free, communal and creative work which expert-controlled institutions deprive people of. And it would put other and more important values in place of those consumer society forces upon us. It would also create, for the first time, broad scope for men to come into contact with the values that have generally been reserved for women, and this would give women, men and children a new experience of the fellowship and free, independent activity which leads in the direction of a different and better society. And not least, a solution of this sort would save society part of the enormous annual sum that each place in a day centre costs, thus making possible the necessary income compensation for low-income families who would otherwise be dependent on double work.

But above all, this sort of solution – or others based on the same fundamental values, attitudes and principles – would have a *counteractive* effect, because it puts solidarity and fellowship before self-interest and competition for private, economic and professional status.

Further examples could be given of the need to link action for change to consciously held counteractive values – but they should not be necessary. It seems self-evident that, in a society which is primarily dependent on everyone competing for narrow, material, private gain and status, the prerequisite for change is anything that amounts to the antithesis of these values.

What does need to be stressed is that action for change which favours the interests of one's own group alone forms no part of a counteractive process. It may be justifiable and right, but it has nothing to do with social change. Fighting for one's own interests alone is so little counteractive that it is simply part and parcel of the competitive principle of established society. Action only becomes counteractive when it presupposes and furthers the reverse of established social values: the values of solidarity and fellowship *in place of* individual and group competition.

As I have said, there are reasons for expecting members of certain élite groups to oppose change from below and general liberation from the value system on which our society is based. It may be necessary to prepare for the likelihood that master thinkers from the various new classes that monopolize power and ideas in modern society will actively oppose attempts to think and act counteractively. And their opposition will probably grow as there is a more conscious mobilization around the values which provide the movement for change with a wide counteractive strength.

This opposition will be an expression of the *external* conflicts of power and class which still exist. But it would be both psychologically naive and an example of unrealistic thinking in terms of 'models', to reduce the *conflict of values* at the root of the whole thing to a simple matter of class. Just as Marx himself came from a bourgeois background, there will be members of both bourgeois and radical élites who will side with the majority in the popular process of transforming values. Strategically, it would also be stupid to define all members of élites and groups with power as opponents, thus rejecting the support of those of them who share the basic values of the movement for change and are willing to accept their consequences.

Similarly it is unrealistic to think that all 'ordinary people' support the counteractive values. Even though there are many indications that the lives of most people are lacking in human fellowship and solidarity, it is clear that a conflict of values also divides the general public – indeed that the conflict exists in every individual. However reactionary it may sound, and however difficult it may be to make it accord with schematic social models, we cannot escape the fact that we are facing not only an outer, but also an inner, spiritual struggle for liberation.

If it is true that all efforts for change will be absorbed by the existing system unless they express values that are the opposite of the system's, everything ultimately comes down to a struggle for a choice of values and the *consequences* of this choice, which no individual can escape. We must accept that, in a society where the majority's material demands are no longer in conflict with the existing order but rather its precondition, change requires a struggle to express other values, both in oneself and in others.

In a process of this sort, vulgar Marxism's one-sided concentration on the owners of capital as the system's 'scapegoats' can serve to disempower ordinary working people by depriving them of their responsibility for this personal choice. The conservative attack on all radicals, as though they were responsible for all suppression of freedom, has a similar effect.

A movement for change from below should be aware of which groups have positions to protect and can therefore be expected to mount a particular resistance to the process. But the movement's own power will be sapped if everything is reduced to a question of pointing out the 'guilt' of others. If the ordinary person is without guilt, that does not mean he or she has no responsibility. Responsibility for one's own choice should not be represented as an indictment but as a self-evident right. A movement for change should therefore be open to support from anyone willing to share this responsibility – whether the person in question belongs to 'the innocents' or to those who are expected to resist.

In his account of 'one-dimensional man',[55] Herbert Marcuse makes the same point: both materially and ideologically, he points out, the classes which once represented the absolute negation of the capitalist system are now more and more integrated into that system. In his view, a transcendence of the existing conditions requires a transcendence *within* these conditions, an act that the one-dimensional person in one-dimensional society is prevented from performing. If development towards the individual's complete integration into this one-dimensional society is to be obstructed, then the oppressed classes must liberate themselves from themselves as well as from their masters.

The same basic idea is expressed by many, perhaps the majority, of the new thinkers who have freed themselves from obsolete ideological schemes. 'The Westerner of today is "split into two people" and is busy exploiting himself,' says Glucksmann.[3] 'If one is aware of this inner division, it ought to be impossible to imagine a final and unique revolution in which the good and the bad clash in a decisive battle.' Glucksmann asks us to start asking questions, both of ourselves and of the thinkers in our countries. 'Anyone who knows where he is going can take the credit for criticizing them. We have to ask simpler questions in order to find out where we come from, to discover what it is in everyone that threatens to extinguish the spark of resistance for good ... '

We must stop accepting the tendency of 'value-neutral' ideologues always to analyze the simple and fundamental in terms of the complete and complex, as though an all-encompassing theory was valuable per se. We must liberate ourselves from this abstract theorizing by beginning to build our own overall attitude on the basis of a simple, fundamental choice of values: through our acceptance that we are also facing a personal struggle.

Making the word 'idealist' into a pejorative term, as is commonly done in élite circles – as though there were no greater idiocy than evaluating things in accordance with ideals – this is precisely an indication of a flight from the questions which threaten élitist theory.

What matters now is to form a new sense of fellowship around the human principles and values that can create something fundamentally new, on the basis of a desire for cooperation and experiential understanding, and a willingness to put oneself in others' shoes, to step out of the cramped pigeon-holes – political, environmental, occupational and national – in order to see the consequences of our values, both in the immediate context and in the broader perspective. 'Much more than decisions on economic policy is involved,' says Galbraith. 'A system of morality is at stake.'[37]

No élitist theory can appropriate choice and responsibility. The counteractive values must be expressed through the free actions and personal development of ordinary people. The élite may cooperate in this, but they cannot lead. The paradoxical problem is that the moment the process is taken over by someone who thinks they know the way and the goal in detail, the process is killed, because the initiative is taken from the people whose position conflicts most powerfully with the system's values and power structure, and who therefore have the most real motive for change.

On the other hand, what everyone has the right to fight for – indeed what ought to be and must be fought for – are the fundamental values and principles which everyone, regardless of their education and position, can relate to personally. How can this happen without the process being stifled by being 'prefabricated' before it starts?

9. 'The Unfinished'

For some theorists, social change is a matter of ideological discussion and the presentation of complete solutions, a question of having systematically correct opinions which can be justified in terms of a certain complete view of future society. Indeed, in order to be accepted as a participant in the élite's debate on social change, one must often be able to present a comprehensive solution of this sort, with built-in answers to everything. The question of how élitist thought structures of this sort actually affect public opinion is scarcely discussed. As has been said, élitist thought tends to induce passivity in the majority, thus obstructing social change.

As an alternative to the total and complete, Thomas Mathiesen[50] proposes 'the unfinished' – an *outline* of something wholly new, bound by almost nothing except the counteractive principle. Incomplete alternatives of this sort are far more threatening to the existing system; in practice they have a far greater counteractive effect because they are more difficult to dismiss. A message that is alien to the system but pre-formed is in far greater danger of being rendered ineffectual or 'non-competing' in relation to the established view: 'Because it is clear ... that the message, in being put into practice, does not belong to the old system, the satisfied member of the old system can dismiss the message as being inapplicable to him- or herself or the system, as irrelevant, as having nothing to do with the system. The opposition's contradiction of this can be rejected as being permanently "external" and thus set aside.'

The actual effect of the dismissal of total, ideological solutions is demonstrated every day. The defenders of the system can use powerful arguments to convince the public that the preconceived alternative 'cannot function' in relation to the known and established mechanisms. As a result the alternative is seen – and also perceived by the public at large – as an internal concern for ideologues, separate from present reality. In this way, the idea of a new and complete solution can in fact serve to support the existing order by making the concept of real change unimaginable for ordinary people.

An alternative to the complete and established is not something else complete and established, but the *unfinished* – which remains revolutionary because it is never rigidly confined, but always *on the way* towards something new and unknown: 'The choice therefore is not between different versions of complete clarification, but between complete clarification and the unfinished. What the choice emphasizes is tolerance for a lack of clarity as the antithesis of the status quo.'

The dynamic, counteractive element in the unfinished resides in the fact that it represents a constant challenge that cannot be dismissed out of hand. The contradiction's lack of clarity as far as further consequences are concerned means that no one can be quite sure that the contradiction is in fact an outside view – incapable of being put into practice. Contradiction and competition are united – in the alternative. And this, says Mathiesen, is the definition of 'the unfinished'. 'Counteraction, and hence the transition to the unfinished, is set in motion through creating a consciousness that we are necessarily facing a *dilemma* – through the conscious experience that we in fact have to *choose* between a continuation of the existing order (possibly with minor changes) and a transition to something that is not known.'

However, the approach to transformation is obviously not only through the presentation of a sketchy alternative. Change requires counteractive action. But if it is to contribute to the process of change, action need not – must not – be confined and tied within the limits laid down by the detailed, 'complete' solution. What is important, if the action is to contribute to change, is that it arises from counteractive principles and attitudes. In this way, and probably only in this way, is space created for multiformity – for broad, popular cooperation for change from below.

Nonetheless, says Mathiesen, 'there is an immense political pressure towards completing the sketch as a finished drawing, therefore towards completing the growth of its product.' This pressure is felt in two ways. In the first place, demands will be raised by master thinkers on the inside that the movement for change must commit its members to an acceptance of the systematic, ideological understanding they themselves represent – in order to avoid the risk of sharing a pigeonhole with people who represent 'incorrect ideology'. By merely linking such a movement to a set of basic values, they claim, there is a risk that rank and file members will misunderstand and draw 'wrong conclusions'. But this didactic defining effectively kills the gradual and personal process of developing a consciousness concerning the implications of values, which 'the unfinished' facilitates.

This demand for ideological clarification is something every popular movement is exposed to sooner or later – and giving in to such demands always has the same result: the movement becomes organized according to the usual pyramid pattern, the 'conscious' theorists take over the leadership, construct an ideology on behalf of the great number of ordinary members and ask for a mandate to determine strategy and action on the basis of this ideology. And since only a very few people feel competent to take part in advanced ideological debate, a mandate is given and active participation from below is reduced to training in élite theory and control strategy. Those who are not ready for the advanced theoretical understanding, and those who prefer to think for themselves, drift away. The movement shrinks because the dynamic of 'the unfinished' is gone.

Another source of pressure towards completing the sketch comes from outside, from the established political party structure. This may take the form of an attempt by a particular party to identify the movement with its own established policies. But if the movement's questions represent a threat to the party's ideology, attempts will be made to render it harmless by defining it as belonging to the opposing political camp. The movement will be painted 'red' by conservatives and 'blue' by radicals. In this way the party avoids taking its challenge seriously. If those involved in the movement insist on sticking to the unfinished alternative, independently of established ideologies, attempts will be made to define them as irrelevant in terms of the dividing lines the different parties have established as the 'real' ones.

An important factor contributing to pressure in this process is the political media élite. The experience of political journalists consists largely of defining and interpreting events in society in terms of the established party structure. A movement for change has to be put in this context if it is to be treated as a novelty. Demands for party political standpoints are therefore made of the unfinished. If the movement sticks to its unfinished challenge, it will soon be dismissed as uninteresting by large sections of the press. It is stifled as information channels to the public are blocked.

But capitulation to the demand that objectives and problems be predefined in the language and on the premises of the various parties with power results in annexation by the existing structure. In such circumstances, the power and authoritarian nature of this structure is used 'to locate emergent organizations more definitively, and thus to render them harmless,' says Mathiesen. 'As long as no definitive choice has been made and the movement has not been "placed", the emergence is still in progress and the organization is contradicting and competing. And even inasmuch as a choice is made, it is in any case essential to retain clearly the right to develop out of that standpoint and to change it.'

The solution lies in maintaining the initiative through constant direct action for short-term counteractive objectives which continually challenge the existing order – and, at the same time, in always keeping a grip on the long-term, unfinished objective. But 'the point is that these short-term objectives do not become the final ones, but remain steps on a road that is still unfamiliar and no more than intimated – unfinished.'

> We get counteraction, then, at the breach with the existing order, where *at the same time* we stand facing an open field. This is to say that counteraction, and the very first phase of the unfinished, are one and the same thing. The moment of freedom is in entering that open field ... The alternative society is the society in which the old social order is in the process of fundamental change.

The real alternative to the existing order is *always* unfinished. The answer to the usual question of how long the sketch's unfinished character is to be preserved lies in 'the conflict between the counteractive and the system-creating forces, and in constant counteraction, construction, new counteraction, on one level after another. One can speak of a cyclic transition through constantly renewed states of incompletion. I experience this as the process of life itself,' says Mathiesen.

Sticking to 'the unfinished' as a principle for a transforming movement does not of course mean opposing the political standpoints and outwardly directed arguments of those involved in it. But it must be accepted that the participants stand at various levels of political consciousness, that their perspectives are always developing, and that one form of counteractive action must not exclude another. Only with this acceptance that the movement does not stand for something final and rigidly determined, but for a *process* of creating a consciousness of the consequences of values through independent activity and discussion – only in this way can the movement avoid stagnating and turning in on itself. And only in this way can the overall movement for change avoid being weakened by ideological battles among its different groupings. One of the most important advantages of 'the unfinished' is that it allows room for cooperation and free, constructive debate on all basic matters.

This process of development through debate, broad cooperation and many-faceted action based on a growing consciousness of the implications of the counteractive values, is precisely what is obstructed by capitulating to élite demands for completion and ideological control.

'The unfinished' produces development from below. Complete ideologies inevitably produce élite control. A revolt against society's pyramid structure must be built according to another model – a 'flat' structure of individuals and groups in which none has power over others, where the controlling factor is not leadership and preconception, but a common counteractive principle.

The danger that someone may 'misunderstand' the implications of the given values, or misuse their freedom by participating in the movement for change on the system's premises, is inversely proportional to the strength with which the counteractive values are made clear as the basis of debate and action. Those who wish to take part from the standpoint of other values will be exposed in the concrete debate over values which 'the unfinished' encourages. And debate with those who seem to have a different value perspective can itself work as a constructive, consciousness-raising element.

The danger of accepting complete, binding conclusions is greater than one might at first think. Sometimes the conclusions may be so inescapable, as logical consequences of the fundamental, counteractive values, that they simply cannot be contradicted. The problem is that once the principle of rigidly determining logical consequences is established, there will always be theorists in the movement constantly claiming new 'logically necessary' consequences of the initial premise. This leaves the way open for an unstoppable battle involving increasing ideological particularization which finally – and as usual – places power and control in the hands of a few élite thinkers. The process of creating consciousness stops as soon as individuals become 'consciousness-receiving' rather than independently perceiving, as the 'pedagogue of liberation', Paolo Freire, emphasizes so strongly. The development of consciousness, Freire points out, is a process in which people, not as receivers, but as perceiving individuals, achieve a deepened consciousness both of the sociological reality which shapes their lives and of their capacity to change that reality.[56]

The revolt against the society of planning is a revolt for the right to think for oneself, to become conscious of what one stands for. To try to control it from above is to go against the revolt itself. People who are not encouraged to believe in their own capacity to judge will always be more inclined to listen to those who represent what is customary rather than those who argue for change. Seeing that what one is accustomed to can and should be changed requires a liberation from those who make judgements and the freedom to come to conclusions on one's own behalf.

A particular danger with 'complete' ideologies is that they often tend to move in the direction of the existing structures of power and opinion in the established party political apparatuses. As Mathiesen says, definition will always be necessary in the language of the established apparatuses of power. This makes it more difficult to highlight conflicts and demands that are not given expression in the structures of the established parties and organizations. This is probably especially important today, when the counteractive values seem to cut right across most parties and organizations.

The fundamental conflict of values which characterizes industrial society at the crossroads divides the parties, if not in the middle, then into two parts of varying size.

In the socialist parties, the division is between, on the one hand, those who want to guide the working majority forward to revolutionary or reformist change through increasing economic and material demands under centralized leadership, and, on the other hand, those who want to contribute to change from below by mobilizing a general resistance to materialism and competitive mentality in the interests of national and global equalization and solidarity.

On one side of the conservative parties are those who want to defend capitalist industrial growth and the conditions it requires: competition for economic self-interest and the winners' rights of property and leadership. On the other side, there is a small but increasingly articulate group of 'value conservatives' who want to promote the human fellowship and majority freedom which this system suppresses. They are increasingly conscious that the conservation of values conflicts with the system that demands constant radical upheavals in values, traditions and conditions of life. They are in practice seeking a new system where both freedom and the right to own the means of production and property is fairly *distributed*, both nationally and internationally.

But a clear division also runs through the new, more ecological and populist parties – between those who regard global justice primarily as an automatic, future result of ecological, non-exploitative, self-sufficiency politics, and those who have a broader perspective of solidarity and recognize that the consideration shown to our own populations during the restructuring must also be granted to others.

Time and again, discussions with people in all the three areas of party politics, who share the same fundamental commitment to values and wish seriously to put them into effect, have revealed an important fact: they are much closer to one another than their ideological leaders (and often they themselves) will admit.

In 1977, the Future in Our Hands movement arranged a press conference in Oslo which demonstrated this need for new political dividing lines cutting right across the established party structures. Present at the conference were members of the new, value-conscious sections of all parties currently represented in the Norwegian parliament. They all declared publicly that they considered the primary question of global solidarity, on which they had a common view, as more important than the party lines which divided them.

And this amounted to more than a verbal unity. They were agreed on a series of crucial questions, in opposition to the official policies of their parties. But this fact, which would undoubtedly have interested large sections of the public at large, was almost completely omitted from press reports of the conference. Most political journalists appeared to have little interest in drawing attention to this sign of a departure from the party battles they are normally concerned with.

How fundamental this internal conflict in the parties is, and how much closer to one another the 'new' factions are, can be illustrated with statements from the two largest parties in Norway. Trygve Bratteli of the Norwegian Labour Party wrote, in 1976: 'The most pessimistic ... seem to fear that resources are being exhausted, that we are becoming too materialistic, and that we are taking resources from developing countries ... It is remarkable that people today are worried about a scarcity of resources and energy when, for the first time in history, we are standing on the threshold of a technology that is overcoming the scarcity problems of former times.'[57]

But as a representative of the same party, Einar Førde, said at about the same time: 'Sooner or later we will not escape the question of a more just distribution. It is clear that our own economic and social standards will be directly affected if we are to help developing countries ... we may soon be in a situation where it is the politicians who are pushing hardest the demand for higher and higher private consumption, while public opinion is in fact prepared for a change of direction.'[58]

On the Right, the conflict in the Norwegian conservative party (Høyre), between capitalism and value conservatism is expressed just as clearly in the following statement by Helge Ole Bergesen, former vice-chair of the National Association of Young Conservatives and later editor of the value-conservative periodical *Kontur*:

> The only area where one can say that the party is promoting consistent conservative policy is in the attempt to protect the position of certain groupings. This applies particularly to the leaders of private enterprise, whether they are owners or professional managers ... The party wants to limit expansion in state bureaucracy and enterprise but seems to have no misgivings about major industrial development in the private sector or the concentration of power which inevitably results from it ... The contrast between our affluence and the poverty of the poor scarcely exists for the Conservative party ... Sooner or later it must choose its course: either a continuing combination of power conservatism and developmental radicalism, or a value-conservative direction which aims at preserving central values in today's society and rejects the social-democrats' growth experiments.[59]

But attempts to present these vitally important new political dividing lines have so far run into almost insurmountable obstacles put up by the master thinkers of established party attitudes – in political groupings, in the party apparatuses and in the mass media. New ways of thinking are thus suppressed. The public are faced with a choice between outdated and preconceived alternatives.

But now and then the new way of thinking breaks through to reveal a surprising, repressed interest in a fundamentally new *starting point* for political judgements, as when the book *Revolt from the Centre*[48] was launched in Denmark. And sooner or later the pressure from below will finally break through the barriers.

10. Change and the Demand for Freedom

A major obstacle to change is the artificial division – created by dogmatists on both Right and Left – between social change and freedom. On the whole, it is easy for the forces protecting the status quo to spread the idea that a radical transformation of what exists now is synonymous with subjection to a centralized state power or communist dictatorship. The rationale for this is the classical Leninist model which new-thinking socialists have long abandoned, but which the dogmatists still see as the only alternative. General freedom – is the broadest sense – is not, however, a characteristic of the modern system of industrial growth. On the contrary, freedom as a right for all will only come through a *transformation* of the existing order.

There is little point in opposing revolutionary change by referring to the revolutions that have occurred in poor countries and the unfreedom they have brought with them. The revolution that is now gathering force in the affluent society represents liberation from quite a different form of oppression. When this revolution begins to have a counteractive effect on the system, it will do so precisely by *breaking down* élite power; it will not be like previous revolutions, a revolt in which the majority allow themselves to be led, but a majority revolt against being led. And the political guidance involved in the process will not be forced upon it from above, but created from below. If this revolution comes about at all, in the way that this account supposes, it will in itself be a guarantee against élite oppression.

This move towards revolution in the rich countries is without historical parallel. It is the first revolution for other values and rights than economic ones, a revolution *for* freedom, not for the few and select but for the many, not just out of individual self-interest but primarily out of a demand and a desire for fellowship and solidarity. Even if this is not yet always equally articulated or equally conscious, it seems nevertheless to be the counteractive power of this unique revolution – a power which will be felt ever more strongly as the system's opposition to these values becomes increasingly apparent to the general public.

'Freedom' is a concept that has been misused perhaps more than any other at the extremes of both political wings. The demand for freedom must be taken more seriously – and interpreted more comprehensively – than the dogmatists have wanted. It seems as though hitherto both political camps, in order to escape the demand for freedom which challenges the system they believe in themselves, have concentrated exclusively on their opponents' oppression and forgotten their own. Neither the warnings of political coercion under communism, nor the evidence of the violence and oppression capitalism creates for the global majority, should be explained away. The opposition to unfreedom which is being expressed here by both sides ought, on the contrary, to provide a generally accepted principle for the analysis of our own society's future. But then the idea of freedom must also be liberated from the restricted interpretations that it has usually been given.

The liberal concept of freedom

Classical economic liberalism generally links the concept of freedom narrowly to two conditions: freedom for private initiative and competition for economic input, reward and property; and freedom of thought from political oppression. But its interpretation of these aspects of freedom seems to rest on narrowly materialistic thinking. Both ignore the problems of freedom that are typical of industrial society – the restricted freedom to give personal expression to other goals than economic self-interest, and the equally restricted freedom to shape society's production, consumption and development according to a different fundamental outlook than that which the system's normative influence on values contributes to.

None of these limitations of freedom is absolute, but they arise from a clearly oppressive exercise of power over people with other values, goals and capacities than those to which the system gives priority.

Freedom for private economic initiative shapes liberal society to suit only those who put economic and other narrow forms of self-interest before solidarity and fellowship. It creates power and potential for those people with the greatest motivation, ability and opportunity to procure privileges and individual positions of power, and it correspondingly hinders those with other motives and talents. The system of marking in schools, the system of reward and promotion to power in industry and public service, the principles according to which the management of organizations is conducted – all these give priority to the freedom and power of the one-dimensional competitor to gain at the expense of those who put fellowship and companionship higher. And as a result of this priority, a division of power is promoted which expresses the same distortion.

Arguments for the unequal distribution of ownership of the means of production are typical of this view.

It is said that economic liberalism's competitively selected business management will always be the best suited for efficient management and the growth in production. This of course ignores the selection that occurs through inherited position, capital and environment, though such is not the primary objection today. The fundamental fault is in the very principle of selection that liberals argue for – leadership is handed to those who give higher priority than others to what affluent societies must now move away from – economic reward as the motivation, exclusively material judgements, growth for growth's sake. The liberal argument for the selection of leaders today turns against the ideology itself. It makes production and work input into activities whose value is measured only in money, while production directed according to social motives (like the Lucas plan) becomes an impossibility.

And the freedom for personal initiative which this is supposed to provide is *not* promoted, but is restricted, for the majority. This freedom and the intrinsic value of work is the preserve of only a minority of proprietors and managers, while the work of the majority becomes meaningless. If the freedom to own the means of production, and the potential for creative initiative and development which this involves, are to be credited with the social significance attributed to them in liberal theory, then society's first task ought to be to secure this freedom and right for all. The right of determination over the means of production should be decentralized and linked everywhere to the work itself – so that everyone can experience the liberal right of personal development for the good of society. Then social production as a whole would reflect more varied motives than the single-track money motivation which today's selection of leaders serves to perpetuate.

Liberalism's stunting of the concept of freedom also applies to the highly exalted choice of goods. Without the narrowly materialist mentality which seems to lie behind it, this too would be an argument *against* liberalism. All we have is a free choice within materialism, in relation to a meaningless mass of inessentials, while the fundamental *choice of values* is largely obstructed. This is simply the freedom of a minority to spend billions on the *suppression* of the majority's freedom of choice through the powerful influence of marketing on values. The system gives proprietors the right to burden the majority with the costs of this influence, which adversely affects the majority itself – while those who want to promote other social values have no access to equivalent financial resources. What would liberalism say about a society which granted similar privileges for the financing of propaganda to one particular *party* at the expense of all others?

Adam Smith's economic liberalism 'replaced the ideal of the freedom of the human being with the ideal of freedom of trade', says Poul Bjerre in his book *Cooperative Society*.[60] 'Over a long period, liberalism came to stand for the freedom of the big fish to eat the small. The small also had the right to eat the big, of course; there was freedom for all, but it was the small that were eaten.'

The concept of freedom is equally abused at the opposite political extreme. There too, true freedom is regarded as the right of an élite, while the freedom of the majority supposedly consists in allowing themselves to be led by those who define both their choice of values and the meaning of freedom for them, during the period of transition and also, in practice, in the centralized society of the future towards which this extreme wing is often aiming.

And between the extreme positions stand other leaders defining people's freedom on their own premises – at the tops of the pyramids of the technostructure, the labour movement, the bureaucracy and other organizations – always as a freedom to subject oneself to the correct leadership, the leadership which has most cleverly formulated its ideology concerning the good of the people, the means to perpetually increasing material wealth. It seems equally inconceivable to all of them that people's own choice might perhaps be in the direction of greater equality and *less* wealth, if they could thereby escape the insecurities and upheavals in the conditions and traditions of life which result from industrial growth and constantly advancing technology.

Studies by the German company Siemens indicate that by 1990, 40 per cent of office work will be performed by electronic, data-controlled typewriters. By the same time, General Motors expect 90 per cent of production to be fully automated.[61] Who has thought of asking the workers who are to be replaced by these machines about their freedom and choice? Is it surprising that a revolution for new values and guiding principles is gathering strength from the base of the affluent society?

Anarchism

In many respects anarchism, much abused and often misunderstood, is one of the ideas which has taken the demand for freedom most seriously and has most consistently advocated autonomous development from below towards a society with freedom for all.

In the foreword to his anthology of anarchism, the Danish writer, Christian Mailand Hansen,[62] says that the rebellion of youth in the industrial countries has shown 'the necessity of new human values and other evaluations of these. With its individualistic and partly non-theoretical point of departure, anarchism might be resuscitated – and even used by other political tendencies as "therapy" ... ' One of the characteristic features of anarchism is:

its anti-authoritarian attitude even towards its own teaching, which for anarchists is more of a moral attitude than a programme ... Anarchism has no wish to put into practice any social doctrine, since social doctrines subdue the individual. The idea of power would be the same, whether it were exercised by socialists or capitalists.

Most of the famous anarchists were not primarily writers, but men of action, for which reason anarchism is often called 'the philosophy of action' ... Where Marxists often start with the questions, 'What is society, what processes of production operate in it, what are the social and political constellations?' anarchists begin with the question, 'What is the human being, in itself and in its social relations?'

Of course anarchism too has had its master thinkers who have tried, to a greater or lesser extent, to 'prefabricate' it through mutually conflicting ideologies. There is disagreement, for example, about how the ownership of means of production is to be distributed. What all anarchists seem to agree on, however, is the rejection of *the state* and its takeover of the means of production. In this respect it conflicts clearly with Marxism and Leninism.

Even though individual anarchists may have a tendency to dismiss all organization, even when it arises from a conscious popular demand, anarchists willingly accept the interaction between the commitment to values and the political transformation of society which is brought about through popular action. The development of a consciousness of the fundamental values of human fellowship is the principal motor of change, but this transformation of people

does not only lead to, it also presupposes to a certain extent, the transformation of society ... Thus the anarchist concept of revolution is also more 'evolutionary' and less calculating, since no social theory is being followed ... The rejection by anarchists of the 'scientific' character claimed by a line of socialists, results from their thinking that people cannot be generalized and animated by drawing up statements of account for economic absurdities ... The anarchist sees the necessity of a re-evaluation of things, new value judgements – before systems and structures can be changed.

Anarchists reject no religions but oppose the churches' religious monopoly. They believe in directly experienced 'universal human love'. They believe in shared responsibility for others, but not in institutionalized marriage. They believe in parental responsibility and oppose institutional childcare. Parental rights will not be abolished and parental responsibility must not be palmed off on others.

Some of anarchism's more dogmatic extremists have probably contributed to many people's fear of its ideas. But the central anarchist ideas seem to accord with the concept of free change from below, created through popular action and mobilization around counteractive values in the direction of the unfinished alternative.

Proudhon referred to of all those who throughout history have called 'for revolution *from above*. Instead of teaching people to organize themselves, instead of appealing to their experience and reason, they demand power and violence of them. How do they distinguish themselves from despots?' The anarchist, Landauer, also rejects the authoritarian prefabrication of the process of change which occurs when it is linked to a single type of action and a single and rigidly determined solution. He criticizes the dogmatic Marxists who dismiss the many alternatives that are developed on the way and who 'do not want to know anything about peasant cooperatives, credit unions, workers' cooperation ... ' Kropotkin, another renowned anarchist, writes:

> If a revolution is to be set in motion it must be in the form of a widespread popular movement, in which every town, every village is invaded by the spirit of revolt, and in which the masses themselves tackle the reshaping of society on new lines. The people – both peasants and urban workers – must themselves initiate the constructive work ... Perhaps they are not – they are certainly not – a majority in the nation. But if they are a numerically significant minority ... then they will be able to follow their own course. In all probability they will pull a considerable part of the country with them ... During a revolution, new forms of living will always take root in the ruins of the old forms, but no government will ... be able to express them, as long as these forms have not taken final shape during the work of reformation, which must go on in thousands of places at the same time.

Not as mere ideology, but as an idea inspiring fresh thought and action, anarchism ought to give important impulses to the process of transformation which we are facing. The point is always to combine the counteractive values as the point of departure for action with 'the unfinished' – the outline that may be drawn on the basis of these values, but which must never be allowed to harden into a controlling ideology which drains power from the popular development of consciousness and action.

But what are the unfinished distinguishing features of this outline? Can anything be said about any of its fundamental characteristics without, in this way, completing it?

11. Some Features of a Human Society

At this point it is worth recapping briefly what has been covered in the previous chapters.

Firstly, it has been emphasized that every analysis necessarily starts from a certain view of values and human nature, whether or not this is declared. The moral goals of solidarity, human fellowship and the equal right of all to freedom, influence on society and personal creative development have been specified as the basis of what follows.

From this wider perspective on whose threshold we are now standing, these seem to provide certain guidelines for the sort of development we in the rich countries can permit ourselves. Without dogmatically tying ourselves to any of the major theories of global solidarity that have been discussed, it looks as though the right to 'development from below' is a precondition if our values are to embrace the world's poor majority, and this inevitably has consequences for the rich countries.

This form of independent development means embarking on a course actively contrary to the economic objectives of the industrialized countries: the greatest possible material production and consumption, i.e. growth in wealth as the aim of production, whether or not this can be realized at any given time.

The point of departure for our evaluation of the driving force behind this growth imperative lies in Marx's historical analysis of the conditions of power and conflict in the capitalist system, because his work is concerned precisely with the conflict of interest between the few and the many that we are faced with. In applying Marx's conclusions to our own period, we found that his belief in revolution through the majority's material antagonism to the power of the élite's property was not realistic in our society, because this antagonism is now used as a motive force in the system itself. We have seen, however, that Marx seems to suggest a cause of the growth imperative: the fact that a minority control the means of production and can only secure their position by competing for growth, and the fact that the majority do not have the means of production at their disposal and are therefore compelled to cooperate with the controlling élite on its premises, and to hand over part of the product of their labour for investment in growth and demand production.

Our analysis went on to show that the antagonism between the worker and the owner of capital has today been overtaken by the antagonism between the majority and a specialist élite who have status and power through being able to plan the production and behaviour of others and who therefore oppose change.

What followed pointed towards a further extension of the concept of power and the idea that oppression today is exercised by all the élite groups competing to think, plan and direct on behalf of the majority. The principal external conflict is between the élite groups who wish to preserve the pyramid structures and the many who want to break with them.

It seems, however, that there is also a clear internal conflict here, between the values of economic competition, which the system's growth requires, and their antithesis – the will to put solidarity and human fellowship before personal gain. It therefore seems that the counteractive power of the revolution must lie in a mobilization around these values in protest against control from above and the attitude to values and human nature which goes with it.

If the entire movement for change is not to lose its multiformity, initiative and transforming power, and if it is to avoid being kept passive, narrow and fragmented by being bound to élitist, total theories, it seems important to stick to the idea that the goal must remain incomplete – an outline that is shaped from below and is always in the process of change.

Taking our point of departure in the concept of freedom, linked to the values of solidarity and equal rights, we arrived at the view that these, even when they are applied to industrial society alone, suggest the same conclusion that the broader perspective clearly leads us to: those who use the means of production ought themselves to gain full control over the content, organization and social consequences of that production.

A controllable technology

The last point suggests that the choice of technology is itself important if the given values are to be taken seriously – because later industrial society's complex technology obviously makes popular control impossible over the organization, growth and social consequences of production. Today, as we enter the age of microprocessors, this has become clearer than ever. The introduction of this new technology will force people into an inescapable process of upheaval in work and society – occupational dislocation, the disruption of the conditions people are used to, insecurity and increased demands for planning and control, in relation to which the ordinary worker will be completely powerless.

The coerciveness of this technology was confirmed in several lectures on microelectronics given at the Norwegian Technical Research Council for the Natural Sciences in 1979.[63] Here it was said, among other things, that:

> Microelectronics and the products which follow in its track will confront industry and the rest of society with a perpetual readjustment. The microprocessor has given the first clear warning of this. Norway must play an active part in this development ... We must act as quickly as our competitors; otherwise we will experience only the negative consequences. Microelectronics will affect virtually every area of society's life, and the demand for new skills, new patterns of work, new products, etc. will become far more common than before.

It is quite widely believed that even the most advanced technology could be used to benefit the majority if its use were to a greater extent controlled by workers themselves. Reference is often made, for example, to the possibilities that automation offers for a further liberation from hard and monotonous work. No absolute or dogmatic position is going to be taken on this point, but one vital question concerning this technology should be raised in the light of the demand for an equal right to influence on society. The question concerns power.

Until recent decades, it could be said that the demands of technology in terms of organization, principles of control and social adaptation were largely comprehensible to most people. This is now changing at an accelerating pace. We can already see today how computer programmers can demand the adjustment of operational and working routines to suit the needs of electronic data systems. A report entitled *Work Forms in System Development* published in 1979 by the Norwegian Institute of Productivity says, for example, that with increased technology in an organization, an information gap can easily develop between the top and the bottom. It goes on to say that the increased use of technology creates a greater division of labour which in turn leads to increased control over the individual's work through the need for greater coordination. One of the report's conclusions is that development may lead to a greater inequality of power, something which may be due to corresponding differences in skills, general understanding, dependence and supervision.

This applies today. We can only guess at the way this problem may grow with the immensely complex microelectronics that are now being introduced. It is constantly being emphasized in industrial circles that this technology requires the adaptation not only of the individual company, but of society as a whole. The futurologist Per Benterud has compared its consequences with a global revolution.[65]

It is frequently stressed that in future workers will have to be prepared to move, both geographically and occupationally, according to the scope for industrial development, and that education must be more closely aligned with the needs and interests of business.

What this suggests is that technology places a power in the hands of the experts which stands outside the ordinary possibilities of popular control. For the sake of a technology which only the specialist-educated understand, an adaptation may be demanded which the general public must simply submit to once the technology has been introduced. In such a situation, the equal right to freedom and social influence easily becomes an illusion, whether or not the right of government is formally attributed to the people themselves.

There seems to be only one premise on which complex and uncontrollable technology can be defended – that a further growth in wealth is more important than equal rights to freedom, personal development and control of one's own society – i.e. in direct contradiction of the values we are building on here.

'An alternative solution', says Illich in *Tools for Conviviality*, 'could be to define individual well-being in terms of the freedom of the individual member of society to determine his own life and to plan his own future.'

People will rediscover the value of joyful sobriety and liberating austerity only if they learn to depend on each other rather than on energy slaves .. The issue at hand is not the juridical ownership of tools, but rather the discovery of the characteristics of some tools which make it impossible for anybody to 'own' them. The concept of ownership cannot be applied to a tool that cannot be controlled ... [We must] devise tools and tool systems that optimize the balance of life, thereby maximizing liberty for all.

This suggests a general principle concerning what we can aim at and what alternatives campaigns for change can realize – and have realized, on a small scale, here and now. It does not of course preclude the possibility that demands for more human control, content and use of *existing* advanced production may be important counteractive steps on the way. Here again, the Lucas action may be an example.

All told, certain features of a future society are emerging which seem to arise directly from the set of basic values.

We glimpse a society where no minority is able to procure position and privilege by its power over other people's labour and means of production, neither through possession nor state control.

– Where technology does not deprive people of work but is an aid to their own creativity;

– Where the scale of operations is such that they can be monitored and controlled locally – as far as possible so that they serve immediate local needs;

– Where the content of production and the organization of work in a given enterprise is determined locally through cooperation between the workers and consumers concerned.

In this way, work would become a creative, social activity in the spirit of human fellowship; unequal economic reward would become less necessary as an incentive, and the competitive scramble could be counteracted through equality of income.

A major part of what is now paid and institutionalized care could be left to the companionship and cooperation of the local community, and much public administration could be decentralized and made a matter of local responsibility.

At the same time, the overall national framework could be clearer: for an equal distribution of land to independent farmers, and for the provision of sites for homes and recreation for other citizens; for the equalization of income, both nationally and in the form of a progressive national taxation to the benefit of a global equalization; for the protection of the nation's combined resources, biological production capacity, and other fundamental social conditions.

In practice this would mean a balanced economy, probably at a lower level than today. For pioneer nations, it would again require liberation from any international trade that constantly forces new technology on them through international competition. And it would necessitate new, less destructive and resource-hungry forms of defence.

National self-determination

The last point, the need for a liberation from international trade, needs particular discussion, because it looks like a major requirement for change in the direction we have indicated.

In the present circumstances, most economists would regard a halt in national growth as an impossibility. As long as our economy is dependent on export to other industrial countries, the balance of trade will force us to keep up with their technological development. It is said, for example, that we cannot avoid introducing modern microelectronics without falling behind in the competition for exports. As has been said, this would greatly reduce the demand for labour. If we are to avoid unemployment, we are faced with three possible solutions, all of which conflict with our chosen objectives.

Either the available labour-power must be used through perpetual industrial growth and an increase in production that can only be offset through further appeals to materialism and competition – or this labour-power must be re-channelled into non-productive, public service activity. This alternative presents the obvious danger of a further institutionalization of people's lives. We risk being subjected increasingly to control by professional 'carers' and its disempowering appropriation of our independent activities.

The third possibility is for the reduction in work due to technological competition being compensated for by reduced working hours. In practice this may mean that wealthy-creating social effort is largely left to experts and leaders, while most people are given thoroughly organized work tasks complemented by a 'leisure' devoid of productive, socially influential activity.

There are of course other possible solutions, but in all cases they would force on us a development – a revolution – on technology's terms. This upheaval would not be guided by the wishes and conscious choices of the majority, but by competitive considerations of international corporations, based on quite other values than our own. And this enforced development would reduce the possibility of adapting our economy to the needs and wishes of the impoverished world majority.

The most important question is whether this whole revolution is not totally unrealistic as long as we are unwilling to make ourselves less dependent on the competitive international economy. If this is so, work for social change must go on in parallel with work for increased national independence, the greatest possible degree of self-sufficiency, and the development of trading links with less developed countries and with states whose objectives and values correspond with our own.

The principles listed above as being central to a human society *seem* to be natural objectives in terms of our basic values. Nevertheless, guidelines of this sort for future society are not of crucial importance to the revolution we have discussed here. The crucial factor is the process of transformation itself: fresh thinking, experiments, campaigns, examples and counteractive action – everything that begins to shape the future from below, here and now – everything that results in ordinary people experiencing what it means to be *able* to control development, to stop it, to redirect it, to think about where it is we want to go, to begin to consider what the purpose of it all is. In this process of transformation predetermined principles for future society are no longer so important; they become possibilities, ideas concerning the transformation of what exists now, something to compare the structures of growth society with, but not something that binds and restricts the most vital factor: *participation* in the change, getting something started on the basis of conscious values – from below.

Nevertheless, ideas concerning what today seem to be the future consequences of the basic values can be useful and necessary in order to put flesh and blood on the bones of what we are aiming at and to strengthen the belief that there can be something better than what we have.

The fact that the ideas, laws, institutions and technology that will be needed in such a society do not exist does not mean that they cannot be developed over time. This indeed is one aspect of the shaping process – and whether development towards our given objectives takes a longer or a shorter time is of less significance. Before we have achieved them, it may be that these objectives are no longer the ones we want – they may have been outdated by the new thinking and possibilities that people have developed on the way.

All that can and should be stated clearly is what is fundamentally wrong, in terms of our basic values, with the existing situation – the reason why it must be and will be changed. Whether one starts from the ecological limitations, our capacity for psychological adaptation, the increasing acuteness of conflicts, an evaluation purely in terms of values, or the fear of a coming nuclear war over the sources of raw materials, it is clear that the system of industrial growth cannot survive in the long run. Like all historical epochs, the age of capitalist big business is also subject to the laws of change, and there have never before been such clear arguments for hastening the process of change. Never has an extrapolation of our present lines of development indicated so clearly the breakdowns and catastrophes that are, in fact, inevitable if the revolution does not come in time. But no prophets of doom are needed to advocate revolution in the affluent society. The countless positive and exciting possibilities that arise from a breach with the status quo ought to provide adequate arguments for participation in the formation of the alternative. And this is not only the freedom to come, but also the freedom to be seized now, in what exists, in cutting across the system's inbuilt laws. For the participant, the alternative is also here and now.

12. The Many Possibilities

For many people, putting a name to the alternative seems more important than the transformation itself. The necessary revolt against our inhuman system is clearly of no interest to these label enthusiasts if they cannot call the alternative something, whether socialism, anarchism, populism, communism or eco-politics.

Let's call a spade a spade, it is said. The trouble is that these spades often dissolve into pure fog the minute one begins to ask the representatives of the various beliefs what principles their ideas are based on. The concept of socialism, in particular, has been used as a popular designation for so many conflicting ideas concerning the society of the future that it scarcely says anything more than that one is against capitalism. Hiding behind this term are beliefs both in centralized élite leadership and in decentralized local control, both the most extreme infatuation with large-scale enterprise and the ideology of craft production alone, both takeover by the state and the complete distribution of property, both total materialism and equally absolute anti-materialism, to say nothing of countless definitions of the concepts of class and conflict, and the most varied ideas of how change is to come about, whether through democratic means or a minority coup, the demand for greater wealth or alternative struggles for other values.

Nevertheless, it often takes little more than the use of the word 'socialism' to gain acceptance in radical company.

The problem with 'socialism' and the other labels is that for many people they become a substitute for deeper thought; for those who choose to use a label, it creates an illusion of having taken a position on something – and for those who reject it, the result is often that they don't really know what they are rejecting. In practice, such terms are often used primarily to express a wish to belong and to be accepted by a particular label group – it is then left to the leading ideologues to specify what the bottle's contents are to be.

Like rigid ideologies, group terminology and the established party pattern, these labels tend to camouflage many of the true conflicts of modern industrial society. Worse, they also prevent cooperation between people who could work together on counteractive change and fundamental objectives. Only by stating clearly the essential basic values for the transformation we want can we arrive at a meaningful debate with respect and understanding for other people's viewpoints.

What we have covered so far indicates not a single solution but many possibilities. Cooperation in working for counteractive change requires that we do not exchange what we want for an overly rigid determination of how it is to be organized and developed. If process and counteraction are the decisive factors, the movement for transformation will need to have a multiform character, consisting of countless revolts, campaigns and individual actions side by side. And different ideas concerning the society of the future can be tested against one another without this leading to the disintegration of the movement itself.

In an interview in 1975,[8] the Norwegian centre party politician Bjørn Unneberg declared his anticapitalist position but chose another term than socialist for his views. He maintained that there is an important difference between the property which gives a right to the fruits of one's own labour and that which demands a right to the fruits of *others'* labour. He favours the 'cooperative' which is known both from consumer cooperatives and from the field he is particularly concerned with – agriculture – where it refers to voluntary cooperation between independent proprietors. 'I think it must also be possible to develop the cooperative form much further in other areas, such as small-scale industry, crafts and trade,' says Unneberg.

Even though consumer and producer cooperation, in the same way as socialism, has leaned towards big business thinking and pyramid organization, the cooperative idea is also practised on a smaller scale in independent cooperative enterprises and in local cooperation between smallholders. If one builds on the basic idea of economic equalization, the distribution of power, popular freedom, social influence and the right of disposal over the fruits of one's own work and one's own means of production, there should be no objection to using both terms, 'cooperative' and 'socialist', for a society based on the fundamental values we have discribed.

The Danish writer Poul Bjerre also uses the term 'cooperative society' for similar ideas in his book of this title.[60] In his view, the right to know that one's work has a meaning for others, and the ability to control the results of one's own effort, are of vital importance to people. No one is happy in their work if it is done only for the sake of money. The enjoyment of work comes with our work being valued by others – valued in a broader sense than in money terms.' By institutionalizing and industrializing the work we might do communally, for ourselves and others, it becomes tied to money instead of to pleasure, says Bjerre. And the result is that people must 'do more of the kind of work which means less to them personally in order to earn money to pay others for what they would rather do themselves.'

Obviously the followers of writers such as these do not all stand for exactly the same thing. Without doubt they disagree on many important points. But they do represent different ways of achieving the same human goal. And most importantly, they represent the same break with the existing order. Before *any* of their theories have been realized, however, their premises will have changed – as a result of the popular revolt having created future possibilities that are not visible to any of us today. Shouldn't they and their supporters be able to cooperate for the revolution from below in which they all believe? Is there any need for the various labels to fragment those elements of the broad movement for change which at least have the same *direction*?

Any disagreement between cooperating partners in the revolt from below and the revolution in values need not weaken the movement for change; it may also represent a strength – the strength of multiformity and breadth, the strength of showing that within the counteractive and the unfinished there are many ways forward, all of which it will ultimately be up to people themselves to decide on.

13. Intellectuals and the Popular Revolt

If we accept the need for change from below, and that the process should not be 'led' except through a struggle for the fundamentals which everyone can relate to, then what can the intellectual contribute?

It is self-evident that popular movements can benefit from the knowledge and analytical methods that sympathetic researchers and theorists can provide. Encouraging a general antipathy to intellectuals only harms the sense of fellowship and cooperation for change. Being an intellectual is not the same as being a 'master thinker'. The conflict is not between the intellectual and the popular, but between those guardians of opinion who always 'know best' and those who accept the majority's free right of determination. For many academics, it has already become a matter of importance to put their research and their knowledge at the disposal of grassroots campaigns, in the form of 'counter-expertise' in opposition to the established experts' information and their assertions concerning 'the only possible solutions'. These alternative reserachers do not determine the goals of the popular movements; they analyze consequences and possibilities in terms of the campaigners' own objectives. They show that established experts are *not* value-neutral; that their work could often lead to other conclusions if it started from a different set of values. The traditional prestige of academic research in our society can nevertheless easily undermine the independent judgement that is awakening in new groups, if academics are not aware of certain dangers. Three points are important if academic participation is not to restrict initiative from below:

Firstly, the conclusions of academic analysis should be presented as *possibilities,* as alternatives to consider, not as the single valid answer making all further analysis unnecessary.

Secondly, the analysis and its conclusions should be presented in a language that people can understand. Of course, the results of research first be set out in that research's own terms, with the necessary precision and terminology. The crucial point, however, is that results of research which only appear in this form contribute nothing whatsoever to the new movement for change, because they exclude those who are the true representatives of the movement from below, the antithesis of expertise and specialist training.

In practice, this often means that the intellectual has to use the much-despised 'personal' form of presentation to illustrate the structural and systematic relations that are being presented. Here it is of vital importance to realize that those whom many academics regard as members of the majority actually belong to an educational middle class who are still considerably closer than most people to theoretical models.

Experience shows that the popular, personal form of presentation is difficult – indeed probably impossible for most theorists. It ought to be possible, however, to overcome this problem, as has been done occasionally, through the cooperation of researchers with the journalists and writers who are in contact with a broader public.

To many intellectuals, this may seem both unrealistic and unnecessary, because they are used to discussing such questions in their own intellectual circles, in which society's decision makers also play a part. But the question of who information must reach in order to be of any importance to development is precisely what the revolution from below is about. The closed circuit of research, analysis and planning within élite circles has made democracy an illusion in modern society. We often hear of 'epoch-making' scientific studies and reports on the problems of our time and possible solutions. How many of these have reached more than a tiny fraction of the adult population?

The personal form is not, of course, the only form of popularization. The mass media have a staff of popularizers who have shown that it is possible to communicate difficult material successfully in other forms. The important point is to understand that if it is to contribute to the revolution we are now facing, the popularized form of a researcher's work is just as important as the report itself. New practice in this area is not only desirable for the sake of democracy, it is also a requirement if change is ever to be anything more than theory.

The third condition, if intellectual analysis is to help change from below, is that it should not only represent a model for analysis and planning – but lead to immediate consequences, requirements or possibilities of action for the general public. Far too many analyses confine themselves to presenting a problem or an alternative through an account of structural faults and weaknesses in the existing situation – or through a model of the alternative as it 'ought to be'. The result is that most people are faced with a growing sense of present and future catastrophe and a mass of statements, from those who claim to know best, to the effect that things could be different – but no possibility of participation, of doing anything about the problems, of being able to contribute personally to change beyond accusing those who are responsible and thus laying the responsibility for change on those who least want it.

It is surprising that most people feel powerless and have turned instead to escapism and passive inaction? The enormous interest the Future In Our Hands movement has aroused among many people – far beyond the reach of its members – who had not previously been concerned with social questions, is largely a direct expression of this. The most common reaction was, 'At last, we can start to do something ourselves!' It was not structural and social analysis that people had felt the lack of, but possibilities of alternative action against a course of development they felt they had been manipulated into participating in, against their own wishes. What aroused so many people's interest, and even enthusiasm, was the possibility of taking responsibility for their own choices in situations on which they had their own views and which they could see in terms of simple and understandable attitudes and values. It was a first step in a *process* to which they could relate, and whose potential they probably felt, in quite a different way from most theorists. And the scorn which rose from many élite quarters, where they knew better – where they 'understood' that this was of course a wholly *political* question – that only represented the old outlook, the unshakeable conviction that all development and all change naturally starts from the top.

What many intellectuals did not understand in criticizing the 'lack of analysis' in the movement's information, was that the very link between, on the one hand, a simple overall view and a consciousness of values, and, on the other, the immediate choice of action, is the natural starting point for most people – and that a direct path runs from this beginning to the further growth of political consciousness and participation.

Change and future studies

Perhaps one area where the principles we have set out for the active participation of intellectuals can most easily be illustrated is future studies, or futurology.

Normally, the purpose of such studies is to aid decision makers in industry, bureaucracy and political leadership. The result has often been that future studies have at best contributed to minor reforms intended to help adjustment to new developments, because the groups the reports research consist largely of people who do not themselves feel any need for change – indeed, they often fear change and the consequences it would have for their own position. In this way, too, such studies can serve to strengthen the pyramid structure, making the majority passive and hindering change.

But future studies can also be, and sometimes are, an aid to the majority – helping them to make up their minds, to participate and to act 'counter-actively'. Let us look briefly at one of many possibilities.

In the first place, it is clear that future studies should not be confined to extrapolating trends and analyzing developments that 'await' us. The innumerable projections of how things are going to be in the year 2000 can scarcely lead to anything but apathy, now matter how popularly they are presented. People's expectations, plans and actions are directed towards what is presented to them as a future without alternatives.

But this is already changing. Future studies often now involve the investigation of total alternatives to the established order. But who determines the premises for these alternatives? When will ordinary people be asked by futurologists – through opinion surveys or other means – which basic values, freedoms and possibilities they would give highest priority to from the point of view of their own and their children's future?

Putting such questions to a representative sample would make it possible to establish a basis for realistic alternatives.

- Economic quality or opportunities for competitive advancement?
- Economic stability with fixed prices and incomes or growth in wealth, continued manipulation of consumption and industrial development?
- Centralized control and habitation or decentralization?
- Industrial centralization or the distribution of control over the means of production?

– Continued mass motoring or a predominance of collective transport and bicyles with traffic-free streets and play areas?

– Traditional approaches to defence, or extensive concessions to the development of non-violent alternatives?

– Unchanged or increased aid to poor countries, perhaps on new premises?

These are merely examples of types of questions. In practice, of course, they might have to be formulated differently.

Only by presenting and explaining such questions in popularly accessible terms in the mass media will it be possible to arouse an interest in crucial choices about values and social problems among people who otherwise feel that political debate goes over their heads. By going on to analyze *general images of the future* which might be the consequence of the alternative basic principles, one could link future studies directly to people's wishes and expectations.

A series of traditional academic reports concerning these alternative images of the future would, however, contribute little or nothing to general interest in their conclusions. What could and should be done is to hand over the reports to writers with the literacy skill to convey their basic ideas in popular books and the mass media, putting them in a personalized and accessible form so that ordinary people could see themselves in the context of possible futures. There is every reason to think that this would create considerable interest among the public at large in the crucial choice of direction that industrial society is facing and that has previously been determined largely from above. In quite a different way from traditional research, it would also help groups working actively for change to spread an understanding of alternatives to the existing order.

But this on its own would not serve to set a transformation in motion – to make a change of course a matter of realistic politics with the necessay support of the electorate. Focusing on new objectives does not mean that one is in automatic agreement on the changes that would be needed to start things moving. Reports must also show the main initial consequences, for the various sections of the population, of the alternative courses of development. In this way, ordinary voters would be able to judge the immediate choices and possibilities of action in relation to their long-term objectives. It would be easier to see what one must concentrate on in one's own situation in order to make the alternative realizable. And this would make active participation possible by indicating the types of conduct and action that could help to fulfil the dream of a better world. And finally, as a result of wider public interest in the meaning and purpose of politics, it would eventually become necessary for politicians to state clearly the nature of the society *they* are aiming at – a standpoint that many of them today may not even have clarified in their own minds.

The creation of a consciousness of this sort concerning the consequences of values would also provide a basis for the wider use of referendums – probably the most democratic form of decision making when the public are adequately informed about the alternatives.

The example of alternative future studies is perhaps not wholly realistic in the form presented here. It should also be said that some people, including Ivan Illich, are against any form of future studies because of the undesirable potential for power over public opinion that researchers may derive. What matters, however, is the basic idea at the root of the proposal – the idea of research not as a means of control but as a means by which the public can consider and participate actively in the formation and development of their own future.

It is possible that even this use and presentation of the results of research would not reach a majority of a public that is used to being excluded from such questions. This is not the main point either. The important thing is that it would contribute to a process of increasing participation to the extent that it would enable at least *some* people outside the intellectual milieu to raise such questions in discussions and debates within new groups. Grassroots movements for change would also be an active element in this process of dissemination.

As we have seen, a number of academics in several countries have already given up their élite positions in order to make their knowledge available to such movements and to use their analytical faculties in investigating the possibilities for action on the movements' premises. A Norwegian example is the philosopher Arne Naess who gave up his professorship and emerged from academic isolation in order to be freer to participate in the multitude of popular campaigns for ecology and social change. His fearless action has added weight to these campaigns, and the well-known picture of the internationally renowned professor calmly being carried away by the police from the protest camp at Mardøla has certainly given many good citizens a new understanding that activists are not only 'hysterical extremists'. His books, perhaps especially *Ecology, Society and Lifestyle*,[69] have without doubt strengthened many of the more intellectually oriented campaigners in their understanding of such things as the importance of a holistic approach and of value priorities.

What is still largely missing, and what Arne Næss tried in vain to get help with in writing the above book, is the engagement of popular writers in communicating such facts, overall views, alternatives and possibilities for action in a way that can show the public at large what it all boils down to.

Ultimately the issue is not research but the alternatives that are developed through action and discussion within the broad popular movement for change.

14. Participation and the Way Ahead

Given the principles of change from below – broad cooperation for counteractive action, and 'the unfinished' – the way ahead should not be channelled narrowly through any ideological pigeonhole. Whether or not the many groups working for change regard one another as allies is something it ought to be possible to judge with tolerance as long as there is agreement about commitment to the basic counteractive values.

It is clear, nevertheless, that a campaign for fundamental change must have some idea of the way ahead – of how counteractive action can be taken further politically; of how public support may be maintained. If the many campaigns remain isolated islands in a society where the majority continue to support established policies, change can only occur through the manipulations of a minority, and this would conflict with the demand for the majority's right to shape their own future – apart from which, it would probably prove impossible to achieve anything in practice.

For counteractive social change to be a realistic propostion, the majority must go along with the process. This does not mean that most people have to be committed to a total alternative before anything can begin to happen. That would undermine the dynamic of the process itself. To set the process of change in motion, all that is needed is for the majority of the electorate to support the first counteractive political changes and the basic outlook they express. These initial changes would bring a new situation in which majority support for further proposals for counteractive politics would be strengthened.

One objection to a strategy of this sort may be that it involves manipulating the majority towards extensive long-term changes which only the active minority will have been committed to from the outset. This objection is justified if the long-term goal is seen as being rigidly determined, but not if it is seen as something unfinished, something which can only find its true form in the course of the process. As an example of how collective action can contribute to counteractive political work which in turn supports further campaigning followed by new political moves, let us look at the following hypothetical situation:

Suppose an increasing number of action groups, for example, some of the better paid groups in the labour movement, recognize the conflict between solidarity and selfish competition by giving a fixed proportion of their pay to a solidarity fund, perhaps to provide support for Lucas-type actions among comrades under threat. In so doing, they would be making a radical break with the values and competitive principles that are the basis of the present system.

A general sympathy for and interest in such action would make it possible gradually to increase the majority's understanding of the conflict between solidarity and economic inequality, and political proposals in the same direction could thus gain the general support of the electorate. One such proposal could be an official timetable for the equalization of all wage and income groups and the fixing of maximum differentials allowing supplements only for those in particular social need. This would mean financial improvement for low-income groups, those threatened with redundancy, the old, those dependent on national insurance, and especially for transfers to poor countries. A policy of this sort would lead to an essentially different situation, to new consciousness and increased understanding and interest in other proposals for action – for example, for a campaign against manipulation through advertising.

Economic equalization would mean an end to the rat-race and thus the social costs of halting advertising would no longer be an obstacle. There might be majority support for a gradually introduced prohibition against subjecting people to the influence of advertising, and at the same time an improvement in access to freely available information about commodities. In this way, materialism and the need for growth would be further reduced and the sense of solidarity and fellowship would be strengthened. This could lead to new understanding and greater support for groups campaigning for a more human technology – so that political change in the direction of an alternative to industrial growth and centralized control could gradually become a more realistic possibility.

This example must not be taken as an attempt to tie the process to one of many possible routes. It would not matter if a start in this direction proved unrealistic or undesired. Different ways of starting are as numerous as the various potentially counteractive campaigns. The example is intended to illustrate a dialectical principle in the Hegelian sense: an interplay between counteractive and consciousness-creating action – political activity – increased value-consciousness – new action – and new political activity. This process is guided not by ideological planning determined from above, but by consciousness of values which gradually emerges through action combined with popular political debate, and through the wishes and demands for solidarity which are thus developed in the people themselves.

There is one aspect of this dialectical process, however, that would very likely fail in practice: the broad interest and understanding that needs to be developed among the public concerning the alternatives being presented by campaigning groups. If this is the case – if the campaigns do not change the *majority's* view – no political follow-up will be possible and the process will be stillborn. This is exactly what is happening today; the campaigns are influencing the attitudes and understanding of only a small minority – on the whole only those who feel like participating themselves. For the silent majority, such active participation remains far outside their field of interest.

If the majority see no real possibility of participating, then their feeling of powerlessness, and their consequent passivity, will be maintained. They will remain inclined to be led by the established planning élite and will easily come to regard activists with the eyes of the establishment, as eccentrics with particular behaviour patterns and unrealistic goals which have no connection with the everyday lives of ordinary women and men. Their campaigns may achieve widespread publicity, but most people will regard them as having no relevance to themselves – as something positively 'outside'. No connection will exist between their personal and political wishes and what the campaigns are fighting for. The basis of politics and social development will still be the traditional view. The campaigns will be 'non-competing'.

This is clearly the present situation in every single industrialized country. Nowhere do the combined movements for change comprise more than about 5-10 per cent of the population, and this is probably a generous estimate. And in no country have they won the majority over to support fundamentally *counteractive* political undertakings. All that it has been possible to achieve politically are reforms within the existing structure and on the system's basic terms – or completely isolated victories without influence on the course of development.

This is the most crucial question for any movement for change, and for everyone who supports fundamental change. If no solution is found for the problem of majority participation, of communication between activist groups and the silent majority, then the affluent society's revolution will remain in the realm of theory.

If, for example, the environmental movement is to do anything more than obstruct expansion here and there while the social machinery rolls on as before, it must win over the *majority* to a politics built on other values than today's. If any movement for change is to be more than a private concern of those already active in it, the majority must be brought into the process.

How can this happen?

We shall recognize at the outset one clear fact: alternative activities, campaigns for change and protest movements do not represent a form of activity and participation which the broad majority can identify with. Most people clearly feel themselves to be outside the process of change that these campaigns represent. And because ordinary people are not actively involved in change, their lives are directed towards traditional goals. It is natural, then, not to say obvious, that their political ideas will tend in the same direction. A new political position cutting across tradition and environment is very seldom a beginning in itself, but normally the expression of a desire to make changes in personal goals and values. As long as these are shaped by the existing structure, political attitudes will normally be shaped in the same way.

What sort of activity, what form of participation is closest to most people? The answer is pretty obvious and is a consequence of the common human tendency discussed earlier: most people do not see themselves and their fellow human beings in terms of social structures and political attitudes; on the contrary, they see social questions in terms of their own immediate situation. It would therefore seem natural to start not with participation in campaigns for social change, but with counteractive change in everyday life. This is where most people experience social problems – in worrying about the way their children are growing up and not having enough time for them, in feelings of isolation, insecurity in a competitive society, the pressure to buy things, money worries, the sense of conflict between the wealth one is influenced by and the poverty of millions ... the feeling of being confronted with an inescapable conflict between what one knows in one's innermost self to be best for oneself and others, and what one in fact does.

It is in these immediate contexts, for most people, that counteractive action and liberation become real. The decisive factor is not anti-materialism itself, but what it replaces. In the immediate context, too, action only becomes counteractive when its motive is the antithesis of the established values – human fellowship.

Reducing unnecessary labour and investment only becomes counteractive when it leads to sharing more of life with, and caring more for, children and neighbours. Reducing consumption changes nothing if it is not motivated by the wish to use the means or the time thus made available to the benefit of solidarity and fellowship instead of the advancement of one's own status. A new lifestyle is not counteractive if its motivation is still society's normal motivation – the improvement of one's own position in the narrowest sense. Real change – both in one's own life and in the process this contributes to in society – only happens with a commitment to and the experience of values quite opposite to those of a society based on economic competition; when one emerges from isolation and enters a new sense of fellowship; when other people become companions instead competitors; when one realizes what it means to have something or someone to live for; when one emerges from passivity and begins once again to feel responsible; when one regains the belief that, by freezing oneself from manipulation, one can actively contribute to a development in the interests of humanity.

This concept of counteraction draws only a condescending shrug from those who deprive ordinary people of power by claiming that they will always be what society makes them. It is apparently impossible for them to believe that people today are experiencing a deep loss – of precisely those values of human fellowship and the meaning of life that the system wants to take away from them. This was confirmed by the gallup poll, already referred to, which was commissioned by the Future in Our Hands Movement in 1975.[53] To the question whether they would prefer a simple and peaceful life with a limited income, or a high income and a career with corresponding stresses, three out of four people replied that they would chose the first option ... The typical reaction from the protectors of society was that the survey was demonstrably false, since the majority's replies were contradicted by their actual patterns of behaviour. What these representatives of the élites did not seem to understand – or perhaps did not *want* to understand – was that this conflict between patterns of behaviour and basic outlook is the most profound problem of our time, and a direct expression of the contradiction which now seems to be making a real change possible.

By encouraging simple and immediate counteractive action as a basis of participation in parallel with campaigning groups, understanding can be created between activists and the majority – an understanding that is an absolute prerequisite if the campaigns' objectives are to be realized in truly counteractive politics.

By encouraging such participation, one could help ordinary people towards a greater consciousness of goals and values – and hence of the social conditions which conflict with these. An opinion survey among the members of the Future In Our Hands movement in 1978 showed how this process leads to a new political consciousness: it was precisely through attempting to change to a less commodity-oriented way of life – and through experiencing the obstructions the growth system puts up to such attempts – that a great number of people had acquired a new interest in *political* change towards the same ends. Despite the fact that only about 5 per cent of members have found it natural to participate in the movement's organized groups and campaigns, there is nevertheless a broad understanding and interest in their activities.

Nothing contributes more to raising consciousness than participation, the opportunity to feel that one is co-responsible. For the majority, this opportunity is *initially* in the immediate and the personal. As a result of the consciousness this creates, people no longer have to feel that the pioneering work of campaigning groups is irrelevant to them or a challenge to their own goals and values. They find it much easier to experience the campaigns as an extension of the form of action they contribute themselves, and perhaps as support for their own efforts. The Lucas activists are then no longer 'extremists', but supporters of the same change of course that people themselves are aiming for: Third World support groups are no longer 'idealists' – they are pointing to important alternatives for the use of means which would otherwise go into unnecessary consumption; and political groups campaigning against policies of growth and injustice are no longer 'dangerous radicals', but people suggesting how society can build on the same values that people are themselves trying to work towards.

Interaction thus becomes possible, and the process of *total* transformation is set in motion. The resistance of great numbers of people to consumer society's principal requirement will cut the ground from under the old order – at the same time as a thousand counteractive campaigning groups are sketching the new, and the increasing breadth of consciousness and fresh thinking helps to make realization of the new possible through counteractive politics.

Of course, a counteractive choice of values in daily life should not be seen as an *alternative* to organized campaigns. Taking a personal position in the immediate context is the common element of counteractive action that can unite *all* participants in the combined movement for change into a fellowship that is truly cooperative. If a movement really is to be popular, it cannot exclude forms of action and participation that are most accessible to most people. Only through this value-conscious opposition to the manipulation of consumption will we finally be able to throw out growth society's joker in the game of change – its ability to make every action for change into a new area for production, consumption and growth.

The difficulty of fitting such a strategy for change into the classical theories of revolution, which regard economic antagonisms as the only important ones, has provoked strong reactions from thinkers on the Left: 'Overconsumption isn't a problem for working people – that's a ruling-class problem.' Apart from the fact that we might leave it to working people themselves to decide what their problems are, this is demonstrably wrong. The lower one is on the income scale, the greater is the burden of having to take part in the cycles of fashion and consumer competition in order to live up to growth society's norms, the greater is one's conflict of interest with the consumption planners, the heavier is the financial burden this leads to, and the greater the need for liberation and respect on the basis of other values. This was clearly illustrated in the 'standard-of-living poll' referred to previously, which showed, in *all* the breakdowns of questions concerning attitudes to wealth and growth in consumption, that opposition was greatest among the low and average income groups, and least at the higher-income levels. In reality it is only the ruling class that has the economic strength to escape many of these problems, and who therefore cannot understand what pressure the manipulation of consumption puts on ordinary people.

If encouraging ordinary people to participate, even outside the organized groups, is so important, we have to do something about communication. The *personal* contact and inspiration which people get from one another in action groups is obviously not available to those not involved. It is therefore vital to create channels for a broad exchange of information which will make it possible to maintain contact and a sense of fellowship among the majority. Continuous work will be needed to disseminate information in such a way as to counteract the established means of influencing values; a way that makes it possible to tackle immediate questions of values and the problems of liberation for the public at large; to create understanding for, and interest in, the many grassroots campaigns, their ideas concerning change, and their relationship to our basic values; and to increase people's consciousness of the link between all this and their political attitudes to social development. If information of this sort could get through to the general public, it ought to contribute a great deal to strengthening and uniting the overall social movement for change.

Revolution and party politics

It is clear, from what was said in the chapter on 'the unfinished', why information of this sort, and the mobilization for change which it represents, must be counter-political. Of course, it cannot be *unpolitical;* on the contrary, its aim must be to strengthen the general sense of political responsibility for development. Making everything into a choice of *parties* actually means asking people to hand everything over to one party leadership or another. All this leads to is party debate over reforms and alternatives within the existing framework of development – thus diverting attention from a fundamental choice of direction.

There is another reason why commitment to the usual party dividing lines can weaken and fragment the movement for change. For many people who are only at the start of a process of increasing involvement, indeed probably for the majority, the party voted for is a question not of choice but of identification. For large sections of the labour movement in the industrial countries, the dominant workers' party is a class ally they would be extremely reluctant to desert – in the same way that a bourgeois party may represent a social milieu for other groups. Even if their fundamental outlook clearly conflicts with the principal party lines, they will not be drawn to a movement representing another party position – they may even see it as an attack on themselves.

Nevertheless, social identification with a party need not make people politically passive. If their allegiance is increasingly combined with an overall moral outlook which conflicts with the party's, it may contribute to a social development in which party policies are no longer determined from above, once and for all, but changed from below. And a movement with change from below as a basic principle can and should accept that such a development is desirable and possible.

This is not to suggest that 'all parties are equally good', but it does mean that no party should be regarded as uninteresting or incapable of being influenced. It is important to avoid excluding the many potential participants who might be instrumental in transforming the parties. And if it turns out that a party cannot be changed in terms of fundamental values because control from above is too strong, the result will sooner or later be an exodus to parties which do share the overall view. But to insist that this must be the first consequence of participation will hinder rather than advance the process.

It has become a dogma among many people who consider democratic development from below to be far too much trouble, that 'it's all a question of politics', i.e. the crucial thing is to get people to vote for the right parties. What they do not understand is that it is little use for people to change their choice of party if they do not change the motive behind their choice of party. If their new choice arises from the same dependence on consumption as before, the new governing party will at most be able to carry through isolated reforms in its policy of industrial growth. If it breaks with growth, it will lose votes back to the growth parties. For this reason, too, a counter-political consciousness of values must be developed *before* everything can be reduced to a question of party politics.

A revolt against industrial growth society cannot be led by party leaders and cannot be directed according to ready-made party ideologies. It must take the form of a process – a continual revolution in which participation, and the direction taken, are always more important than a dogmatic goal.

It is useless to hope that the problems we face can be solved by adjustments in the present system, or the course that this system seems doomed to take. No sophisticated analysis is required to see the insanity of the world that modern industrial society has created. What do we see if we just cast a glance over the planet we live on?

We see thousands of highly educated researchers, busy building their careers on the development of weapons with a destructive power capable of annihilating, many times over, the life forms and spiritual values that have evolved over millions of years.

We see economists and politicians of high intelligence securing their positions by strengthening the system that in the space of two generations has destroyed more of the world's natural resources than a thousand previous generations; a system that can only be protected through continued massive rearmament, violence and the exercise of power.

We see countless planners in countless enterprises working totally blinkered to protect their leading role in a development of industry and affluence which prevents the majority of their fellow human beings from achieving basic human rights.

And we see the other inhabitants of the industrial countries seeing and sensing the insanity of this, having collectively the potential to make a choice and act to break with this development – but being made passive by master thinkers of many types who always claim that the highest interests of the people and the world demand subjection to their leadership.

It is a revolution we need. But a revolution must build on the antithesis of what we are struggling to overcome.

A revolt against a world being destroyed by violence cannot itself accept the principle of violence.

A struggle against inequality and materialism cannot be driven by material self-interest.

A protest against lack of compassion for our fellow human beings cannot be motivated by value-neutral scholarship.

A break with the fanaticism which divides innocent people into hostile groups cannot be based on narrow dogmatism.

And a popular revolt against élite control cannot be led by élite groups.

It is therefore a revolution from below that is now in the making.

Not just a revolution *against* insanity, but equally a revolution *for* what we are lacking – for the right of all to act as fellow human beings in relation to one another, for the right of the disempowered to responsibility, for the ordinary person's right to take control from those who are too intelligent to understand the purpose of it all.

The words, 'The Future In Our Hands', encapsulate this.

It is no longer a question of putting responsibility in the hands of the right leaders. It is a development from below that we must make way for.

The majority must at last be allowed to shape their own future, with their own hands, out of the values of human fellowship which have been suppressed for long enough.

This is what a revolution in the affluent society means.

15. The Future In Our Hands – A Strategy for Social Change

If the conclusions we have arrived at are right, this book may seem unnecessary. Encouraging participation by facilitating contact and the spread of information in the ways set out in the last chapter ought to be sufficient. It should not be necessary to *describe* the process and the strategy, because its principal precondition is precisely that it should not be bound to any 'final' goal, nor controlled through any rigid determination of means. And it is in accordance with such ideas that we have tried to work in the Future In Our Hands movement.

But it has become clear meanwhile that just such a 'non-strategy', with its preconditions and possibilities, particularly *needs* to be described and advocated, because it is so fundamentally different from the pyramid structures and planning from above which dominate established society. And it needs to be defended against the innumerable attacks such a strategy will always encounter from master thinkers wanting to finalize it, pigeonhole it and lead it. As for spreading information to the general public, this is also often blocked by the master thinkers – as representatives of the intellectual establishment in the media, and as representatives of the established leadership mentality in organizations and institutions.

It was for these reasons that this book had to be written – not to encourage the process of change from below, but to prevent it being stifled from above. It was written in the hope that it might help free-thinking intellectuals mobilize greater resistance to the master thinkers' hegemony – both by departing from old dogmas and by repelling the attempt to control from above the protest movement that is now gathering strength in so many areas of today's industrial society.

It seemed important not only to the development of the Future In Our Hands but also to the evaluation of any grassroots campaign for a more human society, to take up the idea of development from below, its requirements, its power and its potential, judged undogmatically in relation to the most common established ideologies. And it seemed necessary to show that the caution with which we must approach any concrete conclusions is not due to any fear of radical consequences but, on the contrary, to a willingness to accept *any* consequence that follows from treating solidarity and the right of the majority to freedom and personal development as the highest values.

The Future In Our Hands movement is an attempt to create a broad and open forum for the ideas this proposition has led to. In accordance with the concept of social change through majority participation, the movement uses most of its income from subscriptions for the running of an information centre which reaches out to the public at large through the mass media, campaigns, press conferences and press releases, and through direct contact with major social organizations and political parties. The movement's message is propagated through its own organ, *Folkevett* ('Common Sense'), with a circulation of 45,000.

In accordance with the idea that individual initiatives should not be controlled from above, the movement's groups are independent of the information centre, which does however facilitate contact between groups through a special contact department.

These details of the movement's structure apply particularly to the original Norwegian movement, *Framtiden i vore hender*. Autonomous sister movements in other countries have sometimes chosen different structures.

The movement's unifying basis

To avoid internal conflict and fragmentation, it has proved vital to have a clearly defined set of values as a starting point for debate, activity and the choice of structure for the movement.

It could be said that the moral basis *is* the movement. It was the fundamental idea behind the book which gave the movement its name. It is written into the appeal that all subscribing participants have supported, and it is embodied in the information centre's constitution and as the premise on which autonomous participating groups have the right to use the movement's name. This moral basis requires agreement on the following points:

– That active human fellowship (solidarity based on compassionate understanding and identification with other people) is the highest criterion for judging human activities and goals, and that everyone, given the right circumstances, has a potential for developing active human fellowship;

– That the practice of active human fellowship must be based on the conviction that all people have equal rights to the social and material conditions which allow free personal development (i.e. a development of personal life) – to the extent that this is possible without infringing on other people's rights to the same thing, now or in the future;

– That the preservation of the biosphere, in which the human race is an integral element, is a precondition for the development of the quality of human life and its maintenance in the future (a responsibility which must not be exercised at the expense of the equal rights of all, but which establishes the framework for a similar realization of the other values).

These values are held to be obligatory – not as a moralistic demand, but to indicate the overall direction as a criterion for judgement and action. It is therefore required that, in using the movement's name, participants accept these values not only as direction indicators for building the movement, for participants' campaigns and for political discussion – but also as goals for *personal* development and participation in terms of the possibilities and limitations everyone encounters. In other words, no one may participate merely out of a desire to lead others or to lay down a policy in terms of these objectives; everyone is required to take part in the process on an equal footing, and as individuals. The fundamental belief is that people *can* guide their own, and society's, development according to a deeper moral conviction.

In assessing the practical consequences of the given values, it is imperative that they be adopted without national, regional or other discrimination against fundamental human rights. The poverty of the global majority, and the suppression of their potential for independent development and social influence, is therefore the main problem, and indicates the general direction in which the given values can be realized within a particular society.

It is important to grasp the link between the moral basis and *all* ways of evaluating objectives – including, of course, political objectives. This means that *no* proposal concerning political objectives which arises from this basis can be excluded from the movement's debate as being 'too radical', or conversely because it doesn't accord with received radical ideology. In practice, this has saved the movement from the internal battles over ideology that have fragmented so many movements for change. Participants who are convinced of certain ideologies are obliged *continually* to justify the elements of their outlook – not in terms of the ideology itself, but in terms of the overall principle – the common view of 'the purpose of it all'.

The movement's tasks

It is clear from the movement's moral basis that its main aim is not to present theories of change as an end in itself, but to set in motion a transformation in a given direction wherever it is necessary. In the light of what has been said in the chapter on participation and the way ahead, four main principles have been arrived at for the movement:

– To help start things happening *laterally,* so that a free, dialectical interaction between value consciousness, personal liberation in thought and action, and increasing political consciousness, can begin and gradually help to bring about the necessary identification of the majority with counter-active politics.

– To inspire concrete action for the presentation of alternatives to the existing order, and to increase popular influence on current social conditions and legislation in terms of the basic values. The intention is both to encourage greater participation in forming the alternatives, and to develop an understanding of their merits and their feasibility. With this in mind, breadth and multiformity must be considered an advantage to such action.

– To serve as a medium for contact and cooperation between counter-active campaigns and alternatives, both within and outside the circle of subscribing members, at home and internationally.

– To conduct a dialogue with key figures who express support for the movement's moral basis in organizations and parties, in order to challenge these with new ideas, attitudes and follow-up work.

The structure of the movement

The movement's activity falls into two parts with different structural requirements.

On the one hand, the broad dissemination of information and facilitation of contact, which requires concentrated, planned activity in order to contend with society's powerful influence on values.

On the other, the diverse, independent activity of participating groups and individuals, which must be non-managed and non-organized if it is to liberate the intrinsic power of development from below in the population.

In order to make possible the gathering and coordination of information, which would be difficult or impossible if it were done separately by each of the many groups, participants pay an annual subscription for the operation of a common information and contact centre. The information centre's use of subscription funds is controlled by a broadly constituted council.

It has been important to the structure of the movement that the information centre should have the economic strength to handle information effectively in order to promote the movement's basic ideas – while having no status in terms of organizational leadership. So it does *not* plan or initiate the campaigns and activities of participants, but uses its entire capacity and all its subscription funds for the purpose of spreading information as broadly as possible among the general public.

Like the individual action groups, the information centre and its council are independent of any traditional organizational structure and leadership and the rigidity this can easily lead to. In other words, the information centre and its council can formally be regarded as one of the autonomous groups in the movement. The reason for this is a desire to avoid the usual pyramid organizational structure and its constant tendency to induce passivity.

The concentrated use of the movement's economic resources for co-ordinated, *outwardly directed* communication through the mass media and its own organs, which this arrangement allows, is probably one of the reasons that the movement's ideas seem to have reached a broader public than is usual for traditional organizations.

The only other form of control exercised by the information centre's council is its responsibility for seeing that the movement's name, the Future In Our Hands, is only linked to undertakings that are clearly motivated by and rooted in its basic ideas. It is understood, however, that there can be interference in the autonomous groups' right to use the name *only* when this basis is clearly lacking, or when their action is obviously inconsistent, and that judgements on this point demand broad tolerance given the multiformity of activity and expression in different groups.

The other aspect of the movement's activity – the various groups' campaigns and the individual activities of participants – is therefore unrestricted by any form of control apart from their commitment to the basic values. This has resulted in great variety as far as the size, organization and activities of different groups are concerned. Among the ninety or so FIOH groups in Norway (of which about sixty can be called *action* groups), there are both local groups involving ten, a hundred, or more participants, and nationwide organizations convened for particular types of action.

Free and unstructured cooperation also allows personal activity on the part of the majority of supporting members who do not participate in any of the movement's groups.

In order to keep a firm grasp of the supreme objective – the general transformation of society in terms of the basic values – it is stressed that the movement must not see itself as a closed association consisting only of those who pay the annual subscription, but also as a forum, a meeting place and a connecting link between all campaigns and activities based on the same counteractive values. In FIOH's Danish and Swedish sister movements, particularly, whose members are fewer, this function of facilitating contact and cooperation with other groups has been an important aspect of their activity.

The information centre's activities

Here we shall mention only a few illustrative examples of the information centre's attempts to realize its given objectives.

In order to get information through to the majority, it has proved essential constantly to find new ways of illustrating the general message in terms of 'theme campaigns'. To make the most of media coverage, the movement has made use of an extensive index of interested journalists in most sections of the media. Besides this, the centre arranges press conferences at the launching of new information campaigns. In most cases, autonomous groups and individual participants have been invited to help by spreading information locally.

Among the themes that have been introduced and propagated with the help of such campaigns are:

– A campaign for greater emphasis in education on global solidarity and the values of fellowship, linked to the publication of a specially commissioned survey concerning junior high school students' familiarity with global questions – or rather their lack of it. Appeals in Norwegian newspapers; material to all junior high schools.

– An 'Information Against Racism' campaign.

– An information campaign, aimed especially at secondary schools, about a new international economic order and its likely consequences.

– A campaign entitled 'Recycling Makes Sense', with legal registration of repair facilities, buying things second-hand, etc., and the sale of jute bags bearing the movement's recycling symbol, imported directly from local producers in Bangladesh as an alternative to disposable bags.

– A campaign on the connections between diet and problems of superabundance, self-sufficiency and globally responsible nutrition policy.

– A campaign concerning the political potential of less competitive and less growth-oriented policies, in connection with a gallup poll on attitudes to growth in consumption and to social problems and solidarity.

– A campaign aimed at the Norwegian parliament and the electorate, coinciding with the launch of the movement's books, concerning proposals for more goal-directed, globally responsible policies.

– A campaign on alternative technology and solidarity in connection with the movement's cooperation with the publishers of E.F. Schumacher's *Small Is Beautiful,* published at the official inauguration of the 'Norwegian Ecotech', an independent group in the movement.

– A campaign for the equalization of incomes, for alternative production and an end to growth, aimed at politicians, the electorate and groups in the trade-union movement.

– A campaign to demand public resources for an independent scientific investigation of an 'alternative future' for the Scandinavian countries in cooperation with developing countries. (The Norwegian parliament has now allocated funds for this.)

Alongside these campaigns, a more continuous circulation of information has been maintained around various groups, through a staff of volunteer speakers, posters, mobile exhibitions, articles and discussion seminars examining various themes in terms of the movement's basic values – and through collaboration with participants who disseminate information in schools, the labour movement, the women's movement, the church and other organizations.

The movement's magazine has been important in disseminating more thoroughly information concerning the many possible consequences of the movement's basic ideas. It provides information on national and international social questions and alternatives, on an alternative way of life consistent with FIOH's basic values, and on the activities of FIOH and other movements – to supporters and to other interested people through sales on the street and by subscription.

In order to facilitate contact between the autonomous groups, the information centre has its own contact department and newsletter. A network of contacts has been built up, along with a directory of parallel groups and grassroots campaigns in Norway and abroad, with special travel and contact arrangements for this purpose. Apart from this, the groups themselves have set up their own national assembly and their own regional centres for coordinating their activities.

The information centre also has an information secretary to maintain dialogue and follow up the movement's ideas among interested politicians, local party groups and political youth organizations, trade-union representatives, major organizations and in academic circles.

Special research contacts help to maintain links and circulate the findings of studies connected with the movement's ideas in various fields.

An international secretary works especially with contacts abroad who want to start new sister movements in connection with the publication of the movement's books in other countries.

The activities of the autonomous action groups and other participants

So that new groups can be set up independently by supporters who are not naturally inclined to participate in existing action groups, or who want to start other types of project, no one can claim the sole right to the name of the movement within a given geographical area. In other words, there are no traditional 'local branches' which automatically include all members within a given district.

The majority of the nearly 30,000 supporters of the Norwegian movement are, however, outside the organized groups. They help to promote FIOH's ideas through their support for the information work, and by working for the movement's objectives in their political parties or other social organizations, at their workplaces, or in their families and communities. The groups determine their own form of organization and cooperation.

Each group finances its own activity – either through a special group subscription in addition to the central membership subscription to the information centre – or through funds raised by its own activities. An important source of funds is the income made from selling the movement's magazine.

The groups themselves make their activity, and the values underlying it, known in their own areas. And the information centre helps to spread information about alternatives, and action for change, within the movement and outside it.

Each group is free to present its own views – as long as they are justified in terms of the basic values. The information put out by the groups therefore represents various degrees of social consciousness and 'radicalism'. The main point is that they are bound to the movement not by their conclusions, but by their grounding in common values and the demand for global justice. In this way, the counteractive element in the process is reinforced, at the same time as a free debate about alternative solutions is made possible.

A summary of some of the campaigns and activities conducted in the movement will illustrate the great number of counteractive undertakings that can develop from the same basic values. As has been said, some of these are national organizations, others more specialist.

The School Forum is a forum for people involved in education and others who wish to increase understanding about the values of solidarity in the broadest sense in education. The forum distributes information to schools and classes concerning the possibilities of such education. Members of the School Forum have helped to start special courses at several colleges.

The Norwegian Association for Collective Transport is working for more human alternatives to mass motoring.

Our World and Alternative Trade are two groups working to promote an understanding of the value of local cultures in developing countries, and the sale of their craft products to provide income for local producers in poor countries.

The Institute for Useful Production circulates information about initiatives for conversion to peaceful and socially useful production (such as the Lucas plan) and creates links between interested parties. This group has drawn up a directory of over 400 contacts for alternative production in fifteen countries.

The Development Fund is a major national organization in the movement. The fund's resources are raised mainly through participants deducting a fixed amount from their own income, thus contributing to the twofold objective – reduced dependence on consumption and a corresponding contribution to active solidarity. The fund's committee consists of people with practical experience in developing countries who ensure that these resources do not create dependence, but contribute to independent development on the terms of the local population in poor countries. The fund now has over 500 members, providing a fixed monthly income of about $4,500. Its first project was the financing of a dam installation in Mali which the local population wanted to build to help solve their problems of famine and malnutrition during drought periods. The fund has since financed development projects in a total of twenty developing countries.

The Fund for Alternative Development Projects in Norway is financed in the same way as the Development Fund, but is used to support groups, both within FIOH and outside it, which need resources for projects embodying more human or ecological possibilities for development, alternative uses of energy and resources, organic agriculture, alternative useful production, etc. in Norway.

Norwegian Ecotech is another organization which operates nationally within the movement. In cooperation with the Ecotechs in Sweden and Denmark, it works to collect and disseminate information and to contribute to the practical development of a technology that is more human and controllable, and less energy- and resource-intensive.

The Group for Alternative Housing studies, highlights and tries to realize housing projects based on greater communal use and cooperation, and makes contact with populations in poor countries who practise more communal forms of dwelling.

The Disarmament Group is contributing to the development of alternative, non-violent and less resource-hungry means of defence, and of defence policies that are not aimed at protecting and maintaining the industrialized countries' interests in raw materials and trade in the Third World.

The Hostel Organization is the movement's 'decentralized hotel' for participants in all the Scandinavian FIOH movements. It is based on the idea that 'hotel members' offer each other overnight accommodation on an exchange basis, so that travel can serve as a means to promote fellowship and communal life instead of adding to the number of package tours sold by travel companies.

The Jute Bag Campaign is run by a group who buy locally produced jute bags from Bangladesh, sell them as examples of an alternative to plastic carrier bags and the development of disposable commodities, and transfer the income to the producers.

The Community-Twinning Groups start from the idea that our relations with poor countries ought to consist not merely of donations and one-way help, but also of friendship and contact which can broaden *mutual* understanding of our respective cultures and of what we can learn from our respective social and other traditions and solutions. The Community-Twinning Groups make direct links between local communities in Norway and in developing countries.

The Indigenous Peoples' Group works in particular to promote understanding of indigenous peoples' problems in relation to the growth and advance of industrial culture at their expense, and to propagate knowledge of the values represented in their traditional cultures.

Action for Common Humanity was started by a group of people who wanted to put into effect the movements emphasis on human solidarity by offering contact and support for people suffering the loneliness and other problems of today's harshly competitive society.

FIOH Information for the Blind is run by a group who make tape-recordings of *Folkevett* (FIOH's magazine) for the blind and partially sighted.

The FIOH Study Organization is another independent national group which organizes and raises support for study groups whose purpose is to study the movement's ideas, books and articles, and publications on related topics. Several hundred study groups have been active.

Most groups in FIOH, however, operate on a local basis. A number of these have set up shops selling and exchanging used goods which are run by volunteers to help local people with an alternative to resource-intensive consumption fuelled by fashion and disposability. Profits normally go to projects in developing countries or other undertakings in the cause of solidarity.

Others have rented communal land which is made available to people in the area who are willing to work together to grow their own food.

Others arrange exhibitions, produce material for schools, give lectures, write articles for the local press to follow up debates connected with the movement's ideas, organize independent projects in developing countries, traffic campaigns and campaigns against environmentally destructive development – often in cooperation with other organizations.

During local and general election campaigns, many public meetings have been arranged at which local candidates have been challenged in terms of the movement's ideas and perspectives.

Apart from this, a number of groups are working within the institutions to which they are linked – schools, universities and organizations.

Continuing alongside this relatively organized collective action there is, as has been said, widespread non-organized activity among more private groups and families, and among individuals in the movement. This includes the development of alternatives to established patterns of life and consumption, private support for activity in support of developing countries and liberation movements, work to influence ends and means in people's own workplaces, organizations and political parties, and the dissemination of information in the community, in cooperation with the information centre.

The Future In Our Hands does not compete with other movements working for change with the same basic values. It is an attempt to create a movement for the broadest possible cooperation for change in terms of a definite, shared value basis. It is not solely a movement for activists who want to realize counteractive alternatives here and now. Nor is it merely a movement for a new way of life and liberation from consumer manipulation. Nor is it only a movement for political activity. Since its purpose is to contribute to a fundamental transformation, it has to be all these things at once – bringing them together, because all these forms of activity are necessary elements of the process of change if it is to be directed by the majority.

The vital point – if one accepts the majority's right to responsibility – must be to contribute to a broader involvement, to try to harness more horses to the cart. As long as we are unwilling to team up with one another, and as long as we lack shared values which ensure that we are pulling in the same direction, we are condemned to be dragged backwards, steered by the aims and desires of other forces.

The Future In Our Hands – Manifesto for Membership

Let us work towards a more humane kind of society

We can help to reverse the insane trends prevailing today if we work together.

If no change takes place, more than half of all the children now living are doomed to die of hunger and deficiency diseases before they reach adulthood – because a majority of the world's population does not even have enough food.

Our greatest problems are caused by surpluses, and waste. Our increasing over-consumption is leading towards a catastrophe for our descendants, too. In spite of this, we *still* seek to increase our consumption! We must soon realize that, in a world where the majority are suffering great need, there are more important things we can produce than luxury, fashion and prestige goods. Reason must tell us that we can no longer emphasize materialistic values – if we were to solve the problems of today and tomorrow. By doing this, we can also create a more healthy society for ourselves:

– a society in which the conservation of nature and arable land means more than economic growth.

– a society in which stress, competition and a craving for things are replaced by a natural enjoyment of life, and a concern for those needing help.

– a society in which we can afford to create humane conditions in our schools and places of work.

We cannot go on saying that this is an admirable but unattainable goal. Regardless of how difficult it may be to attain, it is the only human goal which we can strive towards.

We cannot wait for others. If one country shows the way, others can follow.

Within most political parties there are groups which aim at getting this kind of programme accepted by their party. But political action must have popular support; if we are to translate our wishes for saner policies into practice, the majority of us must be willing to accept a reduction in our personal consumption. As long as we allow ourselves to be pulled along by the currents of the consumer society, we support the forces which oppose change.

There are many of us who would like to go in for such a change in our own, personal way of life – if we thought it would be any use. It *will* be some use, if we act together. But we are too divided, belonging, as we do, to different parties and organizations. We lack the support of a larger group. We must unite, across the lines between parties, which have not as yet set their sights on these new goals.

A popular movement based on these ideas should not have the form of a rigid, top-heavy organization. We hope, however, that there will prove to be interest in doing permanent information work also in countries outside Scandinavia. The intention of this information work would be to encourage the establishment of independent groups working throughout the country; to inspire and establish contact between groups and individuals who will support each other in resisting the current hysterical mood of competitiveness. That is to say, those who seek a simpler way of life together with a more humane set of values, and who wish to understand the world situation, which makes this change necessary.

This information is to ensure that people hear of the need for this new development – through radio and tv, the press, in lectures and through the movement's own publications.

We shall not be launching new theories which remain at the theoretical stage. Nor do we wish to be carried along by a wave of emotion. We hope, instead, that as many people as possible will take this seriously, and personally, and do something about it. We believe that this is the only way of bringing about the changes we want to see.

The undersigned give their support to this initiative:

George Borgström   George McRobie
Helder Camara   Gunnar Myrdal
Basil Davidson   Dennis Meadows
Thor Heyerdahl   Arne Næss
Jan Tinbergen   Erik Dammann

For British membership, please write to:
The Future in Our Hands (UK) Information Centre
120 York Road
Swindon
Wilts SN1 2JP

If you want to declare your interest for a possible FIOH movement in the USA, please write to:
The Future in Our Hands Project USA
Box 1380
Ojai
California 93023

Notes

1 Bjørn Unneberg, *Arbeider og bonde*, Oslo 1977.
2 Jens Bjørneboe, *Bøker og mennesker*, Oslo 1979.
3 André Glucksmann, *Les maîtres penseurs*, Paris 1977.
4 Joan Robinson, *Economic Philosophy*, London 1962.
5 Gudmund Vinskei, *Vårt Land*, 22 January 1977.
6 Karl Marx, *Capital* Volume 1, Harmondsworth 1976.
6a Karl Marx, *Kapitalen*, Første bok, Oslo 1930.
7 Karl Marx, *The German Ideology, Collected Works* Vol.5, London 1976.
8 Ernst Fischer and Franz Marek, *Marx In His Own Words*, London 1973.
9 Brynjolf Bjørset, *Etter oss kommer overfloden*, Oslo 1934.
10 *Aftenposten*, 25 May 1979.
11 Julius Nyerere, *Dialogue or Confrontation*, London 1975.
12 Julius Nyerere, *Appeal to the Socialists of Europe*, 1972.
13 ILO, *Employment, Growth and Basic Needs*, Geneva 1976.
14 F.M. Lappé, *Food First*, New York 1977.
15 Helge Hveem, 'Investeringer i u-land', *Norkontakt* 8, 1973.
16 Gunnar Myrdal, *Miljö och ekonomisk tillväkst*, Stockholm 1976.
17 *Aftenposten*, 25 June 1979.
18 Gunnar Myrdal, *The Need For Reforms in Underdeveloped Countries*, Saltsjöbaden, Sweden 1978.
19 Karl Marx, *The Revolutions of 1848*, Harmondsworth 1973.
20 Jan Bredsdorff, *Kina – Revolusion tur/retur*, Copenhagen 1978.
21 Keith Abercrombie, *Aftenposten*, 19 April 1979.
22 Julius Nyerere, *Fattigdom og frigjøring*, Oslo 1976.
23 *Aftenposten*, 25 February 1976.
24 Mihaljlo Mesvoric and Eduard Pestel, *Mankind at the Turning Point*, New York 1974.
25 *Aftenposten*, 14 January and 6 June 1975.
26 *Dansk Gyldendals Leksikon*, Copenhagen 1978.
27 Jan Karlsson, *Om Arbete*, Stockholm 1978.
28 Karl Marx, *Capital* Volume 3, Harmondsworth 1981.
29 Karl Marx, *Capital* Volume 2, Harmondsworth 1978.
30 E.F. Schumacher, *Small Is Beautiful*, London 1974.
31 J.K. Galbraith, *The New Industrial State*, London 1967.
32 Arthur Svensson, *Fagbevegelsens rolle i arbeidet for større global solidaritet*, Olso 1978. (FIOH publication.)
33 Odd Højdal, interview in *Ny Livsstil* 3, 1975.
34 Jahn Otto Johansen, *Russisk naerkontakt*, Oslo 1978.
35 *Aftenposten*, 21 September 1977.
36 Gunnar Garbo, *Opprustet og forsvarsløs*, Oslo 1975.
37 J.K. Galbraith, *The Affluent Society*, London 1961.
38 Georg Lukács, *Lenin*, London 1970.
39 Mao Zedong, *Selected Works* Volume 5, Beijing 1977.
40 Gudmund Hernes, *Makt og Avmakt*, Oslo 1978.
41 *Uken*, 10-17 March 1979.
42 Ivan Illich, *The Right to Useful Unemployment and Its Professional Enemies*, London 1978.
43 Dag Osterberg, *Et førord til Kapitalen*, Oslo 1972.
44 Stein Savik, *Aftenposten*, 11 May 1977.
45 Alex Haley, *Roots*, New York 1976.
46 Mike Cooley, *New Technology: Whose Right to Choose?*, London 1978.
47 Matts Heijbell, *Åsiktsbok om alternativ produktion*, Stockholm 1978.
48 Niels I. Meyer, *Revolt From The Centre*, London 1980.
49 Alain Touraine, *La Voix et le regard* and *La Lutte étudiante*, cited in *Dag og tid* 23, 1978.
50 Thomas Mathiesen, *Det uferdige. Bidrage til politisk askjonsteori*, Oslo 1971.

51 Dieter Duhm, *Varestruktur og ødelagt mellommenneskelighed*, Copenhagen 1978.
52 Retranslated from an interview in *Ekumeniska u-veckan's tidsskrift*, November 1977.
53 *Ny Livsstil* 6, 1975.
54 Jörn Svensson, *Du skall ta ledningen och makten*, Stockholm 1974.
55 Paul Mattick, *Kapitalistisk og proletarisk arbejderbevaegelse*, Copenhagen 1975.
56 Paolo Freire, *Cultural Action For Freedom*, Harmondsworth 1972.
57 Trygve Bratteli, *Arbeiderbevegelsen's handbok*, Oslo 1976.
58 Einar Førdelin and Sverre Jervell, *Vår velstand og vekst til debatt*, Oslo 1976.
59 Helge Ole Bergesen, in *Samtiden*, Oslo 1976.
60 Poul Bjerre, *Andelssamfundet*, Copenhagen 1979.
61 Per Benterud and Per Morten Vigtel, *Norges Industri* 21, 1979.
62 Christian Mailand Hansen, *Anarkismen. En Antologi*, Copenhagen 1970.
63 Lars Monrad-Krohn and Haakon Sandvold, lecture at the 1979 annual assembly of the Norwegian Technical Research Council for the Natural Sciences, in *Aftenposten*, April 1971.
64 'Computers Create a Greater Information Gulf in an Organization', *Aftenposten*, 22 August 1979.
65 Per Benterud, 'Microelectronics Must Be Taken Seriously', *Aftenposten*, 3 August 1979.
66 Ivan Illich, *Tools For Conviviality*, London 1973.
67 Hartvig Saetra, *Den økopolitiske sosialismen*, Oslo 1973.
68 Bjørn Unneberg, interview in *Ostlendingen*, 29 October 1975.
69 Arne Næss, *Okologi, samfunn og livsstil*, Oslo 1974.

heretic books ℔

for publication Autumn 1984

Peter Tatchell
Democratic Defence: a non-nuclear alternative

Millions of British people today support unilateral nuclear disarmament. But millions more, though concerned by the nuclear threat, are held back from accepting the CND case by a sense that some form of military defence is needed in a dangerous world.

Peter Tatchell argues that unilateralism must be combined with a credible non-nuclear alternative if it is to win majority backing. He proposes a non-imperialist and non-provocative defence system which would be self-reliant, distinctively democratic and strictly defensive. This alternative to nuclear weapons would be territorial in character, based on a radically civilianised and democratised citizens' army. In arguing the feasibility of this proposal, Peter Tatchell draws on the Swedish, Swiss and Yugoslav models of territorial self-defence, as well as the experience of the Home Guard in 1940 and the democratic impulses that swept through the British army during the Second World War.

Peter Tatchell
The Battle For Bermondsey
paper £2.95   US $5.50

Preface by Tony Benn MP   cased £7.95   US $15.00

The Bermondsey by-election of February 1983 has gone down in history for the campaign of character assassination waged by Fleet Street against the official Labour candidate, in which sections of his own party happily joined. Vilified as an extremist, foreigner, draft-dodger, homosexual and traitor, Peter Tatchell presents here his real views on grassroots community socialism, gay rights and a 'new style' of Labour MP. He explains what it feels like to be the victim of a witch-hunt, and details the unprecedented harassment and abuse to which he was subjected.

'One of the most important political documents to have been published about the Labour Party since the war' (Tony Benn).

Rudolf Bahro
Socialism and Survival
Preface by Edward Thompson

paper £3.50	US $ 6.50
cased £6.95	US $12.95

Widely reviewed and debated since its publication in October 1982, this volume of essays by one of Europe's leading radical thinkers argues that the liberatory goals of socialism can be promoted in the industrialised countries today only through the green movement. A book whose influence is sure to grow as the dialectic between red and green finally gets under way in the English-speaking world.

'Rudolf Bahro is forcing a consideration of peace, ecology, global human needs onto mainstream Marxism in ways that radicals cannot dismiss' (*City Limits*).

Louis Mackay and David Fernbach (eds)
Nuclear-Free Defence   £3.95   US $7.50

A symposium with 23 leading figures in the British peace movement, including Frank Allaun MP, Pat Arrowsmith, Joan Maynard MP, Peter Tatchell, Stuart Christie, Ronald Higgins. This book debates alternatives to nuclear strategy that range from pragmatic to utopian, and contains a wealth of ideas whose relevance is by no means limited to Britain.

'The editors have performed a vital task in revealing the true condition of the peace movement, and the strands that have to be pulled together if it is to advance further and with credibility' (*Time Out*).

Die Grünen
Programme of the German Green Party
Preface by Jonathon Porritt   £1.50   US $2.95

'Die Grünen' — the West German Greens — are today the most dynamic force in the worldwide Green movement, and the most successful in terms of their electoral performance. This is a translation of the Federal Programme on which they fought the general election of March 1983.

'A challenge to all radicals to renounce the wasteland of contemporary industrial politics and to stake a claim in the politics of the future' (Jonathon Porritt).

Kit Mouat
Fighting For Our Lives
Preface by Sheila Hancock   £2.50   US $4.95

A book on the pioneering work of Cancer Contact, a mutual aid network formed by people who are not willing to see themselves as passive victims. It centres around their personal stories: how they've been treated by the orthodox medical system, their experiences with complementary and alternative therapies, and the strength to fight back which they draw from sharing their problems.

Jan Myrdal and Gun Kessle
India Waits
paper £6.95   US $10.95★
cased £15.00   US $25.00

Beneath the pretensions of the 'world's largest democracy' lies a turmoil of conflicts moving ever closer to revolutionary explosion. Written with a deep understanding of India's past, this book offers a panoramic vision of this great country, and an invaluable guide to the storms now impending.

o

★Titles marked with an asterisk are published in North America by Lake View Press, P O Box 25421, Chicago, IL 60625, USA. Our other books can be ordered in North America from Carrier Pigeon, 40 Plympton St, Boston, MA 02118, USA.

Elsewhere in the world, order all titles from Heretic Books, P O Box 247, London N15 6RW. For personal mail order, please add 10% for postage.

o